Management for Professionals

More information about this series at http://www.springer.com/series/10101

Radu Atanasiu

Critical Thinking for Managers

Structured Decision-Making and Persuasion in Business

Springer

Radu Atanasiu
Bucharest International School
of Management
Bucharest, Romania

ISSN 2192-8096 ISSN 2192-810X (electronic)
Management for Professionals
ISBN 978-3-030-73599-9 ISBN 978-3-030-73600-2 (eBook)
https://doi.org/10.1007/978-3-030-73600-2

This Springer imprint is published by the registered company Springer Nature Switzerland AG
The registered company address is: Gewerbestrasse 11, 6330 Cham, Switzerland

For my loved ones

Contents

Part I
Overview

1 Introduction

We all know how to think, just as we all know how to run. However, if, you want to finish a marathon rather than merely catching the bus, there is a structured way to upgrade many aspects of your running: the pace you run at, the way your foot touches the ground, the way you breathe, the frequency of your training sessions, and even the way you dress. All these aspects can be improved for better results. Similarly, the way a manager thinks can benefit from a structured upgrading process.

Two important roles as leaders are decision-making and persuasion, and this book addresses both. Each has a dedicated section, illustrated with clear business examples. By employing the latest research in behavioral economics and management and organizational cognition, this book aims to help improve strategy, planning, and decision-making by protecting against thinking traps such as hidden assumptions and cognitive biases and by providing easy solutions for testing hypotheses and solving dilemmas.

Thinking critically is not only useful for analyzing incoming information in decision-making; it is also crucial for structuring outgoing information in persuasion. When trying to convince a client to buy your service, the board to fund your project, or a peer to change a procedure, you—the manager—can use principles described in this book to prepare for a successful meeting, an effective pitch, or even a constructive debate. In this sense, this book discusses critical thinking as a tool for humane leadership, presenting tested methods to cope with disagreement and to make ourselves and others a little more flexible in changing our minds.

Thinking like the android Data from Star Trek or like Sheldon from The Big Bang Theory (all reason, no feeling, no instinct) is not ideal for a manager today. Increasingly, the business environment is characterized by the VUCA paradigm (volatility, uncertainty, complexity, ambiguity), with tsunami-like spikes such as the 2020 pandemic. Our capacity for reasoning is limited. Herbert Simon famously introduced the *bounded rationality* paradigm, stating that, in real life, the perfectly rational agents described by the theory of rational choice do not exist. In real life, managers do not have the time or the bandwidth to thoroughly analyze each

R. Atanasiu, *Critical Thinking for Managers*, Management for Professionals,
https://doi.org/10.1007/978-3-030-73600-2_1

decision, while the problems posed by everyday business are rarely well-structured. Under these conditions, good managers use experience-based intuition to devise simple decision rules while purposefully ignoring some of the available data when making efficient decisions. What, then, is the recipe for using reason and gut feeling in the right proportion? This book argues for allowing non-rational influences alongside reason, with two conditions: acknowledging them (we will discuss extensively how to do so), and having a solid, structured rational process in parallel (covered in the chapters on decision-making and problem solving).

After a short overview, this book is structured in two parts that reflect its subtitle. The first part focuses on the use of critical thinking for managerial decision-making, discussing how to identify hidden assumptions behind business plans, how to test them, the right proportion between our reason and our intuition, and how cognitive biases can influence both our own and customers' behavior. It then introduces a structured approach and several practical tools for decision-making and problem solving. The second part focuses on the use of critical thinking for persuasion and presents tools and structure for verbal and written persuasion in a business setting, some tips and tricks for having constructive disputes, and insights about fallacies and the use of fair play in argumentation. It ends with uncovering several psychological mechanisms that prevent us from challenging old beliefs and changing our minds. These topics are treated in a relaxed manner and illustrated with business examples. Often, theoretical concepts are well understood, but not internalized if we do not connect them to a practical and personal use. Throughout this book, therefore, I often prompt the reader to answer a question, to imagine a personal use for a certain tool, or to perform a mental exercise.

In this book, I have adapted and used content from some of my articles published in various practitioner magazines, from my platform—thinkinginbusiness.com—and the script of my online courses (MOOCs) on iversity.org.

Who Needs Critical Thinking?

2

Critical thinking is on everybody's lips. Employers think it is one of the most important skills employees should have (The World Economic Forum, 2016), schools increasingly include it in their curricula, and self-actualizing people read books such as this one or attend online courses about it. But what is it? And what is it not?

Comprehensive definitions are good for approaching a matter in a scholarly way. When we define terms for scientific purposes, we need to know exactly all their aspects and how they differ from neighboring constructs. In the case of this book, however, which has a focus on practice, it is less important how critical thinking differs from decision-making (it does). Instead, I open a large umbrella for the concept and then offer different precise methods of application, which readers can employ consciously when confronted with an important decision or with a complex situation.

What is critical thinking? Critical thinking can be loosely defined as thinking purposefully and carefully, while avoiding cognitive traps. The points in this book are illustrated with examples, and we can start with two of them to clarify this concept:

A while ago, some British classrooms had a sign above the blackboard that read: "Your teacher might be wrong, learn to think for yourself!" I consider this an epitome of critical thinking in education, especially while many schools and teachers today still consider themselves as exclusive sources of knowledge in the era of Google and Wikipedia. A student who asks a clarifying question pays purposeful attention to the discussion and is careful to avoid the trap of being convinced by the authority of the instructor alone.

In another example, a manager carelessly signs a new contract with a long-term supplier without reading it, assuming (wrongly) that the conditions remained the same. The manager soon finds himself, to his surprise, in breach of contract and liable for penalties. The manager has fallen into the cognitive traps of hasty generalization and failure to identify and question assumptions.

R. Atanasiu, *Critical Thinking for Managers*, Management for Professionals,
https://doi.org/10.1007/978-3-030-73600-2_2

This second example leads to an important aspect of thinking critically: Most of us know how to do it but often fail to. The manager in question surely knows how to read and analyze a contract, but he does not do so. A primary takeaway from this situation is that, along with the acquisition of critical thinking skills, we should (and this book aims to) increase our inclination to use them when the situation requires it. The human brain is lazy, and it pushes us to use it as little as possible. It may use shortcuts, it may ignore reason, it may rationalize gut feelings after the decision is taken, and it may look differently at identical situations, depending on where we stand. Although we might know how to approach a matter, our brain might be too lazy to use the tools it has, and this is why we need to train our inclination to use them. A CEO might be fully aware that herd behavior (*argumentum ad populum*) is a fallacy when he tells his daughter that "everybody else has the latest iPhone" is not a good argument for buying her one. And yet he might later that day decide on implementing the latest management practice just because "all our competitors did." The key to preventing this trap and enhancing our inclination to think critically is to force ourselves, when the stakes are high, to meta-think: to think about our thinking. A good way to do that is to ask ourselves, when faced with an important decision, "how will I decide in this matter?" and then follow through. Later in this book, I will advocate for the adoption of an even more powerful tool: a decision journal.

What, then, critical thinking is *not*? Some people react with a frown to their first encounter with the concept. They say that the world is negative enough without us teaching how to criticize. They are wrong. Critical thinking is not about criticizing. Both words have the same etymology, but in "critical thinking," the word "critical" is more loyal to its Greek root, *κριτική* (*kritikē*), which means to discern, to examine. The perfect illustration is this: Before a movie is launched, there is an advanced screening where film critics, after seeing the movie, examine it and give their expert opinion, which does not necessarily criticize the film, but analyzes it carefully, in detail, and hopefully without bias. This is how we should employ critical thinking when confronted with an argument: without jumping to attack it. We should check that its mechanism is valid and that the facts it relies upon are true. Most people display a healthy degree of such rational skepticism, especially when analyzing the arguments of others; but we, as managers, should purposefully train our self-reflection and metathinking in order to also identify our own patterns of bad reasoning.

How rational are we? Classical economics is based on the model of unbounded rationality, which endows decision-makers with perfect knowledge of all aspects of the problem, infinite computational capacity, infinite time, infinite resources, and a single aim: to maximize their expected utility (von Neumann & Morgenstern, 1944). Other models of economic rationality, such as optimization under constraints, stem from this ideal model without doubting its premises. After observing that the behavior of real decision-makers is far from that of the perfectly rational agent, Herbert Simon introduced the concept of *bounded rationality* (Simon, 1955): Real people have limited knowledge of the market, limited time, limited computational power, and limited resources, and their decision-making does not aim for the perfect solution (optimizing), but for a good-enough solution (*satisficing*: a term coined by Herbert Simon as a portmanteau of *satisfying* and *sufficing*). Numerous subsequent empirical studies have confirmed that, in reality, managers forego the costs of optimizing and make use of satisficing techniques (Bauer et al., 2012; Busenitz & Barney, 1997; Fodor et al., 2016). We are not fully rational, and we should embrace that (more on embracing it in further chapters).

An often-quoted example of real people ignoring the principles of the perfectly rational agent involves Harry Markowitz, an economist who received the Nobel Prize for his modern portfolio theory in which he explains how to allocate funds, when investing, across several vehicles. His complex mathematical algorithm involves a technique called *mean–variance analysis* and is a good example of classical economic theory. However, when he retired, Harry Markowitz was asked about the way he personally distributed his savings across a portfolio of investment funds and admitted that he ignored his Nobel-winning method and relied instead on the simplest rule: He allocated the same sum to all funds (a heuristic called 1/N, as this is the proportion allocated to each vehicle in a portfolio of N funds). We all use this heuristic when the bill comes and we decide to split it evenly.

Let me ask you a question:

Question What percentage of your business decisions is based on reason? Please, think about it and put a number down: We will return to it later.

When asked this question, the managers I work with usually give a wide range, but a significant subgroup gravitates around 60–80%. There are, of course, those who choose 0–20% without blinking; I tend to believe that such people are actually less prone to error. By contrast, a manager who thinks of himself as mostly rational will not doubt his own thinking and will not look for personal blind spots, leaving no room for improvement. Overall, there is insufficient empirical research to answer the question above. A small study performed on students (Wood et al., 2002) found that between 35 and 43% of behavior is not based on thinking.

Another obstacle to accurately measuring how often we do things that are not based on reason is rationalization, a defense mechanism through which we explain rationally, *post-factum*, decisions that were based on feelings, habit, or bias. We have the tendency to subconsciously decide what to do before figuring out why we do it, and then we need to explain ourselves to ourselves and others. Jonathan Haidt, in his book *The Righteous Mind*, famously uses a metaphor to describe this mechanism: The press secretary, who was not even in the Oval Office when a decision was made, has the job of defending and explaining that decision no matter what, without having the power to change it (Haidt, 2013). Similarly, our reason explains (to ourselves or others), in logical, defensible terms, decisions in which it was not involved at all. Should I ask you about important decisions, such as how you chose your career or your current employer, I might receive tales of weighted criteria, decision trees, and pros and cons. Should I dig deeper, past the rationalization, I might find decisions based on single (and often silly) criteria, like "my friends went there," "my father told me so," or "I liked the building" (these are real examples). We do not like to look silly; therefore, we (consciously or unconsciously) invent rational foundations for our behavior.

But could it be that we employ more reason in our decision-making when the stakes are high? A famous study by Danziger et al. (2011) shows that it is not. Judges represent the profession that relies (or *should* rely) the most on reason. This study researched the factors that influenced judges' decisions to say *yes* or *no* to inmates' requests to be released on parole. One would expect hard criteria to be employed: the gravity of the crime, the family status, and the length of the sentence already spent in prison. To the researchers' surprise, to the surprise of the judges themselves, and to outrage in public opinion, the most important criterion was how long had passed since the judges' last break. The benevolence peaked immediately after a break (an average of 65% of the cases received positive verdicts) and decreased to nearly zero positive rulings before the next break, only to rise back to 65% immediately after judges ate their breakfast and drank their coffee. This study shows that even experienced decision-makers are influenced, without being aware, by irrational factors.

Let me ask you again: What percentage of your business decisions is based on reason? Would you like to re-estimate your use of reason in business decision-making? Or will you stick with your original percentage? Our thinking and decision-making are prone to error, and the first important step is to acknowledge and accept this. Then, we can make better decisions after acquiring and using critical thinking skills and methods; a large part of this book deals with exactly that.

The other important section of this book discusses how we argue and persuade. New research proposes that the reason our neocortex is so large (as compared to our ape cousins) is not in order to facilitate better decision-making but to deal with increased cooperation and competition within and across groups. In plain English, we developed a large brain to better influence others. A hasty conclusion from this statement might be that a) we must be good at it and b) we persuade using mainly reason, as that is the work of a neocortex. Both these statements, if not wrong, at least convey an incomplete image of reality.

As we will discuss in a chapter devoted to the issue, humans are reluctant to change their minds. There are many psychological mechanisms at play, and we will further describe methods for overcoming each of them, but the reality is that most efforts of persuasion fail, at least initially. Research with functional MRI has even shown that attacking somebody's point of view creates the same reaction in the amygdala as an approaching tiger. As for whether we persuade using mainly reason, sound arguments are rarely used in commercial, political, or domestic attempts of persuasion, as one can freely see in advertising, in political campaigns, and in private quarrels. And, anyways, nobody persuades anybody else. When we are convinced and change our mind, we always convince ourselves; the others only provide context.

This book describes how simple changes of focus can make the difference in a pitch being accepted or rejected. An example is the following: When trying to persuade, people focus exclusively on reasons for a potential *yes*, while ignoring their counterpart's reasons for saying *no*. If I want to persuade you to buy a can of juice by showing that it is fresh, cold, and healthy, my plea will have no effect if you have no money or if you recently drank a carton of juice. A technique that deals with this aspect is described in the persuasion section, along with other useful tools and methods. This book also contains a chapter on the use of fair play in both decision-making and persuasion. I argue that fair play does more than making us sleep better at night; it increases our chances for good decisions and having more open-minded negotiation partners. For instance, the use of empathy and concession will increase your chances of success by conveying a more open-minded image of yourself.

We all think fairly effectively, and getting where each of us is today surely involved many good decisions, clever persuading, and fair leadership. However, even good things can be improved. This book organizes disparate knowledge, various management techniques, and concepts from different sciences into a coherent pathway toward a more efficient and purposeful managerial thinking.

References

Bauer, J. C., Schmitt, P., Morwitz, V. G., & Winer, R. S. (2012). Managerial decision making in customer management: Adaptive, fast and frugal? *Journal of the Academy of Marketing Science, 41*(4), 436–455. https://doi.org/10.1007/s11747-012-0320-7.

Busenitz, L. W., & Barney, J. B. (1997). Differences between entrepreneurs and managers in large organizations: Biases and heuristics in strategic decision-making. *Journal of Business Venturing, 12*(1), 9–30. https://doi.org/10.1016/s0883-9026(96)00003-1.

Danziger, S., Levav, J., & Avnaim-Pesso, L. (2011). Extraneous factors in judicial decisions. *Proceedings of the National Academy of Sciences, 108*(17), 6889–6892. https://doi.org/10.1073/pnas.1018033108.

Fodor, O. C., Curşeu, P. L., & Fleştea, A. M. (2016). Affective states and ecological rationality in entrepreneurial decision making. *Journal of Managerial Psychology, 31*(7), 1182–1197. https://doi.org/10.1108/jmp-07-2015-0275.

Haidt, J. (2013). *The righteous mind: why good people are divided by politics and religion* (Illustrated ed.). Vintage.

Simon, H. A. (1955). A behavioral model of rational choice. *the Quarterly Journal of Economics, 69*(1), 99. https://doi.org/10.2307/1884852.

The World Economic Forum. (2016). *The future of jobs*. https://reports.weforum.org/future-of-jobs-2016/

von Neumann, J., & Morgenstern, O. (1944). *Theory of games and economic behavior* Princeton University Press.

Wood, W., Quinn, J. M., & Kashy, D. A. (2002). Habits in everyday life: Thought, emotion, and action. *Journal of Personality and Social Psychology, 83*(6), 1281–1297. https://doi.org/10.1037/0022-3514.83.6.1281.

Part II
Critical Thinking in Business Decision-Making

3 Hidden Assumptions

False assumptions are the main cause of projects that fail. The problem is not that we cannot assess the assumptions as false, but that *we do not even realize we make them.* When presented with clearly articulated assumptions, managers are usually perfectly able to validate or reject them; the problem is that incorrect assumptions are hidden and usually pass unnoticed. A real-life example is the following: The decision, in an entrepreneurial company, to incentivize salespersons exclusively by commission (percentage of sales) led to sales agents working hard for only 3 weeks each month, until they reached a comfortable, self-set threshold income. The underlying (false) assumption that went unnoticed and unchallenged was that "a potentially unlimited income will motivate salespersons to maximize their effort." This chapter will discuss methods for identifying hidden, unvoiced assumptions behind business plans.

I will start with a short WWII story that illustrates how identifying false assumptions can even save lives. Abraham Wald was a Transylvanian-born genius in mathematics and statistics. Educated in Cluj and Vienna, he emigrated to the USA in 1938, fleeing the Nazis. During the war, he was part of the Statistical Research Group, a structure in the service of the US Army. One day, air force generals presented him with the task of calculating the optimum amount of armor for fighter planes. The generals observed that planes returning from battle had an unusual distribution of bullet holes: There were more bullet holes in the wings and the fuselage and fewer in the engines. As a result, they decided to add armor to the affected areas. The problem was that armor adds weight, so Wald was asked to calculate the optimal quantity of armor to be added to each area of the wings and the fuselage. After hearing the request, Wald said that he would not perform the calculation. What? Wait a minute! Why?

Question What made Abraham Wald refuse to calculate the thickness of armor for the wings and fuselage? Take a minute to come up with an answer before reading on.

R. Atanasiu, *Critical Thinking for Managers*, Management for Professionals,
https://doi.org/10.1007/978-3-030-73600-2_3

In fact, Wald did not say he would not do so; he famously replied that armor should not go where the bullet holes are; it should go where the bullet holes are not. Why? The air force officials built an action plan based on an assumption that passed unnoticed until Wald saw through it: that the planes they examined are a representative sample of all planes. They were not; they were the planes that *returned* from battle, which means that the affected areas (wings and fuselage) were not vital for flying. Missing from the sample were the planes that were shot down—such planes were usually shot in the engine, which is therefore where the armor should be added. Abraham Wald identified a false assumption, and this was crucial for changing the initial plan. Armor was added underneath the engines, and this saved the lives of many US pilots, making the statistician a war hero.

Note that the generals would have been perfectly able to correctly answer whether the returning planes were a representative sample or not. They would indeed have recognized the assumption as false, but they did not even realize they were making this assumption. The same danger lurks in managerial offices today: Managers, perfectly able to qualify an assumption as bad, build doomed plans on hidden false assumptions without even acknowledging their existence.

This chapter discusses the important step of identifying underlying assumptions in business plans: in those presented to us (in which cases we are better at spotting weak points), but most importantly, in our own plans.

Question Please think of a failed project that you know of. Can you identify the hidden false assumption that caused the failure? Think like this: "They/We initially thought that (insert hidden assumption). But after the project failed they/we realized that (insert why the assumption was false)."

What, then, is an assumption? In logic, an assumption is an unstated premise—one that is believed to be true—that supports a conclusion. We make assumptions every day, in trivial and important matters alike, in business or in our personal lives. We are aware of some of these unspoken beliefs, but most run under our radar, shaping our behavior and decisions without us even noticing. We often realize that we relied on a false assumption only when reality contradicts it, which is usually too late.

What about business assumptions? Present-day managers commonly have the skill to identify flawed assumptions in their business plans, but having a skill does not necessarily mean employing it. Being involved in several businesses, I can provide firsthand examples of ignored business assumptions that led to rather large failures. In each example below, the first sentence is the business decision made by a manager or a board and then, in brackets and italics, the assumption they relied upon unconsciously:

Examples Business is going well, so we will expand to City Y. (The project that eventually failed was based on the unidentified false assumption that *being successful in City X means that we will be successful in City Y as well.*)

We will move all our sales online. (The decision, eventually reversed, was based on the false hidden assumption that *customers will continue to buy our products even if we switch from selling them in-store to selling them online.*)
The business plan includes a financing round in October. (Most start-up business plans presented to investors mention the next round of funding in the spreadsheet. The round never happens at the time and the value predicted, as the founders unconsciously rely on an assumption that is usually wrong: *A venture capital (VC) fund will be interested in investing in a second round, and we will close this round by October.* An even harsher hidden assumption is that *this company will survive until October.*)
This year we will focus on consolidating and developing the platform. (In that board decision, the whole group ignored this assumption: *While we stop growing and concentrate only on consolidating the technical platform, the competition will relax and do nothing.* Obviously, the competition did not relax.)
It is time we increased salaries. (If the symptom is the lack of motivation, the hidden false assumption is that *increasing salaries will sustainably increase motivation.*)

All these assumptions passed unnoticed until reality contradicted them and made them obvious in hindsight. However, most of them, if acknowledged in time, could have been quickly dismissed as false by the managers, and the rest could have easily been tested. The trap lies, therefore, in the assumptions' inconspicuousness. The manager who decided to expand from City X to City Y did not question his assumption that the respective markets are similar because he was not aware of having it. The assumption was hiding somewhere in his mind, but from its hiding place, it was able to influence his decision-making. I asked him what would he have done if asked, before expanding, "Do you believe that the markets in these cities are similar?" He said that he most likely would have said *no* and, consequently, would have done some market research for City Y. He then said that he wishes someone did ask him that question. In City Y, after a sizable investment, he needed to close shop for a few months, scrap everything, and adapt the business model to the local market.

Question Do you have such assumptions in your business strategy? Is your latest plan free from untested, hidden misjudgments? What is an important assumption that you, your organization, or even your whole industry is not aware of holding? Please take a minute to think, identify the assumptions, and write them down.

In their bestseller *Super Thinking: The Big Book of Mental Models*, the authors Gabriel Weinberg and Lauren McCann identify five main assumptions that tech start-up founders make (Weinberg & McCann, 2019):

My team can build our product.

People will want our product.

Our product will generate profit.

We will be able to fend off competitors.

The market is large enough for a long-term business opportunity.

I will take this further. Each of these five main assumptions is based, in turn, on many more secondary assumptions. The assumption that *My team can build our product* is based on the following:

I can build a team.

I will know, when hiring, what to look for (skills and attitude) so that my team can build our product.

I will be able to pay them.

I am good at managing and motivating people.

My employees will not quit after 3 months.

My employees will not take my idea and their work to the competition.

... and so on.

If each main assumption is based on five secondary assumptions, then there are at least 25 make-or-break assumptions like the set above. These are assumptions that all start-up founders have and base their business plans on. Here, therefore, is my question: When start-up founders come whistling from the trade registry, after incorporating their new company, confident and smiling, how many of these 25 assumptions have passed through their minds? How many have been examined for at least 1 min? My guess is that, on average, the answer is less than 10.

There is a famous *bon mot* from Cicero: *epistula non erubescit*, meaning *the letter (paper) does not blush*. Cicero wanted to say that one can communicate more boldly in writing than face to face, but the saying was converted in management circles into *spreadsheets can endure anything*, meaning that the software does not protest if the business plan is not feasible. When the plan eventually fails, the cause is usually an unidentified false assumption at its foundation. But how is this possible? Most business plans contain a separate tab called *Assumptions*, so why does the existence of this tab not help unveil hidden flawed suppositions? (Fig. 3.1).

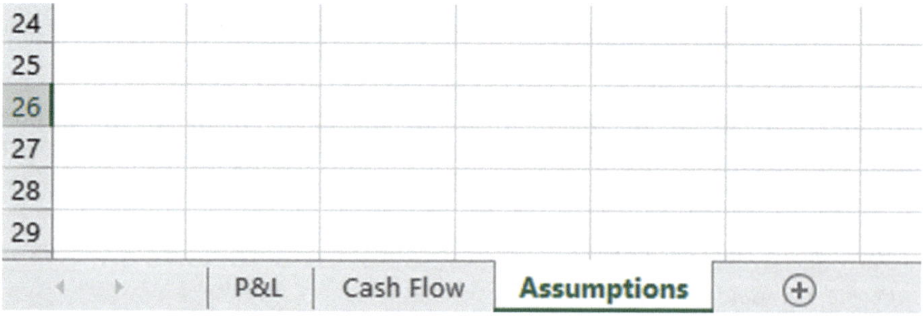

Fig. 3.1 Every business plan has an assumptions sheet

The answer is simple: We mainly fill the Assumptions tab with numbers, not sentences, including price estimates, timeline estimates, sales estimates, and growth estimates. Numbers are set here and then populate the other tabs of the business plan. Make-or-break assumptions, as those seen in the examples above, are not made of numbers, they are formulated in words. There is no number in *Customers will continue to buy our products even if we switch from selling it in-store to selling it online*. Word-based assumptions—written in clear, testable sentences with subject, predicate, and clear boundary conditions—are missing from the Assumptions tab. A potential solution for this conundrum could be to create two Assumption tabs in our business plans: one titled *Assumptions Numbers* and the other *Assumptions Words* (Fig. 3.2).

It is not easy to identify one's own hidden assumptions before it is too late. Still, techniques exist that can help:

1. *Talk to someone and make a list.* It sounds presumptuous to advise identifying hidden assumptions by making a list because them being hidden precisely means that they cannot be placed on a list. In a post on his blog, the psychologist Gary Klein —author of the bestseller "Seeing What Others Don't"—considers the effort to make an assumption list useless: "Some proponents of critical thinking have noticed how often people get trapped by flawed beliefs and recommend that decision-makers list all of their assumptions up front, in order to detect the faulty ones. I am not aware of any evidence that listing assumptions results in better reasoning, so I think this assumption-listing strategy is bad advice. Even worse, if the person is unaware of the assumptions—if they are hidden—then there is no way to list them" (Klein, 2013). In my experience, though, trying to make a list has two advantages: First, it makes us acknowledge that, indeed, there may be hidden assumptions in our plan; consequently, we become more likely to start looking for them. Second, writing things down is an exercise that helps shed light on our thinking, and this book will constantly recommend it. It seems that the top of each pen contains extra neurons, and each time we write things down they become better structured.

It should also be noted that the technique is not only to write the list; it also involves talking to someone. A conversation adds necessary triangulation to our perspective, and often we accomplish this even before the other has a chance to say anything by realizing—while we explain our point of view—that there may be a flaw in our thinking.

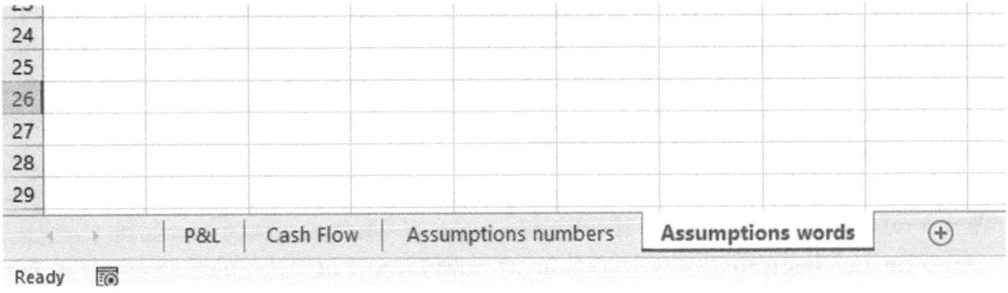

Fig. 3.2 We should introduce a separate sheet for make-or-break assumptions

The easiest way is to gather the project team around the table with the specific task of identifying hidden assumptions. If, however, the decision-maker is alone in this endeavor, then a board member, a colleague, a coach, or even a friend who is not involved in the business can be good discussion partners. If there is absolutely nobody to talk to, try to write in a journal or to think out loud. In my experience, talking to someone and making a list have worked in many instances. However, in cases of doubt, one can always employ the next method—*premortem*—invented by the same Gary Klein whom I have quoted earlier.

2. *Perform a premortem analysis.* We usually realize we were holding a false assumption when reality contradicts it, which is too late. In order to hack the timeline, we can imagine that we are already in the future (say, one year from now) and our plan has already failed. We next need to think of possible causes for the plan's failure. I have led premortems with numerous teams, and this process is indeed able to unveil hidden assumptions. It usually leads to *aha* moments. The process is performed immediately before the launch of the project, when all details of the plan are clear. It is done in a group—with the whole project team—and it usually takes less than two hours. The project manager assembles the team and proposes the following scenario: "It is a year from now and our project failed spectacularly. Why?" Then, each person writes down 2–5 potential causes of failure and the false assumptions that led to them. The project manager continues the process by asking all members to tell what they wrote, one assumption at a time, and aggregates them on a white board, clustered on two or three big topics. In the second part of the meeting, the assumptions that can be evaluated on the spot are discussed and validated or rejected, and various testing methods are proposed for the others; the plan is then adjusted accordingly. Let us work on an example—like all examples and case studies in this book, this scenario is fictional.

Case InterSites.fr, a French online publisher with 10 successful nationwide websites in https://www.merriamwebster.com/dictionary/website its portfolio, is looking to acquire the most popular restaurant review platform in Lyon, restos-a-lyon.fr. The purpose is to widen the existing spectrum of interests by including the food and drinks sector, in order to offer advertisers in this sector a suitable channel for their ads.

Lyon is regarded as the world capital city of gastronomy, and restos-a-lyon.fr has done a great job over the last 5 years of showcasing the best chefs, menus, and restaurants, mainly through the efforts and passion of its founder, Greg LaRoche. The 48-year-old Lyonnaise has developed the platform as a hobby while being a successful tax consultant. His reviews—based mainly on a mystery shopping technique—have gradually gained popularity, and the website has become important for food lovers choosing their place of indulgence, for restaurants aiming to attract new customers, and for the fragile egos of Michelin-starred chefs.

An offer has been made by InterSites.fr, and Greg LaRoche has accepted it. Mr. LaRoche told the acquiring company that he is not a good businessman (exemplified, according to him, by the total lack of advertising on his platform) and therefore leaves all transition plans to them. InterSites.fr, after internal discussions, decides to keep Mr. LaRoche involved only for the following year, but then to standardize the reviews and have them written by a team of freelancing contributors, in order to make the platform less personal and scalable at the national level in 2 years. A more commercial approach will also replace the general not-for-profit feeling of the site.

The publisher is represented in this deal by a team of four people, including the CEO, the new business manager, the CFO, and the future editor in chief of the site. The business plan has been crafted, and the numbers add up—even in the most pessimistic scenario, imagined after the company's experience with the other 10 websites. A GANTT chart is constructed for the integration of the site and then for the expansion at the national level. Everybody involved is excited to sign the deal and to add this valuable website to the portfolio. A few days before the signing is scheduled, the CEO assembles the team in a room and says: "I learned about this cool technique called *premortem.* Would you please do an imagination exercise with me? Let's suppose that this meeting is a year from now and we just had to close the website. Despite our initial confidence, our project went totally wrong: it was a huge failure. Does everyone visualize this situation? OK, now I want you to tell me what went wrong. What did we overlook? What assumptions did we make at the beginning that turned out to be false?"

After a minute or two, the editor- in chief is the first to offer an answer:

I think we assumed that even without the personal style of Mr. LaRoche, the content of the site would still appeal to its readers.

The new business manager then ventures his opinion:

We also assumed that the traffic numbers will stay high and even go up after we introduce advertising.

Question Before reading on, can you identify five more hidden assumptions in this plan?

Other potentially fatal assumptions identified by the team were the following:

We will be able to hire and train good food critics in all major French cities.
We will be able to ensure a consistently high quality for our standardized reviews.
We will be able to conquer new markets (in new cities) even without the charming style of Greg LaRoche.
The rebranding process will not fail (the site currently has "Lyon" in its name, unsuitable for scaling nationally).

The experience InterSites.fr has with its other 10 websites is relevant when planning for a gastronomic review platform.
Competitors such as Tripadvisor, where reviews are written by customers, not food critics, will not make the expert review system obsolete.
Advertisers will be happy to pay for ads, even if they might appear alongside bad reviews.
Mr. LaRoche will be motivated after signing the sale and will continue to write interesting reviews for another year.
Mr. LaRoche will not create another platform.
Proud Parisians will be happy to use a review platform that originated in Lyon.
A business model from the world capital city of gastronomy will work in other cities as well.

And, thus, the list went on. After gathering all the assumptions that could be challenged, the team decided to postpone the signing for a month to have time to analyze and test them all. The findings made them change the plan dramatically. Eventually, the publisher asked Mr. LaRoche to stay onboard as a minority shareholder, to continue writing reviews, and to help grow a network of independent restaurant-rating platforms all over France that only use the publisher as a sales agency.

Premortem can help a team identify and manage the hidden assumptions behind a project before the project is launched. The timeline trick—imagining that we are in the future and failure already occurred—helps members of the team spot and voice weaknesses that might not be uncovered if the question were "Why could this project fail in one year?" Despite its grim setting, the actual experience during a premortem is enjoyable and relaxed. Its inventor, Gary Klein, advises the manager who leads a premortem exercise to encourage all participants to voice their identified assumptions and to create a special prize for the most uncomfortable one (Klein, 2007).

Question Which of your projects in the making could benefit from a premortem?

3. *What would an investor say?* This technique is also applicable before the implementation of the project, and it can replace or complement a premortem analysis. Investors risk their money and are therefore forced to be skeptical and inquisitive when presented with a business idea. On many TV shows, start-up founders present their business plans to investors (in one notable case called "dragons") who, after intense and harsh scrutiny, might invest in those plans. The dragons are encouraged by TV producers to be skeptical, inquisitive, and doubtful. When you have planned a project in detail, a tool for identifying weak spots and hidden assumptions is to imagine you need to present it to someone like such dragons—intelligent and inquisitive people with a skeptical eye and a tendency to refuse. Imagining this situation and the questions these people might raise can uncover deeply hidden assumptions. If the plan is the result of teamwork, you can

design a group exercise. Instruct your team to act like ruthless investors and to ask questions about every aspect of the business plan while the project leader presents it in detail. The only condition is to have an open culture, where fear of failure is low and freedom to challenge the boss and the status quo is high. Of course, the role of the investor may be replaced with any other character that may legitimately question the project: What would the CEO/the board/the head of purchasing/the bank say? Let's practice with a realistic case.

Case The ecosystem of start-ups, angel investors, VC funds, pitches, accelerators, and incubators has grown extensively in Europe over the last years. The setting is a pitching session in Warsaw, Poland, where a series of start-ups each have 5 min to present their businesses. One of the start-ups is about an organic food store, Bionline. Please go through the presentation below, first imagining that you are the founder of Bionline. Knowing that you will present in front of investors, you scan the plan for hidden assumptions that may prove false and kill the business. Can you find any? Then imagine that you are an investor. Is it easier this time?

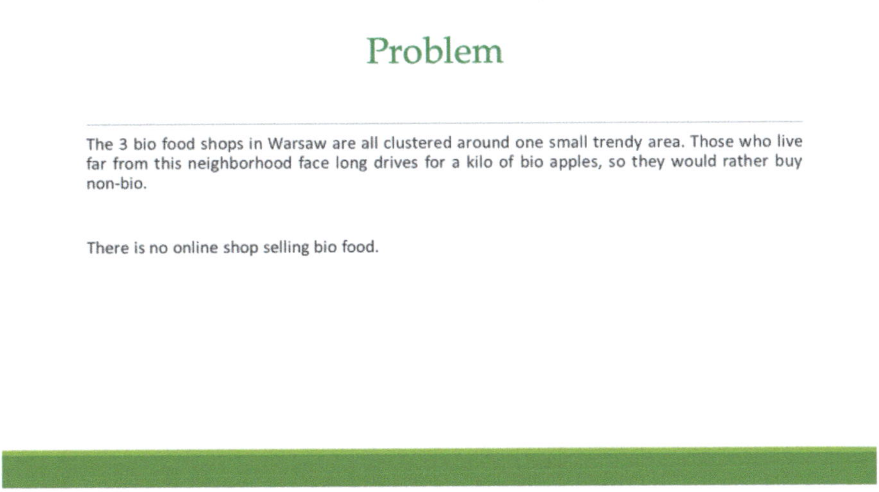

Solution

We have built a platform that connects bio farms from a 50 km radius around Warsaw with the increasing number of people interested in eating bio food.

Although this solution was not tested before in Poland, it is bound to work because it is already the default way of selling bio food in Western Europe and in the US.

Tech

We have used the latest programming language in building our platform, thus ensuring its quality, stability, and endurance.

Customers

We address young, college educated people, with a corporate job.

When we will make bio food accessible online, the long-drives problem will disappear, and people who prefer bio food will have no obstacle in buying it.

We will provide free transportation for first-time customers.

Current Status; Plans

We are in testing beta. We have 3 providers that help us test and we use our friends as paying customers. It is working well.

We plan the public launch for next September.

We had a poll (on the bionline Facebook page, 723 people answered it) and it suggests we concentrate on Warsaw for 2 years, until break even, and then expand to Krakow.

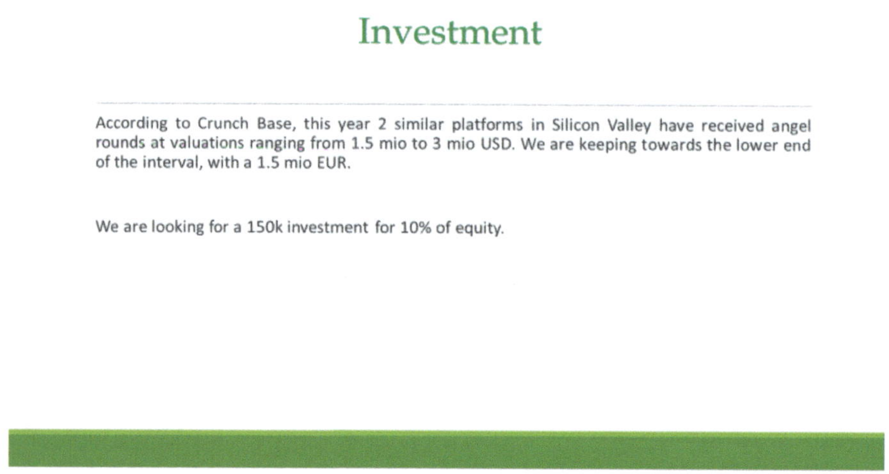

Well? How did you do? There are several assumptions that, if proven to be wrong, can kill the business. How many did you find? Please find some of them below:

Organic food can only be purchased in a specialized store or online. (In fact, there are many other places. For instance, most supermarkets have organic food corners.)

Distance is the only obstacle for buyers interested in organic food. (In fact, the largest obstacle is the high price.)

If it works in Western Europe and the US, it will work here as well. (Not necessarily; this assumption must be tested.)

The latest programming language ensures the quality of the platform. (In fact, the person coding it is a more significant factor.)

The main target audience consists of young, educated, corporate employers. (This must be tested. A more likely target audience is mothers.)

Free transport for the first order will make people buy again. (In fact, they may then be irritated that the transport is no longer free.)

It is wise to plan for the future of the business based exclusively on Facebook polls. (Upon seeing that slide, I—as an investor—would have left the room.)

The valuation of similar platforms in Silicon Valley can be applied to a Warsaw startup. (In fact, the markets differ in investment potential, in the purchasing power of clients, in the number of clients interested in organic food, in the quality of software developers, etc.*)*

Questions Did you identify some of these critical (and likely false) assumptions? Did you identify different ones? What perspective suited you better: that of the founder or that of the investor? What perspective will you use while scrutinizing your own projects?

4. *Look for early inconsistencies.* In contrast to the previous three methods—performed before implementing a certain plan—this technique is done after the implementation starts. Reality has the peculiar habit of contradicting our plans, and inconsistencies usually appear early on. But our instinct is to discard these early warnings by either explaining them away, normalizing them, or even ignoring them altogether.

Indeed, ignoring them altogether is the most encountered situation. People make plans but never expect things to turn out exactly as planned, so they usually say "OK, we budgeted based on 60 clients in the first 4 months. We actually only have 12, but, oh well, we will do better next quarter." Explaining them away would be an upgrade: "I guess the first months are harder, but we will soon recover." And a devious way to deal with inconsistencies is to normalize them without questioning: "OK, 60 divided by 12 is 5, so generally we must expect 20% of what we budgeted." A sad example of normalizing is illustrated by Maitlis and Christianson (2014) in their seminal paper on sensemaking: NASA experts discovered that the Columbia shuttle shed pieces of isolating foam every time it reentered the atmosphere. After several occurrences, instead of being investigated, this phenomenon was normalized: "OK, we know it sheds foam" and perception of risk diminished. This continued until 2003, when—after completing 27 flights—a large piece of foam fell from an external tank and damaged the wing, leading to the disintegration of the shuttle and the death of its seven astronauts.

The key is to always try to explain early inconsistencies and to do so actively. If clients on your e-commerce platform stop halfway through the buying process, avoid saying, "oh, so that's where they always stop, when we have them fill in their details"! Have some friends try the process, go through it yourself, or identify clients who abandoned halfway and ask them why, you may find out that people are usually reluctant to fill in their card details before making any purchase. You can then eliminate that step and, at first purchase, when it feels normal to be asked for card details, ask them whether they want to add the card as default.

Obviously, the four methods described above are not the only ways managers can scan their projects for flawed hidden assumptions. The inclination to discover hidden assumptions behind our plans is as important as the method we choose. This inclination must fight our irrational tendency for overconfidence. Most of the times, questioning our plans feels uncomfortable because we have already invested effort, time, and other resources in creating them. This is a side effect of a cognitive bias called *sunk cost*, which I describe in detail in a future chapter. The key here is to purposefully step (for a short while) outside our comfort zone and scrutinize our plans for questionable assumptions using one of the techniques described above or simply common sense.

I will conclude this chapter by repeating that false assumptions are the main cause of projects that fail and that the problem is not that we cannot assess the assumptions as false but that *we do not even realize we make them.* Actively looking for hidden assumptions is therefore a skill that any manager should develop. After identifying assumptions, they must be tested. The next chapter discusses how managers can test their assumptions.

References

Klein, G. (2007). Performing a project Premortem. *Harvard Business Review, 85*(7), 131–132

Klein, G. (2013, October 29). Hidden assumptions. *Psychology Today*. https://www.psychologytoday.com/intl/blog/seeing-what-others-dont/201310/hidden-assumptions-0

Maitlis, S., & Christianson, M. (2014). Sensemaking in organizations: taking stock and moving forward. *Academy of Management Annals, 8*(1), 57–125. https://doi.org/10.5465/19416520.2014.873177

Weinberg, G., & McCann, L. (2019). *Super thinking: The big book of mental models*. Portfolio.

Test Your Business Assumptions 4

The last chapter helped us identify (and write down) hidden assumptions in our business plans. What then? What should we do with them? When written down, some assumptions are easy to evaluate (whether they are wrong or not) by a manager with some experience and common sense. Most assumptions, however, need to be tested. From focus groups and surveys to A/B testing, evidence-based management uses the tools of the scientific method to empirically discover which assumption is solid and which is not. Often, managers are late to realize that they need to test their business assumptions, if they ever do.

Proceeding to a plan based on untested assumptions can have dire managerial consequences, as in the example below, inspired by a real case:

Case Despite its solid business model, an entrepreneurial company had cash flow problems because most of its clients paid with a delay of a week to a month after the due date of the invoice. As the company paid all its suppliers on time, the involuntary credit to clients created a need for a cash buffer that induced financing costs and other inconveniences. More importantly, the owner and CEO of the company felt great discomfort in being paid late. He had the sales department investigate the matter, so a few senior salespeople asked their clients what situations caused them to pay late. They discovered that the clients had cash flow issues of their own, which they chose to solve by not paying their suppliers on time, especially when the paying terms were short. As the company's standard paying term was 30 days, the CEO thought that it was better to align with the market and modified it to 60 days. He hoped that the few clients who paid on time would continue to pay within the original 30 days and that the others, if not paying earlier, would finally be within the provision of the contract and would at least appreciate the gesture.

R. Atanasiu, *Critical Thinking for Managers*, Management for Professionals,
https://doi.org/10.1007/978-3-030-73600-2_4

A few months after the change was implemented, the CEO was puzzled to see that things did not go at all as he expected. The clients who were usually late continued to be late, despite the double payment term. And now they were late by more days! Nobody appreciated the gesture, and the clients who paid on time continued to pay on time but just before the new 60-day due date. In the end, the move incurred significant costs and problems for the company. The CEO tried to return to the initial 30-day policy, but that proved to be much harder than the move in the opposite direction. He then realized that he should have tested his assumptions with a small number of clients or, even simpler, by analyzing the situation in the market.

Based on this case, in 2016, a group of MBA students conducted a small piece of research and analyzed payment data in companies from seven industries in Romania. They split payment due dates into three categories—0–7 days, 8–30 days, and more than 30 days—and analyzed the payment delays by category. In accordance with the case described above, they discovered that the time periods correlated positively: The shortest due date (1 week) incurred 2 late days on average, the medium one (8–30 days) incurred 7 late days on average, and the longest terms (more than 30 days) incurred—on average—10 late days, supporting the counterintuitive hypothesis that the longer the due date, the longer the delay in payment. The small study, done by five students as an MBA assignment in less than 2 weeks, could have been done—with little effort—by the CEO in the original case.

However, most managers do not have an instinct for testing; they trust their intuition a little too much. This chapter is meant to groom our instinct for testing. Evidence-based management—taking after its precursor, evidence-based medicine—is in fact an attitude guided by the intellectually humble principle "I could be wrong." There are two situations in which testing is especially beneficial: (a) when we think we know exactly how to solve a problem and (b) when we have no idea, so we spend valuable time agonizing over multiple alternatives.

Often, managers rush to apply a solution to a problem they do not understand well. This is a description of the *plunging-in bias*, a systematic error in problem solving and a bias that characterizes many experienced managers. It is especially encountered in entrepreneurs. Experience-based intuition is a valuable tool for any manager, but it cannot compensate for the complete lack of rational analysis. I suspect we have all met the proverbial all-knowing boss who tells you how a problem can be solved even before you finished the sentence describing it. But we also do this ourselves, without realizing. We all are, from time to time, the all-knowing boss, and we often plunge in with a solution long before completely understanding the problem, let alone gathering more data, finding alternatives, or testing. We just do not realize when we do this.

The opposite situation to the plunging-in bias is often encountered in group decision-making, when an urgent problem is over-discussed. This can also happen in individual decision-making, especially with managers who are naturally over-analytical. The key, in both group and individual settings, is the same: to test early. An entrepreneur I interviewed as part of my research developed his own rule against over-analyzing: "Just do it! When I see we are trapped in sterile discussions, I move to piloting the project. I know that I'm naturally oriented toward double-checking and spreadsheet analyses, so this rule helps me change my approach." To avoid over-thinking, managers should establish a clear timeline from the beginning, allocate a limited period for analysis, and move rapidly toward testing the proposed solutions. Testing is therefore the answer to both these opposite attitudes: the plunging-in bias and over-thinking. Evidence-based management uses experiments to prevent errors that may happen when we act too soon or when we tend to over-analyze.

So, how do we test a project? The worst way to do so is by implementing it. If you thought that a specialty coffee shop at the corner of your office building would be a successful venture, don't test that assumption by opening the shop! There are plenty of rapid and cheap tests that one can do. For instance, you can ask your colleagues about their coffee-drinking habits. You can survey, at the main entrance, people who go out in search of coffee and compare them to those who just use the office coffee machine. You can analyze other office buildings and the location of other specialty coffee shops. With proper permits, you can organize a free coffee-tasting day in the lobby—by bringing in a barista and a professional espresso machine—and see whether it generates a long queue or almost no interest. You can even put a fake sign on the door advertising a new coffee shop and see how many people want to go in. Do not sign the lease, buy equipment, decorate, and hire people based solely on assumptions! Test!

All the critical assumptions that are identified before a project is launched should be subject to investigation. Some may be solved with less than formal testing. For instance, many assumptions behind your plan to open a specialty coffee shop might be illuminated after talking to an owner of such a shop. A more reliable method is to find, analyze, and understand base rates in your domain. What is success in the coffee shop industry? Is it the number of people served a day, the average ticket, the total profit? Or is it how many such shops survive or for how long? Gathering this kind of data is not difficult, and combined with the humility to accept that we are similar to others, analyzing base rate data gives a good idea about the future of a project.

But the best way to build on solid ground is to perform actual experiments, like scientists in white laboratory coats. For millennia, humanity validated knowledge with arguments from authority. However, based on principles from Aristotle, the Western world began—during the Renaissance—to use another, more-precise tool for validating beliefs: the scientific method.

The scientific method is based on curiosity and on the human instinct to infer causality. It works according to a few standard steps:

1. *Make observations.* For example, a manager in an online retail shop might observe that accessories for gaming are often ordered as single items, while books are usually part of a larger basket.
2. *See a pattern.* After focusing attention on this issue, the manager discovers that, generally, tech items are often ordered one at a time, while non-tech items are often sold together.

3. *Formulate a hypothesis* or several competing hypotheses. The manager thinks about these patterns and comes up with two possible explanations: (a) Tech items are more expensive, and clients might prefer buying expensive merchandize as single items, or (b) tech items are mostly bought by young people, who are less organized, while non-tech items are purchased by older people who try to optimize transport by bundling them together. When about to be tested, an assumption becomes a hypothesis. Therefore, we might say that the manager now has two competing hypotheses.
4. *Design and conduct an experiment.* For instance, the manager can look at past sales and see whether the number of items in a basket correlates with price, with the buyer's age, or perhaps with both.
5. *Evaluate the results* of the experiment and accept the hypothesis as theory or reject the hypothesis and think of a better one. In our case, let's say that the manager observes a clear correlation between the number of items and the age of the buyer but no significant correlation with individual prices or total basket price. She might, then, validate the second hypothesis as her working theory and act accordingly.

As we will discuss further below, neither a scientific theory (published in a peer-reviewed journal) nor a working theory inferred by a manager after some observations and a rudimentary test is set in stone; they are both, however, very useful pieces of information. As Weick (1995) beautifully put it, "a good theory explains, predicts, and delights." The working theory in our example above explains why tech items are usually bought as single items. It predicts that the age-related behavior applies beyond the tech/non-tech items, which may prompt the manager to minimize logistic efforts by nudging younger customers to bundle things together in a larger basket. As for the delight, scientific theories (and indeed our day-to-day inferences on the world) often have elegance, symmetry, and wit.

The core of the scientific method is the experiment. Management is a good playground for experimenting because, perhaps after medicine, it is the field where testing yields the most benefit. Managers, however, are less inclined to put their assumptions to the test, compared to doctors and healthcare researchers. This is caused by a multitude of factors:

First of all, healthcare is a kinder learning environment than business. In his 2001 book *Educating Intuition*, the cognitive psychologist Robin Hogarth introduces two types of learning environments: A *kind learning environment* is more stable, has repeating patterns, and provides rapid and accurate feedback; a *wicked learning environment* is fast-changing, patterns are not obvious, and feedback is late or inaccurate (Hogarth, 2001). Kind learning environments enable better prediction and therefore tests are more useful in planning conduct, whereas prediction in wicked environments is trickier, with tests of past or current behavior providing less reliable information for future performance (as investment funds are eager to inform you in small print). From a simplistic view, while doctors are more confident that a treatment documented to work against a disease in the past will continue to do so, managers are right to doubt that past business models will continue to yield profit in the future.

A second reason is that medicine is more regulated, so results from healthcare research are systematically adopted in practice more often, whereas best practices supported by management research are seldom adopted on a wide scale, with fads being more influential than research.

A third factor is psychological and is mentioned above: Managers are often trapped by their overconfidence in experience-based intuition. Doctors sometimes fall prey to the same affliction; in business, however, self-doubt is *rara avis*.

The following are two paragraphs on epistemology, for the philosophy-oriented manager. The principle behind the scientific method is induction, a reasoning method that derives, from observations, general principles of how the world works. Here is an example: A girl goes to the park and sees older people playing chess. She is fascinated by their concentration and starts observing the game without knowing anything about it. After a while, she realizes that there is a set of rules and decides to infer them. She sees the pawn moving forward one step at a time and thinks she has figured out the rule, until the pawn moves diagonally to capture another piece. "Oh!," she thinks, "the pawn can move one step forward and, when it captures, one step diagonally ahead." But after a game is finished and the players start a new one, she sees the pawn moving two steps from its original position, so she updates the rule to include this. After watching a few more games, she is certain that she has inferred the correct rule about the movements of the pawn until one player gets one of his pawns to the opposite end of the board and promotes it to be queen or bishop or any other piece. And the rule changes again. Science does the same thing: It tries to infer the rules of the universe by observation and then updates its theories after additional observations. I use this chess example because the famous physicist Richard Feynman used a similar analogy to explain science: It is as if the universe is a giant game of chess played by the gods, and scientists try to infer the rules of the game just by watching. However, for chess, there is a known set of rules, and the girl in our example can discover how the pawn moves simply by asking one of the players or by reading the rules of chess. Unfortunately, the universe did not come with a written set of rules, and that is why theories are never certain knowledge. A new event, a new method of investigation, or a new insight might update or replace a theory, like Einstein's theory of relativity did with Newton's law of general attraction.

Humankind has derived most of its knowledge by induction, but after we started using the scientific method, our collective knowledge increased dramatically. Based on scientific discoveries, we trust the plane to fly through the air, the aspirin to make a headache go away, and light to appear at the flick of a switch. However, philosophers discovered a logical fracture in the use of induction. The *problem of induction*, popularized by the philosopher David Hume, is that induction is based on two assumptions: that the universe does indeed have a set of rules, and that these rules are uniform in time (the rules don't change overnight) and space (rules in Paris, in Japan, and in another galaxy are the same). These principles may seem obvious and true. The problem is that we have learned them inductively, through observation. Briefly, the problem of induction is that—for it to work—the principles behind it must work as well, and those principles work only if induction works, forming a fallacious circular argument: induction works because induction works. This philosophical conundrum does not stop philosophers, though, from boarding planes, taking aspirin, or using electric light. I hope, then, that the philosopher-managers will also ignore the problem of induction and will test their assumptions.

So, after this short philosophical detour, let us return to our experiments. In order to minimize selection bias and confirmation bias, the clinical trials necessary for introducing a new medication are randomized, controlled, and double-blind, which means that patients are selected and assigned randomly to treatment or control conditions and that the medical personnel who administer the drug and the patients do not know whether they are giving (or receiving) the actual medication or placebo. Should business experiments follow the same standardized structure? Perhaps not, but in order to avoid inferring the wrong conclusion, the basic principles of scientific experimentation should be applied to business experimentation, as well: We need a testable hypothesis, two clear variables, two groups (or more if, for instance, we need to try out a series of prices), and a proper test design that limits bias. Let's examine a case study to see how these principles apply.

Case You run a Volvo car dealer, and your strategy is to direct your marketing efforts toward people that already own a Volvo because you are convinced that Volvo owners are an easier target. You do not base this belief on any data; it is just a gut feeling and it works. You use direct emails to previous customers, offer drive tests to people bringing their car in for service, and so on. Your message is not focused on the benefits of owning a Volvo (because the customers are aware of these) but on new features and discounts. The fact that you limit your own market bothers you a little, but you stick to what you do best. Things are going well, but your whole strategy is based on a hunch and on habit. The hunch may be correct, but to what extent? And what if it is not?

Then, after reading this book, you decide to put your assumption to the test. You want to know if owners of old Volvos are really the better target, and, if so, how much better. You are in luck: Your cousin, who also runs a car shop in the same town—an Audi one—is a statistics freak. He always gathers data and loves analyzing them. You give him a call, and he agrees to give you some help in designing and implementing an experiment to test your hypothesis. He also offers access to his database of Audi clients (OK, let us assume this happens in a GDPR-free parallel universe). How should you test your assumption that Volvo owners are an easier target?

Let's take the elements above in order of mention:

1. *A testable hypothesis.* The assumption in need of testing, "Volvo owners are an easier target," is not yet well articulated. Often, a theory states that *X* influences *Y* in certain ways, under certain conditions. For instance, in our hypothetical example with the online retailer, young age influences clients to buy single items. Therefore, we need a hypothesis that clearly states such a relationship between two variables. We also need to be able to measure them. In order to be tested, a general proposition such as "exercising increases happiness" needs to be operationalized into the hypothesis "30 min of daily moderate exercise increases self-reported happiness as measured using the Subjective Happiness Scale." In our Volvo case, "Volvo owners are an easier target" is not clear and definitely not testable. For instance, if I define "easier target" as "more open to my commercial messages," I might test this through email opening rate, but that might not help me sell more cars. In the sense of the Volvo shop owner, a clear and testable hypothesis would be the following:

   Volvo owners are more likely to be convinced to buy a new Volvo than people who own other brands.

2. *Two clear and measurable variables.* In any experiment, we investigate whether an independent variable *X* influences a dependable variable *Y*. The latter is called dependent because it depends on the former. The easier way to picture the relationship is through a system of rectangular (Cartesian) axes, on which the independent variable is depicted on the horizontal axis, 0*X*, and the dependent variable is depicted on the vertical axis, 0*Y*.
   It is important to identify which variable in your hypothesis is independent and which is dependent, as this will influence the treatment group selection (see below). Sometimes, this is not clear. A classic case is with the relationship between price and supply or demand. Although price is intuitively perceived as the influencer in these relationships, it is traditionally depicted on the 0*Y*-axis. Economists still debate whether—in the case of demand, for example—markets respond to price or marketeers price items as a function of demand. However, in our case, the clear independent variable is the current car (Volvo or not) and the dependent variable is the probability of being convinced to buy a new Volvo. We need to show whether the first influences the second.

   Independent variable: owning a Volvo
   Dependent variable: buying a Volvo

3. *Control group and treatment group(s).* The next items in our experiment kit are the groups. If we were to return to the online retailer example, it is not sufficient to measure and discover that 60% of customers aged 16–24 buy single items. In order to understand the influence of age on the size of the basket, we need to compare that figure with other age segments. In pharmaceutical research, we cannot say that medication M against the common cold is effective after knowing that 60% of the people who took it showed an improved condition after

5 days; we need to compare that with people who did not take anything. That is why researchers need to form two groups: the treatment group, made up of people who receive the medication, and the control group, made up of people who instead of the medication receive placebos: identical pills without the active substance. In some cases—for example, when we test several prices for a product—we will have a treatment group for each price and perhaps the current price as control. The groups are always selected based on the independent variable (in our examples, "taking the medication," "age," "having a Volvo"). One of the major mistakes in experimental design is selecting the groups on the dependent variable. In our case, that would mean making a group of people who buy a new Volvo and another of people who buy another brand and seeing how many of each previously owned a Volvo. The even greater mistake would be to solely look at people who, this time around, buy a Volvo. After seeing that, for example, only 25% of these previously owned the same brand, it would be wrong to conclude that it is better to address people who never owned a Volvo before. We will discuss selection bias and other testing mistakes further below. In our case, we must select two groups based on the independent variable (owning or not a Volvo). For reliability, the two groups should be very similar in all other aspects (size, gender distribution, age, socioeconomic condition, etc.). If, for instance, we decide to form a 1000-person treatment group of people who own a Volvo using the shop's email database, we must convince our cousin to help us with a control group of 1000 Audi owners from his database and make sure that the two groups do not differ significantly in any other aspect.

Treatment group: 1000 Volvo owners from Volvo shop email database
Control group: 1000 Audi owners from the Audi shop email database

4. *Test design.* Once we have a clear and testable hypothesis (of course, we might have several competing hypotheses), measurable variables, and the groups, we need to decide how to test the relationship. Most people, when they see such a situation, propose a survey. The problem with surveys was pinpointed by the "father of advertising" himself, David Ogilvy. In his book *Confessions of an Advertising Man,* Ogilvy wrote that "the problem with market research is that people don't think how they feel, they don't say what they think, and they don't do what they say" (Ogilvy & Parker, 2012) making survey results three times removed from actual behavior. Another solution people may propose to this problem is a proxy: another behavior that correlates with the one we are trying to measure, for instance, the number of people who would sign up for a test drive as a proxy for how many will buy the car. But one important error in experimenting is measuring the wrong behavior. For instance, if one tries to measure whether working out increases productivity, counting people who have a gym membership as people who work out is not reliable, as many people are members of a gym but do not go. For this reason, surveys and proxies should only be used when we cannot measure the actual behavior. If we want to know how many people will buy a car, then that is what we should aim to measure.

How can we set up an experiment to induce people to buy a Volvo? The easiest way is to use back data—if we have access to it. But let us pretend that the two sets of data available do not include the car previously owned, giving rise to the following live experiment.

One idea would be to organize an event—for instance, an open-doors day—during which interested customers can eventually buy a car. If we were to use the launch of a specific Volvo model (for instance, a new 4 × 4), this would bias the experiment by eliminating potential buyers interested in other classes. The selected event could have professional drivers emphasizing novel features of the car (such as the pedestrian and cyclist detection with auto braking), a test drive to get to know the car, and a special discount for people who decide to buy that very day. The invitation should be sent to the treatment group (1000 emails sent to Volvo owners) and also to the control group (1000 emails sent to a similar group of Audi owners). The same discount of, for instance, 10% should be advertised in these emails. As most car owners don't wear T-shirts emblazoned with the logo of their car, the discount code could vary in the two groups—perhaps starting with an "A" in the control group and with a "V" in the treatment group—in order to measure accurately. These two groups will, then, be subject to the usual persuasion methods mentioned above and will receive an offer some cannot refuse. By measuring and comparing the number of Volvo owners and Audi owners that end up buying a new Volvo, the experiment could support or invalidate the hypothesis. Let us suppose that, out of the 1000 emails, you observe that 630 were opened by Volvo owners and 425 by Audi owners. This is a normal finding, given that people would rather open an email from the brand they own and the dealer they know. On the day of the event, the number of Volvo owners who attended—87—is more than double compared to the 42 Audi owners in the control group. Finally, we count the sales of a new Volvo car: 16 to Volvo owners and 12 to Audi owners. As predicted, Volvo owners were more likely to be persuaded to buy a new model than people who own other brands. All the numbers are in Table 4.1. At first glance, the experiment has confirmed the hypothesis, and therefore the owner of the car dealership should continue to base his market approach on it.

However, if we look more closely, the case is not clear. One of the benefits of experimenting is discovering unexpected things. The reality is significantly more complex than we imagine and model; therefore, any richer contact with it conveys a richer understanding. Especially when we try to understand our clients, sitting at the office and reading surveys is not the best tool. Clients must be engaged as often as possible, and testing is a perfect opportunity to do so. After our imaginary experiment, a superficial

Table 4.1 Preliminary results of the Volvo experiment. The number of cars sold (in bold) seems to confirm the hypothesis

	Treatment group (Volvo)	Control group (Audi)
Emails	1000	1000
Opened emails	630	425
Visited the shop	87	42
Sold	**16**	**12**

manager would have validated the hypothesis (although not by such a wide margin) and continued his approach. However, after analyzing the results, our more inquisitive character understands two things. The first is obvious: The manager's approach of addressing only Volvo owners leaves money on the table, as the other side of the market has clear potential. The second conclusion is less obvious: We need to calculate a ratio—the in-store conversion rate, inserted in Table 4.2:

By looking at things from this perspective, the car dealer understands that the two groups are really different: The non-Volvo owners in the control group are 50% more likely to buy a model *after they visit the shop*. Well, that is quite a finding! After validating it with further tests (and perhaps another composition of the control group), our manager plans to change his approach completely. Aside from allocating part of his budget and effort to address people who are not yet Volvo customers, he realizes that one key element in increasing sales is to increase the number of people visiting the car dealership, especially if they are not familiar with the Volvo brand. He could do that, for instance, by placing a large outdoor sign on the main road, in front of the store, to communicate interesting events and activities for the whole family.

What can we learn from this? First, that testing usually unveils a reality that is more complex than what we expected, especially about client behavior. Second, and more generally, we should always clarify the conditions for the test to succeed and to fail. How many times more Volvo owners than Audi owners need to buy the new model for me to maintain my assumption? What should the proportion be to change it? Generally, before any test, we need to set a clear threshold for accepting the hypothesis and a clear one for rejecting it. The two thresholds can be different.

Other interesting elements of the models we create by experimenting are mediators and moderators. Sometimes, researchers identify mediators and moderators in their relationships; businesspeople should account for these in their testing. A mediator is an intermediate variable, Q, that mediates the relationship between X and Y. It may be that X does not *directly* influence Y, but X influences Q and Q influences Y. For instance, we might discover that exercise increases productivity, but on closer inspection realize that happiness is the mediator: Exercise increases happiness and, in turn, being happy makes you more productive. Another mediator for this relationship might be health. People who exercise are healthier, which results in them taking fewer days off, which in turn increases their productivity.

Table 4.2 Results of the Volvo experiment, including in-store conversion rate (also in bold), which gives a different perspective on the results

	Treatment group (Volvo)	Control group (Audi)
Emails	1000	1000
Opened emails	630	425
Visited the shop	87	42
Conversion (in-store) (%)	**18.4**	**28.6**
Sold	**16**	**12**

A moderator is a context-related variable that influences the relationship. It is often a boundary that characterizes the context and the conditions of the relationship. For instance, the online retail manager in our earlier example might initially find that young people aged between 16 and 24 do not differ in the number of items in the basket from other age groups. However, if she separates the young age segment by gender, she might see that boys 16–24 almost exclusively buy single items, while girls almost always buy more than four items—perhaps because boys mainly buy gaming accessories, while girls frequently buy clothes. In this case, gender is a moderator that conditions the influence of young age on the size of the basket, and the manager should discover it in order to figure out who to nudge and how. In our Volvo case, there are no striking mediators or moderators, but it is important to be aware of them.

Testing business assumptions does not always resemble a pharmaceutical experiment, especially when the behavior to be tested happens online. Online platforms use a method called A/B testing to constantly improve their structure and processes. The position, shape, and color of all the virtual buttons that are so familiar, from the Facebook *Like* button to the Google *Search* button, are the result of millions of tests, as are the positions and sizes of ads, the design of card detail requests, newsletter subscriptions offers, and the various prices for online services. Many million-people treatment groups are exposed to a wide spectrum of imperceptibly different shades of blue each day to help decide the color of a header. It is interesting to think, when buying a book on Amazon, that you may—right then—be part of a planetwide experiment in which countless groups are exposed to various fonts that read “Buy now with 1-Click” or “Buy now with 1 Click” or “Buy now with 1 click” or “Buy now with one click” or “Buy now with one-click” on various shades of brownish orange. Dan Siroker writes a particularly interesting account of the power of A/B testing. On his company’s blog (Siroker, 2010), he remembers that —as Director of Analytics for the Obama 2008 Campaign—one of his jobs was to optimize the number of people signing up on the campaign Web site, as most sign-ups ended in donations, with each sign-up contributing an average donation of 21 US dollars. For this, he and his team needed to decide what elements to use on the landing page: the media in the middle (they hesitated between six options: three pictures and three videos) and the call-to-action button (four options), making a total of 24 combinations. The team had a clear preference, but they wisely used Google Website Optimizer to run a parallel A/B test (actually an A/X test with all 24 combinations). The results came in: The combination that users favored was not the same as the one the team favored, but a black-and-white photograph of the Obama family and a button saying, “Learn more.” Extrapolating the difference between the tested option and the team’s favorite to the whole campaign, 2,880,000 more people signed up, resulting in an additional USD 60 million in donations. A/B testing may have helped significantly in electing Barack Obama to the White House.

Other online testing methods are even more interesting. For instance, new lines of online business can be tested with a landing page. If we wonder if our future online organic food shop has potential clients, we can set a landing page with the logo and the promise that the shop will arrive there in *X* months, but until then, interested clients can subscribe to a newsletter. If after one week you have 10 subscribers, perhaps it would be better to give up on the idea. A clever way to test the need for an online service is to make a *Wizard of Oz* test by setting up a platform that delivers the service (let's say to find the best restaurants in an area based on your given preferences), but that instead of an algorithm uses real people to deliver the answer. An example would be the launch—in 2010—of CardMunch, a smartphone app that digitized business card information from snapshots. As opposed to competitors, CardMunch used people on MTurk who could transcribe blurry photographs better than any recognition algorithm. Clients were happy with the accurate, but rather slow service, and increased in numbers, paying for the development of an automated algorithm. The company was later acquired by LinkedIn. This method is called *Wizard of Oz* as a homage to the famous character who performed his magic tricks from behind a screen.

Business experiments can be misleading if we do not perform them right. There are a lot of mistakes one can make while designing and performing a test. The most common ones are listed below:

Selecting on the dependent variable and the lack of a control group. If the selection of groups is done on the dependent variable, the results will say nothing useful. However, in most cases, they will not look abnormal and will therefore be misleading. A classic example is an article in The Economist (2003) in which its authors concluded that risk-taking leads to business success by looking at successful companies. The most significant mistake is to select according to the dependent variable without having a control group. If we want to see whether a call is more likely to end in a sale than an email, we should not look just at closed sales (which is just one group, wrongly selected on the dependent variable), observe that 30% started with an email and 70% with a call, and infer that calls are more likely to cause a sale than email. A good illustration of how this is wrong is the following: After checking the interactions that led to failed attempts to sell, I might find that 80% of those started with a call. Another illustration is this: 100% of successful sales started with a "Hello!." That does not mean that the greeting itself led to the successful sale. I should select based on the independent variable, look at a group of discussions that started with an email versus another group of discussions that started with a call, and compare the percentage of success in both groups. Control groups—or, if we cannot assemble one, base rates—offer a very necessary perspective. Base rates are statistical averages of the market that are often public data (if one searches long enough) or can be inferred from public data.

Ignoring alternative hypotheses or key variables. If the online store manager only thought of item prices as influencing the number of items in the basket, she would not reach a useful conclusion. If I want to test the influence of discount on ice-cream sales and I choose to test on the first hot day of summer, I might validate the wrong hypothesis.

Having samples that are too small or not representative. Confirmation bias is irrational and cannot be detected by the person who falls for it. We are inclined to admit any flimsy proof as evidence for what we want to believe, such as "the first client who tried the new service was thrilled," although a single client is insufficient for drawing any conclusion, especially if she is our friend or if she received the new service for free. That is why we need to establish, before testing, clear thresholds for the size of the sample and—as mentioned before—for the findings.

Looking just for confirming evidence. This is confirmation bias again. The philosopher of science Karl Popper stressed that the difference between science and pseudoscience is that for scientific theories, there is always a way to check if they might be wrong. This is called falsifiability or refutability. Popper urges scientists to design experiments that try to disconfirm—instead of confirming—their hypotheses. If my hypothesis is that all swans are white, an experiment that tries to find more white swans (one or a thousand) does not help to strengthen the theory. What a scientist must do is to strive to find a different-colored swan. We must apply the same principle to business testing. One of the most important ways to do that is by avoiding slanted questions such as "How much did you enjoy your stay?" or "How useful is this online tool in your activity?" Better questions are "Did you enjoy your stay in our hotel? What went well and what can we improve?" and "Did you use our online tool in your activity? In what situation? Did it work?".

Measuring the wrong behavior. As mentioned above, if we can measure physical activity directly, we should not count gym memberships. If we can measure car sales directly, we should do so and not use a proxy such as the number of people registered for a test drive. Still more dangerous is to measure a misleading activity. For instance, we may want to measure the interest in a new service. We publish on our Web site a phone number that potential customers can call and inquire about the new service, and we count the number of calls. But that would be misleading if the number is also used for complaints or inquiries about our other services and we cannot differentiate and count these aside.

Not assigning conditions randomly. If we test two prices for a product, we should make two (or three groups, with the current price as control) and measure sales. However, the groups should not differ in any other way. We should not test one price in one part of the country and another one in another, as the results will be influenced by local specifics. We should assign conditions to groups built randomly with customers from all regions.

In conclusion, although managers are not naturally inclined to test their assumptions, testing can provide a good basis for their decisions. Even if business experiments do not require double-blind random control testing, we should always consider the possibility that our assumptions might be wrong and test them somehow. We can employ more elaborate experiments, such as in the Volvo case described in this chapter, or we can just do a pilot study (implement the changes for just one customer or just one day), start small, go out and speak to our clients, or analyze base rates. Intellectual humility—the constant entertaining of the possibility that we are wrong—is a crucial quality for today's managers and leaders.

References

Hogarth, R. M. (2001). *Educating Intuition*. Amsterdam University Press.

Ogilvy, D., & Parker, A. (2012). *Confessions of an advertising man* (REV ed.). Southbank Publishing.

Siroker, D. (2010). *How Obama raised $60 million by running a simple experiment*. Optimizely Blog. https://blog.optimizely.com/2010/11/29/how-obama-raised-60-million-by-running-a-simple-experiment/

The Economist. (2003, July 17). *Who gets eaten and who gets to eat*. https://www.economist.com/special-report/2003/07/10/who-gets-eaten-and-who-gets-to-eat

Weick, K. E. (1995). What theory is not, theorizing is. *Administrative Science Quarterly, 40*(3), 385. https://doi.org/10.2307/2393789

Reason, Emotions, Intuition

5

There is a growing scientific literature on the role of managerial intuition in decisions: The core finding is that intuition functions best with experience. After years of knowing their industry, managers come to recognize patterns and cues that click into place. Moreover, experienced managers can simplify their decisions by knowing what criteria to ignore in their consideration. This chapter synthesizes this growing knowledge by showing managers the benefits and limits of relying on their intuition.

The paradigm of the perfectly rational decision-maker still haunts us, leaving instinct, intuition, insight, and emotion in a corner of shame, along with Ouija boards and voodoo dolls. The way we decide has not changed much over the history of humankind; the way we *think* we decide is, however, tributary to an idealistic image of rationality, painted by Descartes and Laplace. Mind-as-computer and reason-as-the-perfect-guide-for-deciding are metaphors that have reigned for the last 200 years and still direct the way we make decisions, in business and beyond. People still believe that they decide rationally or at least that they should. In fact, we always make decisions using a complex interaction of several systems. Aside from reflection and analysis, our decisions are influenced by our subconscious (the famous System 1 or Type 1 processing in dual-system theories); by emotions; by various chemicals in our blood (hormones or neurotransmitters such as adrenaline, cortisol, endorphins, and serotonin, but also things we add to the cocktail, such as caffeine or alcohol); and by external factors such as the weather, the sounds and colors around us, whether we are outside or inside, the time of day, and so on. Although the predominant view is that the internal systems are in competition (mind vs. heart), they actually co-operate in our decision-making. Even the most spreadsheet-oriented managers validate their chosen solution with a jolt of satisfaction, as a mark of the affect heuristic.

In their literature review on the role of intuition in managerial decision-making, Dane and Pratt offer a synthetic definition of intuition as "affectively charged judgments that arise through rapid, nonconscious, and holistic associations" (Dane & Pratt, 2007, p. 40). Or, in the words of a CEO I interviewed for my research,

R. Atanasiu, *Critical Thinking for Managers*, Management for Professionals,
https://doi.org/10.1007/978-3-030-73600-2_5

"intuition is when you like an idea" (Atanasiu et al., 2021). Intuition is therefore a solid candidate for bringing together reflection, fast thinking, and emotions for effective and efficient decision-making. Managerial intuition has been studied intensively as a subconscious tool to tap into our past experience. Herbert Simon, the founder of decision-making research, illustrates experience-based intuition with a compelling analogy between managers and chess grandmasters (Simon, 1987). Unlike a novice, who analyzes the chess board piece by piece, grandmasters recognize patterns on the board, and their intuition recalls—without a conscious effort—the solution that has proven most successful in the past. However, in chess grandmasters, intuition is based on extensive experience. Such a champion is documented to memorize and recognize 50,000 different board patterns from past games that they played or studied. Similarly, experienced managers generate—on the spot, and apparently without conscious effort—solutions that are in fact naturally based on patterns found in their extensive experience. The fact that our intuition taps into a database, as Herbert Simon posited, was also inferred by some of the managers I interviewed. One of them said that, in his opinion, "*instinct contains a lot of information.*" Another one had the same insight: "*I think that our intuition consults data and facts in our subconscious and then comes and tells you to go to the left or to the right.*"

The theory on pattern recognition decision-making was refined by Gary Klein and his collaborators in the naturalistic decision-making framework, based on their research on how people make decisions in the real world. Sometimes, these intuition-based solutions are, like in the case of chess grandmasters, very good. Most of the time, they are good enough or—in a term coined by Herbert Simon—*satisficing* (as mentioned before, *satisficing* is a portmanteau word made by blending *satisfying* and *sufficing*). Further, they are efficient: They do not cost much in terms of invested resources (time, money, effort, information gathering, attention, or mental capacity). However, situations in which intuition leads managers to poor solutions are not rare. The best strategy for managers is, then, to constantly groom their intuition into a powerful tool that generates ingenious solutions with little effort and then to switch to their more skeptical self and start doubting the result ("I could be wrong") and consequently take a little time to analyze and test those solutions. The CEO of a tech company I interviewed said that intuitive ideas appeared to her through something like magic but that "*afterwards you might want to check your intuition, so you analyze the numbers, and that is how this magic gets certified.*"

Several top managers I have talked with are on a conscious path to allow intuition to play a greater role in their decision-making. That intrigued me at first. In some cases, that commitment came after they ignored, fought, or disregarded their active intuition for too long (one leader confessed that "*I fought it hard and said to myself: forget this nonsense!*"). However, afterward, they observed that, by listening to their instinct, many negative outcomes could have been avoided (another general manager abruptly said that "*every time I ignored my gut feeling, I failed*"). In other cases, the same commitment was made by managers who did not have any sense of intuition to begin with. An entrepreneur with a rigorous decision-making process, based on data and analysis, was amazed to see business peers he admires making fast, instinctive decisions, "*like shooting from the hip*." After seeing that those decisions proved to be better-suited than his spreadsheet-based solutions, the entrepreneur decided to cultivate and groom his own intuition. Finally, another entrepreneur and CEO consider his intuition to be a valuable decision-making instrument that he uses alongside reflection: "*I have the advantage that my intuition is well aligned with my rational side; I don't have a conflict there like other people have*."

While intuition is linked to emotions, emotions' role in decision-making is not limited to intuition. The most famous case that illustrates the role of emotions in decision-making was presented by the neuroscientist Antonio Damasio. His patient, nicknamed Elliot, a successful businessman, was diagnosed with a brain tumor, which was subsequently surgically removed. Although the patient passed all cognitive tests after the operation (his IQ remained very high), something very subtle changed in his attitude. He kept postponing decisions, and this ultimately destroyed his career and his personal life. In fact, after surgery, Elliot became incapable of making decisions; he kept pondering, weighing, and analyzing every little detail in every little decision. He became pathologically indecisive. That is when professor Damasio had the idea to test not his cognition, but his emotional capabilities; he found that the patient no longer felt emotions and this lack of emotions kept him from making decisions. Damasio continued his research on other patients with similar brain damage and observed the same pattern: Their cognitive capacity tested the same, but their emotional capacity diminished abruptly, and, as a result, they were incapable of making decisions. In his book, *Descartes' Error: Emotion, Reason and The Human Brain*, Antonio Damasio recounts the case of another patient that could not decide on the date for the next appointment, going instead through "a tiresome cost–benefit analysis, an endless outlining and fruitless comparison of options and possible consequences" (Damasio, 2005). As a conclusion of his research, professor Damasio posited that emotions are integrated by certain areas of our brain in the decision-making process and proposed the *somatic marker hypothesis*, according to which our emotions and the way they manifest in our body (e.g., higher pulse) are a key element in decision-making. Reason and emotions are, according to this research, co-operating subsystems in the human decision-making machine. One of the managers in my research recognized the power of the somatic marker and developed the idea further, saying that somatic markers also make instinctive decisions easier to implement: "*When you feel that insight, and you feel it in your body, you become much more invested and this pushes you to give everything so that the decision gets implemented*." This feeling that accompanies the intuitive insight is similar to Archimedes' "*Evrika!*" and puts a genuine validation stamp on our decisions.

Our subconscious is another important actor in our decisions and behavior. Philosophy and psychology have long distinguished fast and intuitive thinking from slow and deliberative thinking (Kahneman, 2012). Following the early writings of Evans (1989) and Stanovich (1999), the names System 1 (fast thinking) and System 2 (slow thinking) became increasingly popular, reaching peak fame with Nobel laureate Daniel Kahneman's bestseller *Thinking, Fast and Slow*. Recently, the proponents of this dual paradigm reverted to a more moderate view, according to which there are not two systems but one system with two ways of functioning: one mind with two intertwined ways of processing. Hence, Stanovich and Evans now use the terms Type 1 and Type 2 processing instead of System 1 and System 2 (Evans & Stanovich, 2013). Beyond these scholastic details, a manager today must understand that our fast way of thinking greatly influences our behavior, leading sometimes to cognitive biases that are discussed elsewhere in this book. As I am sure that most readers are familiar with *Thinking, Fast and Slow*, this book will not outline the basics of the dual-process theory. Instead, it will describe three proposed ways in which these types of thinking work together. Evans (2007, 2008) proposes two models: the parallel competitive model, in which the two types of thinking occur in parallel and can lead to conflict or competition for influencing the results of thinking (we are the judges and we select between the intuitive solution and the analytical solution), and the default interventionist model, in which thinking automatically occurs as a rapid Type 1 process and proposes solutions that later may or may not be checked and validated by a Type 2 analysis (our intuition provides the solution by default and reason comes after and gives the final OK). Sadler-Smith and Hodgkinson (2016, p. 6) propose a third complex model, the analytic intervention model, in which occasionally—in deep analytic intervention—"Type 1 processes and Type 2 processes are coupled, intuition catalyzes deeper analysis, and intuition and analysis are complicitous jointly in decision making" (reason and intuition work together). My own research has found evidence for both the default interventionist model (one respondent said that "*intuition came first, because intuition is when you like an idea. Reason comes second and validates*") and the deep analytic intervention model (another respondent stated that "*reason and intuition make up the same circle. They are not opposite, they inform each other*").

Unfortunately, managerial intuition is a sensitive topic and has a credibility problem. Toward the others, but mainly toward ourselves. Can a manager feel good and even proud about pouring intuition into the decision-making cocktail? And what can a manager do to harness the power of this useful tool while avoiding the common traps? The research done by Erik Dane and Michael G. Pratt can provide some answers:

I have strong instincts. When can I trust my gut feeling? The spectrum of situations that are well-fit for the use of intuitive decisions is counterintuitively large, as long as we double our instinct with analysis, testing, and validation. First, intuition functions best in domains where we have experience and expertise—intuition is based on subconscious analysis of existing schemas and patterns in our memory, so it is effective in the same environment our experience was trained in, not in a new domain. If I am an experienced manager and my intuition seems to pay off every time I listen to it for my business, I would not trust it as strongly when I buy my house. The complex, domain-specific schemas that provide the database for our intuition are better built through repetitive practice in kind learning environments, where feedback is rapid and exact (Hogarth, 2001). Second, intuition works well in complex situations that cannot be well diagnosed with analytical tools and for which a clear, measurable solution does not exist, for instance, in decisions about people, such as whether to hire someone or whether to trust a new supplier with a sensitive and vital service; in decisions taken in uncertain situations, such as during a crisis; or when we plan for a new product, decide on a merger, or redraw the strategy. These less-structured problems (Shapiro & Spence, 1997) do not have a clear set of possible solutions or a clear set of criteria for discerning them. Dane and Pratt use a framework that puts tasks on a continuum between intellective (tasks with a clear and objective definition of success) and judgmental (tasks without objective criteria or demonstrable solution) and propose that the more judgmental the task, the more effective the role of intuition. They also propose an explanation: "Intuition, as a holistically associative process, may actually help to integrate the disparate elements of an ill-defined problem into a coherent perception of how to proceed" (Dane & Pratt, 2007, p. 45).

Should I, then, just go with the flow and listen to my intuition under those circumstances? Not until we also go through a rational decision-making process. If our intuition is strong, the most important thing is to recognize when it manifests itself (the *Eureka!* feeling is a good sign) and to defer the solution it offers to analysis. The first step for that is to write things down. Let's say, for instance, that I am in the restaurant business, I have opened a series of successful restaurants, and now I am preparing the launch of the next one. While visiting with the real-estate agent a series of 10 possible locations, I fall in love with a wonderful house that has an inconspicuous entrance and an amazing back garden. My intuition screams, "This is it! Make an offer now!," and, as I already know a bit about intuition from reading the previous paragraphs, I realize that I should fully trust it, as it manifests in a domain I am experienced in and the task is rather judgmental. However, the house I am visiting now is number 2 on my 10 locations' list and I have not yet even considered factors like contractual conditions, parking, immediate neighbors, permits, pedestrian traffic, other restaurants in the area, the history of the building (past tenants), and—importantly—the price. So, I should decide to listen to my intuition as a first guide, but also—with that in mind—to run a parallel rational analysis. A spreadsheet approach is unlikely (but very much advisable) for an entrepreneur in such a situation. But let me describe a more likely, everyday business, healthy process that would benefit the decision-making process: We need to screen the whole consideration set (to see all 10 possible locations), because increasing the number of alternatives considered increases the chances of success, then we may use a simple heuristic called *elimination-by-aspects* to reach a shortlist of three. Elimination-by-aspects uses a certain threshold or black-or-white criterion to say no to a number of options and is a natural process that most of us employ without even thinking. For instance, I might not choose locations for my restaurant that have no parking places or locations where the rent is higher than 5 days of income. After eliminating 7 of the 10 initial options, I can choose between the three remaining ones using other criteria. The best tool here would be a weighted decision matrix (described further in this book in the chapter on decision-making), in which every such criterion is given a weight corresponding to its importance and then options are graded on these criteria. Whether I might use the matrix or just perform some rough calculations in my head, an option is selected according to this rational analysis. And now, let us return to my gut feeling telling me to choose option number 2. How should I accommodate the intuitive insight with the cold analysis? We usually rationalize our gut feeling: We tend to favor the option we intuitively prefer in our analysis, to grade it higher, and to give higher importance to criteria in which it excels. Most managers who regularly use a weighted decision matrix confess to tweaking the scores or the weights if the option they favor did not win. This is not an optimal approach; it may only serve as a rationalization of our intuitive choice. An option that can offer a better result, especially in a culture that values intuition, would be to introduce intuition as merely another criterion and to give it a pre-established weight. For instance, I may compare the three final options, but the house with an inconspicuous entrance and a magical garden might be the only one to get 10 points out of 10 for "gut feeling," in a setup where "gut feeling" accounts for 25% of the total criteria.

To conclude this long answer, all intuitive solutions must be then run through a rational analysis. There are no studies to correlate the intensity of the *Eureka!* feeling with the power of the intuitive solution. However, as a rule of thumb, I propose that the more intense the feeling, the more likely we forget to run a rational check. Therefore, to counter this, the more intense the somatic marker—the *Eureka!* feeling—the more cautious we should be in validating our intuition with a structured analysis.

I am not a so-called intuitive person. How can I train my intuition? For managers who do not have a strong sense of intuition but acknowledge its value and want to develop it, I believe the best way to train it is to follow the advice of Ray Dalio in his bestseller *Principles. Life and Work.* He suggests that we should approach every problem to be solved not as a one-of-a-kind, one-at-a-time situation, but with questioning ourselves what is the category it belongs to or, in the exact words of Ray Dalio, "*what is this a type of?*" (Dalio, 2017). This can enhance our sense of identifying patterns and train our intuition. As mentioned above, the best training method is repetitive practice, and the best training ground is a kind learning environment where patterns are clear, the environment is stable, and feedback is rapid and exact. According to Dalio, asking ourselves this question, "*what is this a type of?*," is also a method for distilling rules (or, as he calls them, principles) that are applicable to the entire category of similar problems.

I have a strong intuition about a novel situation. Should I just disregard it? As proposed by Dane and Pratt (2007), intuition is suited not only for familiar situations, but also for ill-structured ones. There is actually no such thing as a completely novel situation, and while our analytical sense might be at loss in the face of novel problems, our subconscious can recognize bits and pieces of familiar patterns from different past encounters and reconstruct the novel problem as a puzzle of manageable steps that we have solved before.

I am not comfortable to admit—to myself and my co-workers—that my intuition has a say in my business decisions. Should I continue to hide it or be more open about this? Unfortunately, intuition is not well-regarded in the workplace. And, clearly, there have been many cases in which intuition pointed to a certain solution that was implemented without a rational check and failed. However, any tool may lead to error, especially when it is misused or employed by someone for the first time. An open organizational culture, however, would greatly benefit from exploring what intuition can add to individual or group decision-making. Intuition, for example, is the perfect tool to tap into the extensive experience of senior members of the organization.

As a conclusion to this chapter, our emotions, intuition, and Type 1 processing are valuable tools for our decision-making and we should be aware of the right conditions in which they are effective. In the words of one of the most insightful CEOs in my research, *"managers should acknowledge intuition, test it, and then train it."*

References

Atanasiu, R., Ruotsalainen, R., & Khapova, S. (2021). A simple rule is born: How CEOs distill heuristics (*under review*).

Dalio, R. (2017). *Principles: Life and work* (Illustrated ed.). Simon & Schuster.

Damasio, A. (2005). *Descartes' error: Emotion, reason, and the human brain* (Illustrated ed.). Penguin Books.

Dane, E., & Pratt, M. G. (2007). Exploring intuition and its role in managerial decision making. *Academy of Management Review, 32*(1), 33–54. https://doi.org/10.5465/amr.2007.23463682.

Evans, J. S. B. T. (2008). Dual-processing accounts of reasoning, judgment, and social cognition. *Annual Review of Psychology, 59*(1), 255–278. https://doi.org/10.1146/annurev.psych.59.103006.093629.

Evans, J. S. B. T., & Stanovich, K. E. (2013). Dual-process theories of higher cognition. *Perspectives on Psychological Science, 8*(3), 223–241. https://doi.org/10.1177/1745691612460685.

Evans, S. J. B. T. (1989). *Bias in human reasoning: Cause and consequences: A volume In the Essays in cognitive psychology series* (1st ed.). Psychology Press.

Evans, S. J. B. T. (2007). On the resolution of conflict in dual process theories of reasoning. *Thinking & Reasoning, 13*(4), 321–339. https://doi.org/10.1080/13546780601008825.

Hogarth, R. M. (2001). *Educating intuition*. Amsterdam University Press.

Kahneman, D. (2012). *Thinking, fast and slow*. . Penguin.

Sadler-Smith, E., & Hodgkinson, G. P. (2016). An analytic-intervention model of managerial intuition. *Academy of Management Proceedings, 2016*(1), 11831. https://doi.org/10.5465/ambpp.2016.166.

Shapiro, S., & Spence, M. T. (1997). Managerial intuition: A conceptual and operational framework. *Business Horizons, 40*(1), 63–68. https://doi.org/10.1016/s0007-6813(97)90027-6.

Simon, H. A. (1987). Making management decisions: The role of intuition and emotion. *Academy of Management Perspectives, 1*(1), 57–64. https://doi.org/10.5465/ame.1987.4275905.

Stanovich, K. E. (1999). *Who is rational?: Studies of individual Differences in Reasoning* (1st ed.). Psychology Press.

Cognitive Biases 6

Studies have shown that we make only (roughly) half of our decisions based on reason. The rest are based on habit, emotion, imitating others, tradition, environment, plus a special kind of pirate software in our operating system called cognitive biases. Without us knowing, cognitive biases trick us into behaving irrationally, for instance, by working twice as hard to avoid a loss than to secure a gain of the same amount or by continuing a failing project just because of all we have invested in it so far. This chapter explores the origin of cognitive biases and analyzes a select set that is often encountered in business. By reading about cognitive biases, their mechanism, examples, and ways to counteract, readers will be immunized and less likely to fall into these traps. This chapter also shows how cognitive biases are employed in marketing campaigns.

The term "cognitive bias" was coined by the famous duo Daniel Kahneman and Amos Tversky, and their research opened the door for startling progress in psychology, economics, marketing, organizational behavior, and even criminology. They started by questioning the validity of the model proposed by classical economics—a model that describes how people *should* behave—and proposed a new model that describes how people actually *do behave*. They did it backward: first studying the way people behave in various situations, then observing the discrepancy with the classical model, and then proposing a new model and a new field: behavioral economics. The primordial three heuristics (representativeness, availability, and anchoring and adjusting) and their associated biases were first described by Tversky and Kahneman in their seminal 1974 article in *Science*, titled *Judgement under Uncertainty. Heuristics and Biases* (Tversky & Kahneman, 1974). This title (its second half) ultimately gave name to their famous *Heuristics and Biases Research Program*, which, while recognizing the efficiency of heuristics (rules of thumb and cognitive shortcuts), always underlines their associated biases, which lead to error. I believe that evolution has developed innate heuristics as useful tools for our minds. Problems appear only when we misuse them. Another popular author in this field is Dan Ariely, whose books, MOOCs, and Wall Street Journal column

R. Atanasiu, *Critical Thinking for Managers*, Management for Professionals,
https://doi.org/10.1007/978-3-030-73600-2_6

have seen tremendous success. This evangelization is actually beneficial, as cognitive biases, like fallacies and riddles, lose (some of) their power once you are familiarized with them.

Behavioral economics says that a part of our behavior is outside our control and is caused by pirate software in our head: cognitive biases. As we saw in the last chapter, System 1 or Type 1 processing (fast thinking) is crucial for our proper thinking; however, it can misfire. Cognitive biases are such systematic misfires. This chapter offers an overview of a few cognitive biases that may influence our behavior as managers and consumers.

The what-the-hell effect. Have you ever crossed a self-imposed line just a bit, only to say afterward, "What the hell!," and then go all the way? Please picture this: You are on a self-imposed diet, and your dinner is supposed to be a few crackers with light cheese and a glass of wine, at home. Your friend calls and tells you that the usual gang has decided to have a night out, but, thinking of you, they chose a light dinner at your favorite Italian restaurant. "But I'm on a diet," you protest. "I can only have a glass of wine, crackers, and light cheese." "Well, exactly!" your friend replies, "you can easily have those at the Italian place. Come!" The argument is compelling, so you go, adamant to stick to the original menu. And you start well: You order a glass of Pinot Grigio, bread sticks (they are almost crackers, aren't they?), and a burrata on arugula and cherry tomatoes. The wine is almost gone when the food arrives, and the crispiness goes very well with the cheese, so you say to yourself "There's actually no difference between a glass and two glasses" (note the rationalization of desire: our mind is quick to find reasons to support our gut-made decisions—it is one of its favorite methods to trick us), and order another glass. But now the line has been crossed. You have crossed to the other side, and clearly, the wise thing to do is to forgive yourself for the trespassing, to enjoy the extra wine, and to keep things there, while no real harm has been done. But, again, the line has been crossed. In this situation, what does our irrational mind typically say? "What the hell! My diet is ruined anyway! I can now order pizza, like everybody else!" (please note the rationalization again, seasoned with a little *ad populum* or the bandwagon fallacy—if everybody does it, then it must be a good thing). So you do order pizza. Now the line is crossed *and* the harm is done, so the next thing to do is to order a whole bottle of wine ("Why pay by the glass?! It's much more expensive!"—rationalization again) and dessert. Lava cake and tiramisu! (this is actually a good way out of a false dilemma: have both options).

Has this ever happened to you? *Mutatis mutandis*? Most people I have asked can pinpoint various situations when, after crossing a limit, instead of stopping, they say to themselves "What the hell! The line is already crossed, I might as well indulge all the way!" First described by the dieting researcher Janet Polivy (Polivy et al., 2010), this effect has been aptly named *the what-the-hell effect*. It is a perfect example of a cognitive bias: a systematic irrational behavior—systematic because, under similar conditions, it happens to most of us, repeatedly. This makes it predictable, as in *Predictably Irrational*, the inspired title of the bestseller on cognitive biases by Dan Ariely. It is predictable, so, after learning about cognitive biases, we can foresee our fate at the Italian restaurant and do something about it beforehand. It is predictable, so, after learning about cognitive biases, the charming Italian who owns the restaurant can offer a second glass on the house and kick-start the effect. The what-the-hell effect applies not only to eating, but also to other behavior such as procrastinating or overspending. As with many other cognitive biases, the way to avoid the trap is to know about it and to prepare beforehand. In our case, knowing about it means either seeing and recognizing this pattern in our own past behavior, or learning about cognitive biases in general and the what-the-hell effect in particular, or both. Doing something about it beforehand means using our own irrationality against itself. This is a common feature of most countermeasures described in this chapter. If we consider ourselves rational and in control, we will end up eating pizza and two desserts, while drinking a lot of wine. If we allow ourselves to think that we are sometimes irrational, sometimes vulnerable to cognitive traps, and sometimes a little childlike, then we can devise clever mechanisms to prevent the trap, as we usually do for children. In our case, before leaving home for the Italian place, we need to a) acknowledge that we might be subject to the what-the-hell effect and b) devise a Ulysses pact: a method for the *at-home-me* to prevent the *after-a-glass-of-wine-at-the-restaurant-me* from falling into the irrational trap. Here are some ideas: Just bring money for the intended order, take the car (in countries where just a glass of wine is allowed before driving), have a friend guard your ordering, and so on. Such Ulysses pacts or contracts derive from the Odyssey, in which Homer tells us how Ulysses wants to hear the seductive song of the sirens without being seduced to jump into the water to his death. Ulysses therefore prepares beforehand his passage through the siren-infested sea. He has all his sailors put wax in their ears and tie him to the mast. They sail through, immune to the song, while he is listening in delight, without being able to give in to temptation. A Ulysses pact is us, tying ourselves to the mast before passing through siren territory. I chose the what-the-hell effect example to open this chapter because such a familiar human weakness is perfect to illustrate the topic of cognitive biases.

Loss aversion. The key to Jimmy Connors' success (the number one tennis player in the world for 268 weeks) was his credo: "I hate to lose more than I love to win." At first glance, the discomfort of losing and the desire to win must be the same: two sides of the same coin. But not for Jimmy Connors. And I don't think that is the case for you either. Let us imagine that the boss just increased your salary by 100 euros. Are you happy? Sure! Do you throw a party? I doubt it. It is only 100 euros, after all. Now, imagine that your boss cuts 100 euros from your salary. How upset are you? Definitely more upset than you were happy for the extra money. In fact, it was demonstrated that the pain of losing is twice as powerful as the pleasure of gaining something of the same value. This asymmetry is called "loss aversion" and was first discovered and studied by Daniel Kahneman and Amos Tversky, introduced above. But where does this asymmetry come from? Why is a bird in the hand worth two in the bush? It seems that this bias was written in our operating system when we lived in caves and had few but valuable possessions. What did one of our ancestors risk to lose if he ventured into a fight with another tribe? Something more valuable than 100 euros, certainly: his life, his freedom, a limb—important stuff. Those who valued not losing what they already had did not enter fights and, thus, lived to perpetuate their genes. They are our ancestors. We are the descendants of the cautious ones. This caution—this preference to avoid losing instead of accumulating gain—has been written into our software and transmitted to us over time. Of course, common risks today are radically different, which sometimes leads to absurd effects, but biological evolution operates slowly.

What are some examples of economic behavior resulting from loss aversion? This bias can sometimes prevent us from selling an asset at a loss: some shares, an apartment, or cryptocurrency. Imagine that you bought an apartment for 120,000 euros when the market was high and now its price is about 75,000. You do not use it, it stays empty, the rent would be quite small anyway, and you need money to buy a house. However, you never even consider selling the apartment because that would imply marking the loss of 45,000 euros (the difference between the purchase price and how much you would get on it today). This is not a rational approach: The chances of the market reverting soon to that all-time-high are low, and you need the money now, not in a few years. It is simply that you cannot stand the thought of losing; loss aversion is to blame for this blockage. Is there a way out of this? How can we trick our mind into not tricking us? A mental exercise provides one answer. Imagine that you do not have the apartment, but you have the money. Someone comes and says they can sell it to you for 75,000 euros. Would you buy it? If the answer is "Definitely not, I don't like it and I don't need it! Plus, I need that money to buy a house," it means that between the apartment and 75,000 euros, you would choose the money. In your current situation, there is a simple way to achieve this: Sell it! A clearer variant of this mind trick works with cryptocurrency. Your friend bought Bitcoin when the market was high and now, with its value decreased, refuses to sell. You suspect a clear case of loss aversion, but unfortunately, biases disguise themselves in rationalizations, so he answers that, in fact, he knows for sure that the price will go up again, so he is confident that, after a short wait, he will sell and make a profit. This rationalization, though, is easier to dismantle. What would be a rational behavior when we know for sure that the price will go back up? Obviously, buy some more, which you can safely propose, because your friend will never do so. Perhaps, while examining this cognitive dissonance, your friend will begin to consider that he may be subject to loss aversion.

One of the funniest methods of exploiting loss aversion for a noble cause was Pact, an app that motivated you to go to the gym. We all know of the common behavior of buying an expensive subscription to the gym and then never going. Well, if the large price paid for the subscription does not get people off the couch, Pact did it with 10 dollars. How? You set a number of weekly visits to the gym and Pact checks (with GPS) if you went. If you skip a practice, the app takes 10 dollars from your card for each absence. The mechanism worked perfectly, with hundreds of thousands of Americans becoming more active due to their aversion to losing 10 dollars. My daughter showed me another nice example: The Forest application helps you keep your screen time in check. You set a time slot (for instance, two hours) in which you should not use the phone, and during this time, a virtual tree grows on the screen. If you use any other application, the tree dies. It seems that this is one of the most effective ways to combat mobile phone addiction in teenagers.

A more business-related example is: A good way of motivating salespeople is the use of commissions. Agents get a percentage every time they make a sale, and that is good. But an even better way to do it would be to agree on a high target, to put the next month's commission already in the salesperson's account and—at the end of the month—to subtract the sum they did not earn. When the money is already in their account, the incentive to do anything in their power *not to lose* the commission is two times greater than the motivation to earn it in the first place.

Online stores use loss aversion to counteract a common behavior: The user browses, chooses a product, adds it to the cart, then closes the window and leaves without making the purchase. How can the online retailer make the consumer come back and finish the transaction? One way would be sending a message through which the potential buyer is informed that the stock of the product is low. This will change their perception from "I could buy this thing" to "I could lose this thing," and the sale is much more likely to happen. Loss aversion is the mother of many cognitive biases like the endowment effect, the scarcity effect, and the status quo bias, all discussed below.

Status quo bias. We prefer the current situation. Whether it is our current job or career, our way to deal with contracts, or a software that we have been using for some time, what we have now seems better than what we could have, so why change?! This avoidance of change is also rooted in loss aversion. Can we use the apartment trick here too? We can try. If I imagine that I already have the new job or the new career or that I have already started the entrepreneurial project I keep thinking about, would I go back to what I do now? If my company were already digitally transformed, would I want to go back to the cumbersome systems we use now? If I had already started running or going to the gym a year ago, would I let myself go back to being a couch potato again? I do not know what you cannot change and I do not know whether this exercise is useful or rather uncomfortable, but what I know is this: We rarely regret the things we have done, and we usually regret the things we did not do.

Endowment effect. We value disproportionally more the things we already have. Even if there is a "no-questions-asked" product return policy, stores know that once the item enters your home, it will be much harder for you to return it. This effect, closely linked with the Buddhist concept of "attachment," leads to important bias when we face the decision to part ways with something that we consider ours, whether that is a chocolate bar, a recently purchased product, our project, or our career. One very interesting variant of the endowment effect is called ***the IKEA effect***—we place a much higher value on products we created ourselves. A famous study by Norton et al. (2012) showed that "labor leads to love." Subjects were asked to assemble IKEA furniture and then to price the items they assembled, along with other, pre-assembled IKEA pieces. They were willing to pay 63% more for the pieces they worked on than for other pieces. Therefore, we overvalue the things we already have and the things we built ourselves.

Scarcity effect. We value the things that are in limited supply. When Concorde announced, in the fall of 2003, that it would stop selling tickets for its supersonic flights between Europe and the USA, prices went crazy. In a sweet experiment (Worchel et al., 1975), cookies in scarce supply were rated as more desirable than identical cookies in abundant supply. Very often, a small red note saying, "only two seats left at this price," "last available room in this hotel," or "two more people are looking at this room" can make us hurry and buy without further consideration. In a nutshell, people want things that are in limited supply, even if the quality and the price stay the same. This effect is often abused by marketers in scarcity strategies that announce limited stocks. Similarly, Apple famously releases new generations of products in small batches, in order to have early adopter queue for days in front of the store.

The fascination of free is the fascination generated by the price zero. In math, zero is a number: a special one, but just a number, nevertheless. But as soon as zero becomes a price, minds become clouded and people start forming mobs. In a fun experiment (Shampan'er & Ariely, 2006), the authors used Hershey's Kisses—an average-quality chocolate—and Lindor—a high-end chocolate. They were offered at the entrance of a store at a heavily discounted price: Hershey's Kisses for 1 cent (from about 7 cents, with a 6-cent discount) and Lindor at 15 cents (from about 35 cents, a 20-cent discount). The catch was that you could choose to buy just one of them. People behaved rationally and chose the better chocolate, which also had a larger discount: 73% of them chose Lindor. The next day, each chocolate bonbon was supplementary discounted one more cent: Lindor 14 cents (at a 21-cent discount) and Hershey for *0 cents* (at a 7-cent discount). This should not change the decision, should it? It is just 1 cent. The discounts were almost the same. But now Hershey's Kisses was *free*. And free is magic: 69% of the subjects chose the free Hershey's Kisses, compared to only 27% a day before.

But when something is priced at zero, is it really free? Perhaps the perceived monetary price is indeed zero, but often we pay a non-tangible, but still very real price in future commitments, time, or personal effort. Take, for instance, the Long Night of Museums. In most European capitals, this yearly event keeps museums open for free during one spring night. However, sometimes the experience is not free at all. In Bucharest, although many museums participate in this event, the star is the Grigore Antipa National Museum of Natural History, where adults and children can observe a great variety of plants, animals, and ecosystems. For free. But is it really for free? First of all, the normal price of the ticket is 4 euros for adults and 1 euro for children and students: a small price for an interesting experience. Consider a family with a 10-year-old girl who, despite the small regular ticket price, decides to visit the museum *for free* during the Long Night of Museums. Being the star of the event, the museum usually has a long queue with waiting times of up to 5 h! How is that in terms of cost? Can we estimate it? I think so: Ask the *pater familias* how much is he willing to be paid to wait in line for you and your family and you will get a price for their waiting time. Then, inside the museum, the little girl—already tired after standing in line and perhaps already past her bedtime—will have a hard time observing the beautiful butterflies or the majestic manta ray behind crowds of people. How much would that diminished experience cost? After examining what *free* really means, it is time to look closely at what it makes us do. It sometimes makes us choose the lesser option, just because it is free, although the difference between the better option's nonzero price and the price zero can easily be justified with differences in quality. It can sometimes make us buy things we do not need. I once went to buy a deodorant spray, and seeing that it came with a free razor, I bought two. One may argue that I eventually used both cans, which is true. But what about the razors? I have a very nice shaving kit, which I prefer, so I really did not need them. But the fact that they were free impressed me into buying more than I needed. Eventually, if you really want to know the end of the story, the *sunk cost effect* kicked in—"Now I have the extra razors, I might as well find them a good use"—so I decided to start shaving at my gym and use them there. *Sunk cost effect* is a bias that will be described further in this chapter. By the way, it seems that I don't need to look very far to illustrate this chapter; my own behavior provides enough examples of irrational behavior.

This fascination for the price zero is often used in sales. While pricing a set of items, instead of offering them as a bundle for price *X*, retailers can take one item out, offer the rest as a bundle for the price *X* and, as a bonus, include that item *K* for free. It is the same thing, but so much more appealing.

How do we fight the endowment effect, the scarcity effect, or the fascination for the free? One trick would be to ask the advice of a friend who is not influenced by the effect (who does not know, for instance, that the item you want to purchase is in short supply or free). Another option would be to ask yourself what advice would you give your friend if she was in the same situation. Often, we give better advice to others than we give to ourselves. A third way out would be to wait a bit and sleep on the decision (if time allows) so that the irrational effect fades away.

The default effect is our tendency to—when in doubt—do nothing. I will illustrate with an example, published by Johnson and Goldstein (2003). European authorities did not understand, a while ago, the large difference between countries in the rate of people who declared themselves organ donors. For instance, Germany had a 12% rate, while Austria had an amazing 99%. German authorities even paid for an advertising campaign, which only increased the rate by a few percent. Then, they realized that Germany used an opt-in system, which means that you are by default considered a non-donor, and to become a donor you need to act (to tick a box), while Austria had an opt-out system that means that by default you are a donor, and you need to tick a box if you disagree. Requiring this simple tick can save lives. While confronted with a hard choice (and, I hope you agree, this is a complex one), people usually chose to do nothing: to leave it as it is. They do not tick the box. But in an opt-out system, that is the way to become donors! That is the power of default. You may encounter this system when you agree to receive email marketing, to download additional programs, and so on. But now you know. Like in the organ donor case, the default effect can be put to good use in soft influence policies or in smart business offers. If, for instance, you are a retailer, you traditionally offer clients the possibility to choose between a discount now and accumulating points, and you, the retailer, prefer that they choose points, you can make that the default. Instead of the client choosing between the two options, make the "accumulating points" the default one that can be replaced by the other by request. The numbers will amaze you!

Sunk cost. We have the tendency to continue a losing project just because we have already invested a lot in it: not only money, but also time, effort, or feelings. Did you ever watch a movie and, after seeing the first half, realize that it is really bad, but then choose to watch it until the end just because you paid for the ticket and invested the first half hour anyway? Does your company still offer a service that is no longer needed and keep spending money, time, and effort on new, unnecessary features, hoping that maybe you can rescue that service? Did you ever stay in a job you hate or in a toxic relationship just because you have been in it for 10 years already? There is an English proverb that describes this behavior: throwing good money after bad. Economists call it *the sunk cost effect*. We continue a bankrupt project just because we have already invested a lot in it and we do that because we hate losing or wasting our resources, so it is safe to explain sunk cost by loss aversion. This bias is called sunk cost because the investment (the cost) we made cannot be taken back—it is sunk—but nevertheless, it influences our decisions, often without us noticing. A 2009 survey of 463 readers of mckinseyquarterly.com showed that, as opposed to their subordinates, managers and decision-makers do not realize when their projects are ready to be killed. In response to the question "Does management admit mistakes and kill unsuccessful initiatives in a timely manner?," 80% of C-level executives said "yes," compared with just 49% of non-C-level executives (McKinsey and Company, 2009).

Sunk cost is an extremely common trap, and it is capable of inducing considerable business and personal damage. I know that personal examples are the most effective, so let me tell you how I fell into that trap not once, but twice, in the same context. I teach about cognitive biases, so perhaps you might think that I am immune. I am not—the tendency, for those who know about cognitive biases, to identify them easily in others but not when it is their own behavior is called the ***blind spot bias***. But let me get back to my story. A few years ago, I was training for a longer triathlon, a Half Ironman in Italy, an event that combines a 1900 m swim, a 90 km bike ride, and a half marathon—21 km. It was not my first competition on this distance, and I knew it required a lot of training. As these events are in high demand, I booked my place months in advance, along with (nonrefundable) plane tickets. Immediately after booking, a similar event was announced for the Romanian seaside (at home), scheduled just a week after the Italian one. I booked that as well, thinking that I could kill two birds with the same training period. A few weeks before the first race, my left knee started aching. I used all methods to keep the pain quiet, but just three days before the Italian race I realized that it was unwise to force my knee, so I decided not to go and I stopped training. A week later, perhaps due to the resting period, my knee started aching less, so I thought that I could at least try the Romanian race. This was the first iteration of the sunk cost. We can recognize (and avoid) sunk cost through a little mental exercise: Pretend you did not incur the cost and someone is offering you the project; will you accept it? In my case, let's say that I had not registered for the second race. If, a few days before the event, someone had offered me a free registration, would I have accepted it? Definitely not! I would have said that my knee hurts, that a long-distance triathlon is a bad idea, and that I just gave up on doing one. This mental exercise is a good litmus test for identifying and fighting the sunk cost effect. If you consider continuing a project you started yourself, but would scrap it if someone else offered it to you now, then the sunk cost effect is the force behind your need to keep the project alive. You should end it. If you stay in the same job just because it was your job for the last 10 years, but would never apply for it now, it is time to reconsider your employment. Unfortunately, although I teach this method, it did not occur to me to do this mental test, so I decided to go anyway. But as a weak sign of reason, I pledged to go just for the fun of it, to swim and bike, but to abandon before running, which is the most damaging on the knees. I think you can already predict my second iteration of the sunk cost. I was in the second transition—the place you leave your bike and put on your running shoes and the place where I initially planned to abandon the race. But I thought that, since most of the distance was already behind me (can you spot the sunk cost?), I could at least finish it. I did. I reached the finish line in the penultimate place, with a limp, and soon I had my knee operated on. This example illustrates not only the sunk cost effect but also the fact that knowing (and, in my case, even teaching) about a cognitive bias does not provide full immunity.

How does the sunk cost manifest itself in business? Here is an example:

> **Case** Michael, the manager of the X Mobile (a large telecom company) branch in town *A*, runs a good business, but is troubled by the lack of high street visibility of the brand. Despite the fact that many sales are made online, he cannot help wondering what an X Mobile flagship store on the main commercial street would do for brand awareness. Plus, the main competitor already has a huge store on that street, where customers can try the latest models, play with branded gadgets, and immerse themselves in a high-tech experience. X Mobile also has flagship stores in all important towns in the region, and the perfect retail space has just been freed up and put on the market.

Michael builds a business case to be presented at the next regional meeting. In his analysis, there is an initial investment of 100,000 euros in decorating the store in the brand colors and logos and furnishing it with the latest tech gadgets. This cost may seem a little high, he thinks, but although this is not a break-even type of analysis, the running profit he estimates for the store (25,000 euros per year) will cover the initial investment in 4 years, with brand awareness as an extra benefit. The business case is approved, and soon an X Mobile flagship store appears on the main commercial street in town A. The results are not as expected. The first year ends with a small loss (−1000 euros), the second year gives a little hope when the bottom line is zero, but then the third year ends again with a loss, this time −2500 euros. The estimated contribution to brand awareness is also negligible. At the beginning of Year 4, a consultant from the HQ visits town *A*, looks at the numbers, and asks Michael why isn't he closing the store, to which Michael responds that he cannot possibly do so, not after investing 100 k in the first place.

Question: If you were the consultant from the X Mobile headquarters, how would you continue the conversation?

The answer to this question is not simple. Of course, you could always tell Michael that this is a classic case of sunk cost and dismiss his thinking and argument as flawed. That will not change the manager's mindset an inch. And that is because sunk cost is caused by a combination of factors and they each need to be addressed. Let us try all approaches, one by one:

First, we may try logic. The initial cost is irretrievable and cannot be taken back, so it should not count in any scenario. If we do a scenario analysis on a sheet of paper, with two columns side by side, "close the store" versus "do not close the store," the 100 k will be there under "irretrievable costs" in both columns, so it cannot impact the choice. As a principle, in any decision to keep or kill a project, past costs and past earnings should not be considered. The only relevant ones are future costs and future earnings. It is a bit counterintuitive, but the size of the initial investment should not matter. Although this is the rational thing to say, in my experience it is the least effective in changing people's perspectives. The problem with cognitive biases is that rarely can they be avoided using logic. The best approach is through mind games, mental exercises, uncomfortable questions, and Ulysses pacts. For number-oriented people, though, this accounting-style argument might work.

Second, we must address the hope that things will improve. The cryptocurrency exercise presented above can function in certain situations. Of course, hope is often based on good premises and optimism is a crucial trait in business. However, sometimes hope for some improvement in a losing project is simply naïve. When planning, one must decide from the beginning on clear showstoppers, low-performance indicators that, when reached, signal that the time has come to end the project. They need to be precise, agreed by all, and written down from the beginning, because sunk cost and the IKEA effect will, after a while, make us very lenient with the performance of our project.

Third, there is the emotional attachment: We often simply cannot let go. The thought of closing the store gives Michael physical discomfort. The way out would be to extract the person from the context using various mental exercises: Would you close it if the initial investment were just 10 k? If you were to move as the local manager to town *B* and find a store in this situation, what would you do? Wouldn't you close it? And finally, the killer question is: If your good friend asked for advice in a similar situation, what would you say? Additionally, you can ask for someone's advice. But beware! Do not seek the advice of someone who was involved in the initial decision. Do not ask your oldest colleague, who approved the opening of the store, whether to close it or not. He might be as biased as you are. All these mental exercises would have helped me in my triathlon case.

Fourth, the fear to acknowledge failure must be mitigated. When Michael closes the store, he acknowledges to the whole organization that his pet project was a failure. The key here lies not with Michael but with the organization itself and with the attitude instilled by its leaders. If the norm in an organization is that failure is blamed and punished, employees will do everything they can to hide their failed projects. One way to do so is to make dead projects seem alive, which, in many instances, requires further investment. Throwing good money after bad. If, however, the company culture treats failure as an opportunity to learn and grow together, Michael might be easier convinced to close down the flagship store.

Fifth, there is the anchor of the break-even calculation. While the break-even point is a very useful tool in assessing projects before they start, it sometimes anchors us in a flawed mental model when the project is underway. People usually set their mind on recovering their initial investment no matter what and, in our case, would wait any length of time to get the 100 k back. Of course, useful concepts like the time value of money (money in the future is worth less than money today) or opportunity cost (what else we could do with the same resources) are never considered in such cases. The problem is that the break-even point is a hard anchor to abandon. This kind of thinking, in which I want to recover irrecoverable costs, leads to a related bias: *the pro rata bias*. Here is an illustrative example. My company spent one million dollars in R&D for a new product. Everything went well: The product is ready to launch. The marginal cost for producing one unit is one euro, but in setting the price I do not take into consideration this marginal cost, or the demand, or the price of similar products on the same market. I price it at 100 euros so I can quickly recoup the investment. Is this wise?

The sunk cost trap is extremely common, causing different types of damage, from more and more hours playing FarmVille (as the hooked player cannot let their past investment of time go down the drain) to aeronautical industry projects or to the meaningless continuation of the Vietnam War. One of the trap's complications is an escalation of commitment. Often, in organizations where failure is penalized, the person who can decide to put an end to a project is the same person who decided to start the project in the first place. Ending the project would mean admitting to the initial mistake, which managers in such organizations prefer not to do. They therefore perpetuate the project in the manner described above, but sometimes this cannot happen without adding more and more resources, in a perfect illustration of "throwing good money after bad." One example is offered in the *HBR Guide to Making Better Decisions*. The authors mention a consultancy project they were involved in with a major US bank, which offered many bad loans to foreign businesses. After an initial analysis, they found that bankers who initially approved the loan were far more likely to approve additional funds than bankers who took over the account from a colleague, thus ending in issuing more bad loans. The solution that the bank eventually implemented was to reassign an account to a new banker immediately after any problem appeared. As Warren Buffett once said, "When you find yourself in a hole, the best thing you can do is stop digging."

Our houses are full of old things that we no longer need but that we do not throw away. If they were not ours and someone gave them to us now, we would refuse them or dispose of them immediately. But those things have been ours for so long that we keep them. We often have projects, in our companies and in our lives, that we keep only because we have invested a lot in them. Let us pretend that the spring is coming and we need to do a general cleaning. Or we can make an analogy with the principles of tidying up taught by the famous Japanese consultant Marie Kondo. She advises to only keep things that "spark joy." Similarly, we can make a list of the projects in our company and only keep those that "spark profit." I will not advise here on personal matters, but I am sure that the reader is perfectly capable of extrapolating the analogy.

Anchoring is the tendency to rely too heavily on the first piece of information (the anchor) that we receive. What is the distance between the Earth and the Moon, in kilometers? Can you provide an estimate? Now look back on your thinking process. Chances are that—if you are like most people, not knowing the distance between the Earth and the Moon—you thought of a distance you know (perhaps the length of the Equator, approximately 40,000 km? Perhaps the distance between two cities?) and then multiplied it by an estimated factor. I don't know how well you did, but here it is: The distance between the Earth and the Moon is not constant, as the Moon's orbit is not a circle, but it varies around 400,000 km. This is not important; what *is* important is that the automatic process I described above is employed automatically by our minds when we need to approximate something we don't know. It is called anchoring and adjusting (the anchor is the length of the Equator; the adjusting is multiplying that number with a factor), and it is a very useful tool. The problem appears when we misuse it. One of the ways we do that is through a tendency to rely too much on the information we receive before being required to estimate something. A very interesting experiment, presented in Ariely's bestseller *Predictably Irrational*, illustrates this tendency (Ariely, 2010). In the study, performed on MBA students from MIT, a bottle of '98 Côtes du Rhône (a French wine was chosen because its price is harder to estimate) was auctioned in class in the following manner: First, the students had to write down their social security number. Then, they needed to single out the last two digits (which are completely random) and transform them into dollar figures. For instance, if the two last digits were 34, they became USD34. The third step was to answer a simple yes-or-no question: whether they were hypothetically willing to pay that sum of money (USD34) for the bottle. After they were anchored this way, in the final step, the one that actually counted, students were asked to write down how much would they be willing to pay for the bottle, although not before being warned that in the previous step the number was completely random and should not influence them. Being MBA students at MIT, all participants thought that they could easily overcome anchoring. They were wrong. Those who had social security numbers ending in two digits between 80 and 99 were willing to pay much more for the same bottle of wine than those with social security numbers ending in 00–20: more than three times more! This study illustrates the fact that we are prone to being anchored even when the first piece of information we are exposed to has no relationship to the thing we are trying to estimate.

One of the first business consequences is that, contrary to folklore, we *should* always be the first to propose a price in negotiations, as this initial figure has a large probability of anchoring the rest of the negotiation. Often, after a little back and forth, the final price is an adjustment of the first price mentioned. Here is an example:

> **Case** George is passionate about vintage cars. He discovers that an old model of ARO (a 4 × 4 car built in communist Romania) is for sale by its first owner and decides to give that man a call. A meeting is set. In preparation for the meeting, George searches for prices of similar cars. Unfortunately, the market is almost nonexistent for this model, so he cannot use it as a good indicator of a decent price. His maximum budget is 5500 euros, but he genuinely hopes to buy the car for a much smaller sum, perhaps 3500 euros. However, he is not sure of this price and also not sure how to proceed: Should he start by mentioning the 3500 euros offer, or let the owner open the money conversation?

On the other side of the negotiation is Mr. Popp, who also does not know how to price his car. He loves it, he kept it well, but now he can no longer take care of it. He does not want to sell it below 2500 euros: He has already turned down such an offer. But how much would be a decent price? He does not know. Perhaps 5000 euros?

We have an interval between 2501 euros and 5500 euros where a deal can happen. In scenario 1, assume that George opens the discussion by proposing to pay 3500 euros. This starting price is already above Mr. Popp's lower limit, so the deal can be made. Symmetrically, in scenario 2 Mr. Popp starts the discussion by asking for 5000 euros. This figure is toward the upper limit of George's budget, but still within it, so he will not walk away. The deal can happen here as well.

In both scenarios, a deal is done. By definition, a deal is something both parties are comfortable with. Usually, the mind has strong coping mechanisms that will rationalize the situation into a win. However, the outcome for the two negotiators is radically different: There is a significant difference between the prices. Although this is a fictional situation, being the one to open real-life negotiations often leads to a strong advantage. Also, the case here talks about small(er) sums, but anchoring often influences real-estate transactions or M&As (mergers and acquisitions), where the sums involved have considerably more zeroes.

Another example of anchoring and adjusting is the way companies build their budgets for ongoing business lines. When first creating a budget for a new project, especially when uncertainty is high, multiple scenarios are considered, multiple criteria are built in, and multiple perspectives are consulted. When a project is ongoing, however, the budget for next year is almost always built by anchoring (the budget for the current year) and adjusting (accounting for a bit of growth). This is a perfectly reasonable way to budget; the only downside is that it does not consider the possibility of exponential growth. While the budget for next year is anchored in this year's numbers, the execution next year will be unconsciously anchored in the budget. If a company budgets a 10% growth, it may reach 15%, but rarely 150%.

How can we avoid being anchored? We saw that, in negotiations, we should be the first to make an offer. When we need to estimate something important, it is better to gather data and to sketch a first estimation before asking somebody else's opinion, as most probably that opinion will anchor us more than we know. Similarly, when asking for advice, offer as little information as possible, to avoid anchoring the other. Do not ask "Should I pay 5000 euros for this vintage car?," as that figure will inevitably become an anchor for both. Ask instead "How much would you pay for this car?".

Price relativity. A not-so-distant relative of anchoring is price relativity, the fact that we do not think of prices in absolute values, but rather as compared to other prices or money values we know. For example, during sales, we no longer care about the current price but instead about the percentage discount. To see this, consider buying a car. If you ever did buy a new car, chances are that you paid an absurd sum of money for an unnecessary feature like the rain sensor. Who needs that? If rain starts, you do not need an extra sensor; you can *sense* the rain yourself with your natural vision sensors (your eyes) and start the wipers. When I bought my new car, the rain sensor was where I had my wake-up call. Until the rain sensor entered the discussion, the salesman easily convinced me to buy a number of features that I now confess I have never used. I don't even know what they are!

To illustrate the effect of this effect, immerse yourself in this situation:

Case You are in the showroom, buying a new car you dreamed of. The price of the chosen model starts at 25,000 euros. You are seated at a nice desk, with the list of customizable features in front of you, and you feel that—as the discussion continues—your future car is slowly being born. Then comes the rain sensor, or the signature wheels, or—let's say—the leather-covered steering wheel, priced at 300 euros. Would you buy it? If yes, you probably think that its intrinsic value made you do it. After all, it feels much better, both in winter and in summer, to keep your hands on leather than on plastic. However, the chances are that you said "yes" without considering its price as an absolute value but as a (small) percentage of the total price. A little manifestation of the what-the-hell effect is: "If I already pay almost 30 k on this car, I might as well pay 300 for a leather steering wheel." In order to discern between a reasonable choice and a cognitive trap, we can use a thought experiment. Imagine that the leather steering wheel was not an option at first, so you already bought the car without it. It has been a month, you are very happy with your car; it still has that special smell, but it also feels like home already. In this context, an email comes from the dealer saying that new features are available to install on your car during the compulsory checkup next week. One of the things on offer is a leather steering wheel, priced at 300 euros. Now, the 300 euros is no longer part of the initial buying price, but a distinct price, to be paid separately. Would you buy that, or any other feature?

If you were like most people, you would not. It could partly be the endowment effect—you become increasingly happy with what you already have, but it is also the fact that the 300 euros will now be compared with that city break you were planning and will lose the battle. Please observe that, in this new case, the price is still not perceived as an absolute value but compared to some other sum of money.

I do not have a mind trick to consider prices in absolute terms, but I had students saying that they get out of this trap by applying a universal unit as opportunity cost, for example, cups of coffee:

> Alright, the guy proposes a leather steering wheel. Classy! And for just 300 euros. What is 300 compared with almost 30,000? Nothing! I think I will get a leather steering wheel! But hold on! Could this be a case of price relativity? What if I think in terms of cups of coffee? How many can I buy with 300 euros? Oh, dear! I think I will pass!.

Availability bias is the tendency to overestimate the probability of events that you remember better or that are more present in the media. Availability is another classical heuristic that, with its accompanying bias, was described by Tversky and Kahneman (Tversky & Kahneman, 1973). People estimate the frequency of certain events according to the ease with which they come to mind. A certain health condition must be frequent in the general population if two people we know have it (obviously not a good inference); flying is the most dangerous way of transport (it is not, it is by far the safest according to all statistics) because the media covers all plane crashes but almost never car crashes; bad clients seem (erroneously) to outnumber good clients because—from a management perspective—good clients often pass unnoticed. One interesting variant of availability is the ***survivorship bias***, which leads us to believe that the success stories we see in the media are a good indicator of the respective field. Dropping out of college seems to be a good career and life choice, seeing that Steve Jobs, Bill Gates, and Mark Zuckerberg left college without collecting a diploma, only to become three of the most successful people on the planet. Why is this view biased? Because the media only covers the successful dropouts: It does not tell the story of the millions of college dropouts who did not make it and now regret not finishing their studies. Media also fails to mention that most successful people actually obtained their diplomas; that is not interesting news.

This bias can, for instance, prompt us to start a venture or a project in a field that seems hot because of the successes we read about. Before embarking on that path, we should make sure to know the percentage of silent failures in the field. Availability and survivorship are biases that afflict many start-up founders. Investors often hear proposals like "We need an investment for our new sandbox video game. We will make an open-world game like Minecraft and get rich. Look, Microsoft bought Minecraft for 2.5 billion." Yes, but Minecraft is the one game that succeeded. We normally do not read about the thousands that failed. As we discussed in the Bioline case, start-up founders often propose valuations after reading Crunch Base, a database of recent funding rounds, mainly from the USA. And then, just like that, they value themselves at a minimum of 1 million dollars. Why? With a few slides and not even a minimum viable product (MVP)? Well, they may say, because those US start-ups raise millions every week and their valuations are quite high. Yes, but Crunch Base is the list of start-ups that *succeeded* in raising funds. There is no list of the thousands and thousands that did not get funded and failed! All in all, not all rock singers get "money for nothing and chicks for free." Only the successful ones.

Framing is the tendency to react to a particular choice in different ways, depending on how the choice is presented to us. Let me ask you: How much do you tip on Uber? I am sure that everyone (who tips) has very clear criteria (the quality of service, race's length, the personality of the driver). But are we sure that we really base our decision on these criteria? Isn't it just rationalization? If Uber were to make a statistic, they would notice that the average amount left as a tip for a driver increased sharply in some countries at the beginning of 2019. The reason is not a wave of generosity or a sudden increase in service quality, but a small change in the app. In the past, in Romania you had to choose between 2 RON (Romanian New Leu, the currency in my home country), 3 RON, and 5 RON; from February 2019, you could choose between 3 RON, 5 RON, and 10 RON. Most people, when deciding how much to tip the Uber driver, which size of beverage to buy at the fast-food store, or which insurance to buy, unconsciously choose the option in the middle. This is the influence of the framing effect, in which the way a choice is presented to you influences your decision. We do not, however, have anything to say on the way prices populate this podium of offers. Who, then, is really in control of our choices? Is it us, or the marketers who designed the offers? This leads to a related bias, *the decoy effect*.

The decoy effect is a variant of framing and appears when an additional *unwanted* option influences our preference. Let me give an example. Consider a menu at an Italian restaurant. The antipasti page is filled with delicious offers, from *melanzane alla parmigiana* to *carpaccio* and *caprese*, all ranging in price between 9 and 12 euros. The only exception is *gamberetti in crosta di sale* (5 pieces), which costs 20 euros. Would you buy that? If you were like most people, you would not. Unless you really like to spend on food or really enjoy prawns, you would normally steer clear of the most expensive item on the menu. But, now, imagine that there is another item, printed at the top of the page: *fichi con prosciutto* (3 pieces), 29 euros. And, if you desire, for each supplementary fig wrapped in 24-month cured *prosciutto di Parma* and drizzled with gorgonzola, you pay an extra 9 euros. Isn't, now, this the thing you would never buy? Now, in comparison, the prawns in salt crust seem decently priced, a bargain even, so you would buy them. It all may seem to be your choice, but, in fact, it is the choice of the designer of the menu. The name of this bias illustrates how an option almost nobody wants (the decoy option) will have an effect on the choice between the other options, namely favoring the next most expensive. Nobel laureate Richard Thaler offered the term *choice architecture* to explain how the way a choice is framed greatly influences the decision. From now on, because we know, we will be able to choose on more objective criteria between three subscription options, three laptops, or three software solutions. And we will also avoid jumping to buy the 95% fat-free yogurt while ignoring the 5% fat option.

The paradox of choice. Counterintuitively, after a certain (low) threshold, having more options does not facilitate but rather inhibits decisions (Schwartz, 2005). This bias was described in Barry Schwartz' bestseller, *The Paradox of Choice. Why More Is Less*, and the key concepts can be understood by watching the author's acclaimed 2005 TED talk. The principle behind the paradox of choice is that when —for instance—we choose which laptop to buy, we believe we want to have a consideration set (a shortlist) that is as large as possible. In fact, if we have more than five items to choose from, we freeze and become unhappy. Apparently, the magical number for any consideration set is three. Hence, if you offer two subscription options, add a third one. If you have an online store (where laptops can be bought from, for instance) and customers can narrow their search using different criteria such as brand, price, type of processor, memory, and so on, try to design the choice so that on the final (decision) page, there are between two and four models, ideally three. If there is just one, the client will feel they don't have a real choice, so they will close the browser and walk away. Metaphorically. If there are more than four or five options to choose from, the client will appreciate that cognitively, but their choice process will be soon paralyzed and they will also walk away. Aside from decision paralysis, Barry Schwartz shows that too many options can make consumers unhappier with their choice. How does that work? When forced to buy the only existent option or to choose between two or three, if we end up with a poor product, we can blame the retailer. But when we could choose between 30 options, if we end up with a poor product, it can be only our own fault.

Unintentional heuristics and their associated cognitive biases are evolutionary adaptations that function efficiently in most situations, while occasionally misfiring. Aside from knowing about biases and their specific countermeasures, a useful mindset is to consider ourselves less rational. If we allow ourselves to think that sometimes our mind can trick us into irrational behavior and if we fight the *blind spot bias*—which makes us see biases everywhere but in our own behavior—we will be better equipped to identify and fight these cognitive and behavioral traps.

References

Ariely, D. (2010). *Predictably irrational, revised and expanded edition: The hidden forces that shape our decisions* (Revised and Expanded ed.). Harper Perennial.

Johnson, E. J., & Goldstein, D. (2003). Do Defaults save lives? *Science, 302*(5649), 1338–1339. https://doi.org/10.1126/science.1091721

Kahneman, D. (2012). *Thinking, fast and slow*. Penguin.

McKinsey and Company (2009, August 14). *Strategic decisions: When can you trust your gut?* https://www.mckinsey.com/business-functions/strategy-and-corporate-finance/our-insights/strategic-decisions-when-can-you-trust-your-gut

Norton, M. I., Mochon, D., & Ariely, D. (2012). The IKEA effect: When labor leads to love. *Journal of Consumer Psychology, 22*(3), 453–460. https://doi.org/10.1016/j.jcps.2011.08.002

Polivy, J., Herman, C. P., & Deo, R. (2010). Getting a bigger slice of the pie. Effects on eating and emotion in restrained and unrestrained eaters. *Appetite, 55*(3), 426–430. https://doi.org/10.1016/j.appet.2010.07.015

Schwartz, B. (2005). *The paradox of choice: Why more is less*. Harper Perennial.

Shampan'er, K., & Ariely, D. (2006). How small is zero price? The true value of free products. *Advances in Consumer Research, 33*, 254–255.

Tversky, A., & Kahneman, D. (1973). Availability: A heuristic for judging frequency and probability. *Cognitive Psychology, 5*(2), 207–232. https://doi.org/10.1016/0010-0285(73)90033-9

Tversky, A., & Kahneman, D. (1974). Judgment under uncertainty: Heuristics and biases. *Science, 185*(4157), 1124–1131. https://doi.org/10.1126/science.185.4157.1124

Worchel, S., Lee, J., & Adewole, A. (1975). Effects of supply and demand on ratings of object value. *Journal of Personality and Social Psychology, 32*(5), 906–914. https://doi.org/10.1037/0022-3514.32.5.906

Decisions, Decisions, Decisions 7

Herbert Simon, the father of the decision-making discipline, wrote that "the work of managers (…) is largely work of making decisions" (Simon, 1987). One would say, then, that management science should have a clear idea of how managers decide, individually and in groups. Decision-making is classically understood as a logical process that goes through analyzing the situation, generating alternatives, evaluating the possible outcome and consequences of these alternatives in light of the objectives, and choosing the best solution. According to the classical sequential model of the decision-making process proposed by Simon (1960), strategic decision-making can be thus schematically deconstructed in three phases:

Phase 1. Intelligence, in which the problem is identified and data are gathered
Phase 2. Design, in which a set of alternatives is generated
Phase 3. Choice, in which alternatives are evaluated and a solution is chosen.

Of course, scholars have proposed other, more complex sequential models (Mintzberg et al., 1976; Schwenk, 1984) and yet other scholars have argued against the validity of rationalistic models of decision-making (Etzioni, 1967). For an encompassing view on decision-making models, see the witty *Organization Science* paper by Langley et al. (1995). Non-sequential models have also been proposed. Michael D. Cohen, James G. March, and Johan P. Olsen wrote a famous paper in 1972 in which they showed that in real organizations decisions are made haphazardly, reactively, and chaotically. The paper, titled *A Garbage Can Model of Organizational Choice*, observes that "organizations can be viewed as collections of choices looking for problems, issues and feelings looking for decision situations in which they might be aired, solutions looking for issues they might be an answer to, and decision-makers looking for work." (Cohen et al., 1972, p.1). If this image looks familiar and you can identify traces of it in your organization, do not worry; you are not alone. Acknowledging that managerial decision-making is a process that can be improved is a first step toward improving it.

R. Atanasiu, *Critical Thinking for Managers*, Management for Professionals,
https://doi.org/10.1007/978-3-030-73600-2_7

Deciding is so natural that thinking about our own decision-making style is a bit awkward, like thinking about the way we walk or run. It may prompt us to do peculiar moves at first, but if we take a bit of time and focus to analyze what and how we do it, we can improve both our decisions and our running. This chapter will address some aspects of decision-making that can lead managers toward efficacy, efficiency, and out-of-the-box thinking.

Case Let us start with an imaginary decision: You need to choose between two apartments. One is the one you currently live in. Rent is 500 euros; commuting time is one-and-a-half hours daily (there and back); the building is old, with poor insulation; you have a free parking space; you run (or have a dog, or a small kid), and you need a park, but the closest park is 2 km away; your best friend lives across the street; and the local pub is perfect. The second apartment is more expensive, 800 euros; is much closer to work, with a total commuting time of just 45 min; the building is new; there are no free parking spaces around, but you can rent one for an extra 100 euros; and there is a park across the street. At a first glance, which one would you—personally—choose and why? Please remember or write down your choice and its motivation.

If you are like most people, you have immediately formed a preference, and usually, it is based on just one of the criteria presented above. I use this exercise in class and have participants choose one of the apartments by voting with a show of hands. Most of my MBA students vote in a fraction of a second, choosing one apartment or the other. Questioned on the reason, they usually have just one criterion (price, commuting time, the best friend, the park) or a combination of two criteria in a new one ("The difference in commuting time and walking to the park is worth more to me than the difference in rent"). Few people take more than an instant to analyze all criteria presented. Fewer still observe the false dilemma ("Why should I choose just between these two?") or request more information ("How many rooms? Is the house furnished or not? Are we talking about my own personal situation—salary, marital status, etc.? Which floor is the apartment on? How is the neighborhood?," and so on). What if, after making the choice, you need to explain it to a colleague at work, or to your curious middle-school kid? When asked, people usually develop a full explanation that considers more criteria and makes use of a choice method such as pros and cons or weighted criteria. This is a clear case of rationalization, the often-unconscious process of building a rational post-hoc explanation after we have made our less-rational choice. Rationalization may be triggered by an outside inquiry (like the colleague at work or the kid asking about the apartment choice), but most often is an unconscious mechanism through which we construct some logical explanation for our shoot-from-the-hip choices just to justify them to ourselves. We make many decisions based on our gut feeling, and our reason kicks in afterward and starts building a case for our choice.

Question Can you think of such a decision? An important one, in which you think you made a rational choice but upon a closer inspection you realize you decided instinctively?

7.1 One-Criterion Decision-Making

As detailed above, people usually make decisions intuitively or based on a single criterion and rationalize the process afterward. Ignoring most criteria and deciding based on a single one is our natural way of choosing, and it functions better with experience. Bauer et al. (2012) show that experienced bank managers know the right information to be ignored when assessing clients. A similar conclusion is cited by Åstebro and Elhedhli (2006): "expert auditors are not influenced by irrelevant information while more inexperienced auditors are."

It is hard to acknowledge and accept that we decide based on a single factor when multiple criteria are available. But when we do acknowledge and accept this fact, we will better understand our past choices, the way we may decide in the future, and the decision processes of others. In sales, for instance, the assumption that the customer is convinced to buy for a mix of reasons (for instance, price plus certain features plus brand awareness) leads brands to complicate their communication and puzzle the shopper. If they understand, for instance, that each person looking for a mobile phone has already made a shortlist of candidates and will choose among them based on a single criterion (different criteria for different customers, but still single ones) may result in shorter publicity messages that each emphasize one feature. In his book, *Alchemy: The Surprising Power of Ideas That Don't Make Sense*, Ogilvy's Rory Sutherland pinpoints in his unmistakable style how a single and unexpected criterion differentiates two brands: "Consumers do not choose between brand A and brand B the one they think it is best, but the one with the lowest probability of crappiness" (Sutherland, 2019). For instance, if two vacuum cleaners have more or less the same features and the same price, shoppers will choose the brand that makes them believe that the device will not break too soon. Sutherland argues that the power of a brand acts mostly by assuring the consumer that things will go well. This is an example of the way we most often make our choice: by minimizing the potential loss in a worst-case scenario. Named minimax (minimizing the maximum loss), this seemingly abstract way of making choices is actually very present in our business and personal behavior.

Another natural way we choose based on a single (yet composite) criterion is by minimizing anticipated regret. This is a psychological mechanism that actually introduces opportunity cost into our natural decision-making process. Besides evaluating the potential benefits and risks of the chosen option, a large weight is given to the anticipated regret of overlooking the other option(s). For instance, in our two-apartment example, the decision to move to the new place may be taken by a person who values social ties only after feeling that the pragmatic advantages of moving can overcome the regret of not being able to have a drink with the best friend so often at the local pub. The Danish poet Piet Hein pinpointed the principle behind deciding based on minimizing regret when he wrote in one of his famous grooks (aphoristic poems) a very simple rule that can help us solve difficult dilemmas (Hein, 1969):

A PSYCHOLOGICAL TIP

Whenever you're called on to make up your mind,
and you're hampered by not having any,
the best way to solve the dilemma, you'll find,
is simply by spinning a penny.
No—not so that chance shall decide the affair
while you're passively standing there moping;
but the moment the penny is up in the air,
you suddenly know what you're hoping.

We should note that all these natural decision strategies (minimax, its cousin maximin—choosing so as to maximize one's minimum payoff and minimizing regret) are rather pessimistic and very influenced by loss aversion (see the chapter on cognitive biases). What does that say about human nature?

7.2 Gathering and Analyzing Data

Although the last paragraphs have discussed people's inclination to ignore information while deciding, in important business decisions, we need to overcome this tendency and carefully build solid business cases before choosing one path or the other. Assessing the situation and gathering and analyzing information is a straightforward process; therefore, this section will provide a few perspectives on how and where to look. We will then discuss the balance between considering too much and too little information.

In their bestseller *Decisive*, authors Chip and Dan Heath offer a few tips on how to assess a situation before deciding (Heath and Heath, 2013). One such tip, which they call *laddering* (because of the successive focusing on local, regional, and distant fields of vision), is to start by looking for successful (local) implementations of the decision, which they call bright spots, then to assess the best practices of the field (regional), and finally to see if analogies from related (distant) domains can apply. For instance, if we run a successful bakery shop and we realize we need to scale, we must look around for bakeries that have scaled successfully and understand their model (opening shops one by one? opening more shops at once? franchising? choosing high-street or malls? becoming a supplier of bread and pastries for restaurants?). Then we can analyze the whole bakery business landscape, nationally and internationally, to understand trends, best practices, future opportunities and threats, and how competitors might react to our scaling. Finally, we can look for useful analogies with other domains—for instance, by understanding how franchising might be a viable option for scaling by looking at classical models such as that used by McDonalds.

Another tip proposed by the two authors is to shift perspective by zooming in and out of the problem. Let us take a hypothetical example:

> **Case** A company that offers a subscription to a monthly selection of wines sees a high churn rate in clients and, despite being profitable, is looking to change its business model by employing a more traditional online shop model. Before doing that, the manager assesses the situation by *zooming out* and *zooming in*. *Zooming out* is done by looking at the base rates in local subscription-based business models, from healthcare providers to toys and gyms. He is surprised to see that most such businesses succeed despite many customers closing their subscription each month. As long as the number of clients coming in is substantially larger than the number of clients that walk away, business is good. Puzzled, he then *zooms in*, by meeting face-to-face a few of his active customers and a few customers that just closed their subscription. He invites them for a coffee and his grim assumption that the service is not valued is contradicted by both categories. Active customers are very happy with the service, they actively recommend it to friends and write about it on social media. When asked what would be some reasons for eventually closing their subscription in the future, they listed a variety of reasons that have nothing to do with their satisfaction, like moving to another town or taking a break from drinking. The three ex-customers spoke in equally great terms about their experience with the service and confirmed the speculations of their active counterparts. All have renounced the service for personal reasons and are eager to return as soon as conditions allow. For one of them, who moved to a town nearby, the manager offered to extend the serviced area, and the offer was accepted on the spot. This led to the idea to assume a slight increase in average transport cost per customer in order to increase the serviced area to the whole county. All in all, after *zooming out* by comparing his churn rate with base rates from similar business models and after *zooming in* by talking to active and inactive customers, the manager had a much better grasp of the situation and—instead of changing the business model—decided to expand the current one.

But how much consideration is appropriate, especially during a crisis, when time is crucial? How much time should a manager spend preparing the case for a decision in times of crisis? Most successful managers are experienced in making successful decisions. However, in unusual times, when speed is essential, problems are unfamiliar, and stakes are high, we need to update our decision-making style. The first step is to acknowledge that we have one, and the second is to admit that—while it may have served us well until now—it can always be improved. These two steps require a moment of introspection and a degree of intellectual humility. How, then, do you make decisions? Decision-making styles can be arranged on a spectrum from *plunging-in* to *paralysis by analysis*.

Plunging-in bias is, as mentioned before, the tendency of many experienced managers and entrepreneurs to come up with a solution and to start implementing it long before they read the second half of the memo describing the problem. In the opposite corner lies the manager who needs to have all the data, all the computation, and all the analyses before deciding. Jeff Bezos, the founder of Amazon, uses two simple principles to tackle this tendency. First, he splits decisions into reversible and irreversible categories and has a different decision-making process for each. He wrote the following in an annual letter to Amazon shareholders: "*Some decisions are consequential and irreversible or nearly irreversible—one-way doors —and these decisions must be made methodically, carefully, slowly, with great deliberation and consultation. If you walk through and don't like what you see on the other side, you can't get back to where you were before. We can call these Type 1 decisions. But most decisions aren't like that—they are changeable, reversible—they're two-way doors. If you've made a suboptimal Type 2 decision, you don't have to live with the consequences for that long. You can reopen the door and go back through. Type 2 decisions can and should be made quickly by high judgment individuals or small groups. As organizations get larger, there seems to be a tendency to use the heavy-weight Type 1 decision-making process on most decisions, including many Type 2 decisions. The end result of this is slowness, unthoughtful risk aversion, failure to experiment sufficiently, and consequently diminished invention. We'll have to figure out how to fight that tendency. And one-size-fits-all thinking will turn out to be only one of the pitfalls. We'll work hard to avoid it*" (Amazon.com, 2016).

Then, even for the irreversible ones, Bezos advises in another annual shareholder letter (Reisinger, 2020): "*Most decisions should probably be made with somewhere around 70% of the information you wish you had. If you wait for 90%, in most cases, you're probably being slow.*" I was always puzzled by this precise percentage, but I am sure you get the point. Both types of managers need to borrow a little from the opposite style. While the experience-based intuition of the fast movers is trained in calmer environments, this landscape is new and their intuition might misfire, so they need to insert some reflection and data-based analysis in their decision-making. Over-analyzers need to adapt to the speed of the times and to sacrifice accuracy for efficiency. They should favor action over reflection and try to test scenarios with fast and cheap pilots. Also, over-analyzers tend to search for the perfect solution. An important thing to understand is that—in business—decisions can never be perfect. The perfect solution is a myth. An over-analyzer tends to gather a large amount of information, to think of a large list of good alternatives, to apply all possible criteria, to search for a solution that solves five objectives in one shot, and to please all stakeholders. When they finally choose, they keep worrying that one of the alternative solutions they discarded was in fact better. The key is to give up the myth of the perfect solution, to follow one or two key objectives, to ignore the right information to be ignored, and to please just the most important stakeholders and then, after choosing, to forget all the other good solutions and focus on implementing the good one we selected, in a short, well-defined time frame. A fast and good-enough decision is better than a better one, made in twice the time. What would fast mean? The range is vast. It could mean a month for the board of a large company for deciding where and how to start internationalizing. It could mean 10 minutes for a salesperson working in that company when deciding how to respond to an unusual request from a good client. All in all, management is not about finding perfect solutions, but about moving forward with good, efficient solutions.

Question What characterizes you more: the plunging-in bias or over-analyzing? Which type would you say you are?

7.3 More Than One Option

A decision can be defined as a choice between several options. The number and quality of the alternatives strongly influence the quality of the decision and—evidently—its outcome. However, in their day-to-day decision-making, managers do not consider many options and do not look far to find better ones. Most decision-making meetings are flawed by the lack of a remarkably simple parameter: the number of options considered. One of the most prominent researchers on business decision-making, Ohio State University Professor Paul Nutt, has studied a large number of decisions made by top management teams and found that in 70% of cases, the number of possible solutions they considered is 1 (Nutt, 1993). That cannot even be referred to as "considering." The false sense of choice arises from counting a *yes-or-no* discussion as a decision. If you and your team are considering whether or not to embark on project *A*, that is not considering two alternatives; that is considering just one. Considering two alternatives is comparing project *A* to project *B* (and, please, dare to include *C* and *D*). But, apparently, that does not happen often. Should it? Well, the same researcher studied 10 years of important decisions made by the board of a medium-sized German tech company and found that, when the board had a shortlist of at least two alternative solutions, the final choice was more successful than in cases when they just debated whether or not to go with the only one option considered (Nutt, 2002). How much more successful? Quite a bit: six times more! So, if you consider launching a new line of business, it will have more chances of success if your decision is made between two or three different options.

Chip and Dan Heath (2013) describe several pitfalls in generating and dealing with alternative solutions and offer simple methods to tackle them:

Go/No-go decisions. Most commonly, as found by Paul Nutt, individuals and groups decide while considering just one option, choosing whether to do something or not. In fact, this is a truncated decision. A whether-or-not decision gives a narrow frame and limits the perspective. For instance, imagine that a board considers whether or not to start a new line of business. There is a good business case, but the board acknowledges the fact that there are risks that cannot be evaluated. They therefore hesitate between launching the new line or not, with two camps emerging, each supporting one of the options (*go* and *no go*). One of the parties sees the opportunity and can live with the unquantified risks; the other is more cautious and wants to prevent or at least stall the launch of the new business until new information can be gathered. If they could take a step back, the members of the board might realize that they are actually stuck on one option and that they should increase the consideration set by adding two types of new alternatives: combinations of the *go* and *no-go* scenarios or completely new options. A possible combination might be to test some of the assumptions about risks by launching a smaller version of the business line or to postpone heavy investment and to bootstrap for the time being by using existent resources. A completely new option would be to find another new line of business that the company can launch and to compare the two.

The and/or confusion. Usually, faced with multiple alternatives, people only consider one *or* the another, as if they are mutually exclusive, ignoring the many ways they could do one *and* the other in various combinations. This false dilemma arises in simple one-option scenarios (*"Should we move our shop online?"* is framed as a limited, *yes-or-no* problem, guiding us to think that keeping a physical presence and having an online shop cannot work together) and also in situations where there are more alternatives considered (the question *"Should we expand by launching our platform in a country from the region or directly in the USA?"* is framed so to guide us away from the possibility to launch in both Hungary and the USA and away from considering the possibility to launch first in the Philippines, or to scale without launching internationally). A good exercise would be to list all alternatives previously considered as mutually exclusive and to try to combine them into one new and better alternative.

The vanishing alternative. When a likely solution emerges quickly, consensus seems likely, and a lack of alternatives looms, Chip and Dan Heath recommend a clever trick to increase the number of options: pretend that the favored solution has disappeared. For instance, imagine a small organization that is struggling with sales. The CEO is now considering hiring (for a lot of money) a star salesperson who recently left a job with one of the main competitors. This is a good scenario for using the vanishing alternative trick. Before settling the case (deciding whether or not to hire that person), the CEO can imagine that this option is no longer on the table. What would be the next best alternative? Freed from the shadow of the single option, the CEO might identify other possible candidates and also other methods to increase sales, besides hiring that salesperson.

What would your successor do? This method is best applied when the status quo bias prevents managers from making sudden, drastic moves. When, for instance, the traditional business model is threatened by, say, a new technology, the reflex of a seasoned executive would be to adapt slowly, without sudden turns, and salvage as much as possible from the old way of doing business. The fast-changing business and technological landscape, however, might not be forgiving with this approach, especially in the long run. This mindset can be changed, for instance, if the CEO tries to imagine himself being replaced and then to think of the first move his successor would do. If that is to scrap the old business model, then the next question would be "what prevents me from doing the same thing?"

What would the competitor do? This is a variant of the "successor" method, and it involves thinking what the closest competitors would do to increase their market share to our detriment. Again, the exercise ends with the question "what keeps us from doing the same things?'

Question Please think about a recent or upcoming decision. How many alternative solutions did you consider or are you considering?

How are alternatives generated? Most often, there is no structured approach. When there is one, it is usually a kind of brainstorming, be it formal or informal. While research on brainstorming is ambivalent, some organizations use an upgraded version, called brainwriting, which will be detailed in the chapter on problem solving.

7.4 Decision Tools

Let us say we have reached a shortlist of 2–4 viable alternatives, and we need to choose between them. How do we do that? We discussed in this book the many ways we are influenced by non-rational forces, but reason still plays a strong part in our decision-making, especially in business. What tools can we use to *rationally* evaluate these alternatives and to select one of them? This section will discuss five types of decision-making tools: the pros and cons list, the weighted decision matrix, the decision tree, the fast-and-frugal decision tree, and simple rules.

1. *The pros and cons list.* This is a very popular tool—indeed, it is the most common tool people mention when I ask them to name their preferred method of evaluation—but I only mention it here to argue against its use. Unfortunately, this method is both poor and inadequate. It is inadequate because it is designed to evaluate a *whether-or-not* option, not to choose between several options. The two columns (pros and cons) are about one single course of action. Of course, it can be used in choosing between different options by having four or six columns and calculating a score for each, but doing so is cumbersome. The pros and cons list is also a poor method because all criteria listed are treated equally, which is never the case in real-life scenarios. Its inventor, Benjamin Franklin, actually gave weights to his pros and cons, crossing with a line equivalent factors on each column; for instance, crossing out one important pro and two less important cons. Of course, his method is good for *go/no-go* scenarios, but the better tool to use instead of the pros and cons list is the weighted decision matrix.
2. *The weighted decision matrix.* Remember the choice between the two apartments I proposed at the beginning of this chapter. Or better yet, imagine a situation with more than two alternatives, like the following scenario: You expand into a new market, and you need to choose a supplier for transportation services. The shortlist is made of four transport companies, and, for each one,

your team has prepared a short report that includes their prices, quality assessments, reliability assessments, payment options, and number of vehicles. There is no clear preference; some transporters offer better prices, others agree to friendlier payment conditions during the first two years, and so on. How do you choose? We often face a similar situation in our private lives when we need to choose which car or house to choose from a set of options. To do so, an upgraded version of the pros and cons list is the weighted decision matrix, described in the figure below. The principle is the following: we list the options as rows and the criteria as columns. The second row, below the list of criteria, is the weights line, where we differentiate between criteria, as they are not all equal. Sometimes, people use ranking; for instance, they rank five criteria from 1 to 5, attributing 1 to the least important and 5 to the most important. This method, however, only allows for discrete values and does not permit two criteria to be equally important. A better version is to think that all criteria add up to 100% importance and to allocate a percentage to each. In our case, let us say that the price is the most important and we allocate 40% to it. Next, quality of service and reliability are equally important, each with 20%, followed by payment options, which account for 15%, and the number of vehicles they own, accounting for 5%. Together, these percentages add up to 100%. The next step is to grade the four transporters on the five criteria, without taking the weights of each criterion into account. Although some people use rankings here as well, the best option—in my experience—is a straightforward 1 to 10 scale. For instance, Transporter A scores 6 in price (a bit on the expensive side), 9 in quality (their trucks are new and their drivers are the best), 7 in reliability, 6 in payment options, and 4 in number of trucks. But price has much more weight than payment options, despite the same score of 6. In order to reflect this, we need to multiply the score by the corresponding weight of the criterion. A simple spreadsheet does this automatically. In our case, we get the following weighted scores for Transporter A: 2.4, 1.8, 1.4, 0.9, and 0.2, respectively. The final score for Transporter A is obtained by adding these weighted scores together: 6.7. We do the same for all the other three transporters, and the winner should be the one with the highest score, as depicted in Table 7.1.

I wrote *should be* instead of *is*. I have a good reason for that. The reason is that none of these tools should be used mindlessly to designate the winning solution, but rather as a strong indicator of a good candidate. The matrix produces a favorite that *should* then be analyzed. In our case, for instance, the difference between Transporter A and Transporter C is not large, and we should carefully consider both options, or a combination of the two (as mentioned in the section on alternatives). Also, the option pointed out by the matrix should be further discussed according to risks, timeline, short-term versus long-term goals, and so on. Most of the managers I have worked with have used weighted decision matrices both for business and for their private choices. When used for private choices—for instance, for choosing what car to buy—without having someone else to justify the outcome to, they all admitted to a strange behavior: Once the matrix produced a winner, if it were not

Table 7.1 Weighted decision matrix used to choose between four transporters

		Prices	Quality	Reliability	Payment options	Number of vehicles	Total
	Weights	40%	20%	20%	15%	5%	100%
Transporter A	Score	6	9	7	6	4	6.7
	Weighted	2.4	1.8	1.4	0.9	0.2	
Transporter B	Score	3	7	9	5	4	5.35
	Weighted	1.2	1.4	1.8	0.75	0.2	
Transporter C	Score	8	4	8	2	8	6.3
	Weighted	3.2	0.8	1.6	0.3	0.4	
Transporter D	Score	6	5	5	6	6	5.6
	Weighted	2.4	1.0	1.0	0.9	0.3	

the one they secretly favored, they went on and modified—in good faith—the scores and weights until the rational procedure and the gut feeling indicated the same winner, in a clear example of rationalization. Have you ever done that? We should avoid this behavior in a business decision, or at least be clear and transparent about it. A better option would be, in open-minded organizations, to acknowledge the value of managerial intuition and to include it among the other criteria, with a weight of its own.

Weighted decision matrices are a valuable tool in decisions where there are multiple options, multiple criteria, and there is no time dimension. When, on the contrary, several scenarios can turn out in different ways in the future and we can boil everything down to one criterion (for instance cost), the tool of choice (*sic*!) is the decision tree, described below.

3. The Decision Tree

We can discuss the use of decision trees using a case study inspired by a real situation.

Case Imagine you need to rent a car for a week and there are three insurance policies, which differ in price and in the excess paid in case of an event. The options, inspired by a real situation, are as follows:

Basic, which is free and, in case of an event, you pay up to 950 euros, and the insurance takes care of the rest;
Medium, which costs 100 euros and, in case of an event, you pay up to 450 euros; and
Premium, which costs 180 euros and, in case of an event, the policy covers everything.

Which one should you choose? And how? I wish I had considered this question seriously the many times I have had to rent a car. Usually, this decision (which insurance pack to choose) is influenced by the availability bias: the more recent and stronger a memory of a car incident, the more you will favor higher protection. But there is a tool that can evaluate rationally whether one should pay for extra insurance. This situation has a clear criterion (cost) and an important difference in outcome given two clearly different scenarios (whether there will be a car incident or not). The best tool to be used here is a decision tree in which we use expected value to discern between the three options. Expected value is a concept that, for some, is harder to grasp. It means the average outcome of several scenarios for each option. In our rent-a-car example, the expected value of the Basic option would be the average cost of the two scenarios (*there is an event* and *there is no event*). This can be confusing, mainly because the expected value does not equal the value (in our case the cost) of either of the two scenarios. How do we calculate expected value? The expected value of an option is calculated by multiplying the value and the probability of each of its scenarios and then summing them, as in Fig. 7.1 (simplified for just two options). After calculating the expected value for all options, we compare and select the best one (in the case of cost, the smallest value). A graphical form of this method is depicted in Fig. 7.1, showing its tree-like structure.

Let us work with our case. To do so, we need to know (or to estimate) the cost in all scenarios and to know (or to estimate) a probability for each. The cost is easy to calculate, but what about the probability of an event? Well, I am sure that each of us knows our driving abilities, personal event history, and statistics. These, along with

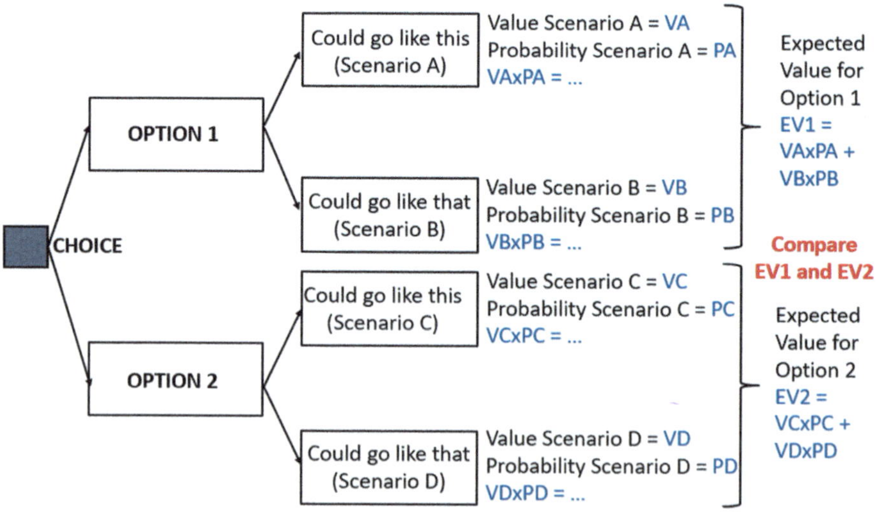

Fig. 7.1 Generic decision tree with two options, each having two possible scenarios

the context (the weather, the quality of the roads, the traffic, and the behavior of the other drivers) can lead to a probability estimate. Let us use, in this case, a 10% probability of an event.

For the Basic option, we will therefore have two scenarios:

Basic without event, where the cost is 0 and the probability is 90% (better written as 0.9)

and

Basic with event, where the cost is 950 and the probability is 0.1.

In order to calculate the expected value of the Basic option, we multiply each value with its probability and then add them up.

$$\text{EvBasic} = 0 \times 0.9 + 950 \times 0.1 = 0 + 95 = 95 \text{ EUR}$$

In the same manner, we can easily calculate the expected value for the other two insurance offers:

Medium no event, where the cost is 100 and the probability is 0.9

and

Medium with event, where the cost is 100 + 450 = 550 and the probability is 0.1.

$$\text{EvMedium} = 100 \times 0.9 + 550 \times 0.1 = 90 + 55 = 145 \text{ EUR}$$

Finally, the remaining scenarios are

Premium no event, where the cost is 180 and the probability is 0.9

and

Premium with event, where the cost is 180 + 0 = 180 and the probability is 0.1.

Given that, no matter what happens, the cost is 180 euros, this option's expected value is 180—we can calculate it as follows:

$$\text{EvPremium} = 180 \times 0.9 + 180 \times 0.1 = 162 + 18 = 180 \text{ EUR}$$

If we put these calculations in the form of a tree, it would look like in Fig. 7.2.

The sums are costs, so we should choose the option with the smallest expected value. We can easily see that, for a self-estimated probability of an event of 10%, the *Basic* option is by far the better choice. The other options become interesting only around a 20% probability of a mishap. Perhaps you can draw a quick decision tree on a napkin the next time you rent a car or you decide whether to buy an extended guarantee.

In a business setting, decision trees can point toward a recommended option in scenario planning. Of course, we need to be especially careful when estimating values and probabilities, but the decision tree is nonetheless a very useful instrument. Like its cousin, the weighted matrix, the decision tree should not pinpoint the winning solution without us double-checking the result.

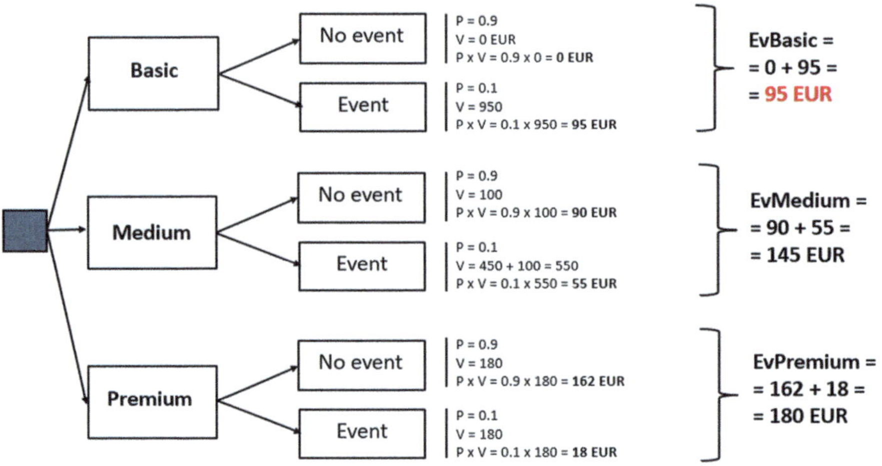

Fig. 7.2 Decision tree for choosing between three insurance options

4. *Fast-and-frugal trees (FFT)*. This different kind of decision tree can be used in situations where different criteria must be evaluated in a cascade of binary decisions. It is a graphical and simpler variant of *elimination by aspects*. These trees are a type of fast-and-frugal heuristic (as described by their theorist, Gerd Gigerenzer) and are called fast because—as decision rules—they point quickly toward a decision, and frugal because they use a small amount of information. FFTs work in stable environments where past decisions can inform future ones. For instance, this tool has been perfected in emergency rooms as a quick guide to deciding on a treatment based on analyzing a series of symptoms. If, when analyzing a criterion, we obtain two more dilemmas—which, at the following criterion, turn into four, and so on, by the power of two—the instrument is hard to use. This is why the fast-and-frugal decision tree is a special kind of decision tree that has an exit at every fork in the road. For each factor it analyzes, it offers an exit (a final decision) and another binary choice. The exception is the last factor, where it offers two exits. In sum, it analyzes a cascade of n factors and, instead of 2^n possible outcomes, it only offers $n + 1$.

In Fig. 7.3, there is a simple FFT, adapted from Fischer et al. (2002), which helps doctors decide whether to administrate a certain antibiotic to children with community-acquired pneumonia.

If, in your line of business, situations do not change significantly and you can quickly classify them based on a cascade of binary cues, drawing a FFT can help in three ways. First, it offers a graphical form that you can follow quickly. Second, it helps you to consider all factors, without losing sight of any of them. And third, it allows you to share your experience-based knowledge in an easy-to-follow way. Aside from emergency care, FFTs have been used in many diverse fields, from judges (to help them decide whether to grant bail or not) to the army (in

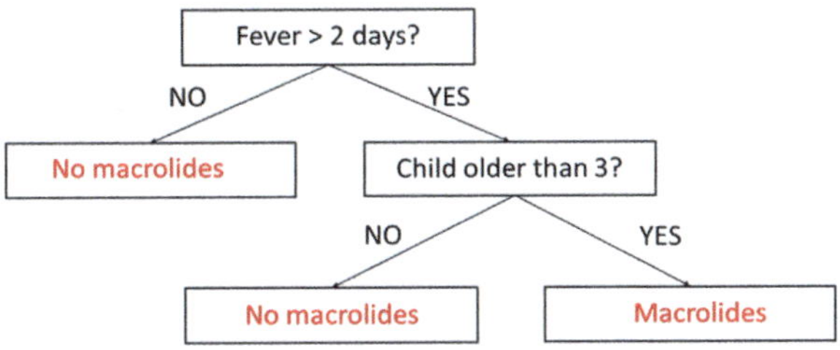

Fig. 7.3 Fast-and-frugal (adapted from Fischer et al., 2002)

Afghanistan, to discern between civilians and suicide bombers). A kind of fast-and-frugal tree is the Vroom–Yetton decision model, which helps managers see how to involve their team in a decision—this model will be mentioned later in this chapter.

How do we build an FFT? First, we need to order the cues to be analyzed; then, we need to make sure that there is an exit at every level; and finally, we put it in a graphical form. Let us build a fast-and-frugal tree for the following case:

> **Case** You are an angel investor, and—after some years of practice—you know when it is worth having a longer conversation with a startup after they pitch. It does not matter if the idea is great if they do not have an MVP (minimum viable product), because you never discuss based on ideas or slides alone. If there is no scalability, even with initial traction, it is better to stay out, as the business will not be able to attract successive financing rounds. After a few sterile talks with startups that have a sole founder, you realize that there must be a team of founders containing at least two people and that they must be beer material. What does that mean? If they are nice enough to drink an imaginary beer with, your relationship might be able to survive future bumps. Only after these criteria are met, you look at a slide with numbers. Usually, their business plan is overoptimistic. But your educated common sense is able to tell you whether adjusting these numbers to reality will still result in a workable business plan. Only if this is the case can you schedule a conversation longer than 5 min. Your friend decided to become an angel investor and asked you to give him a simplified version of this process—a rapid tool in graphic form—that he can use at his first pitching session. How would you do it?

Before reading on, please take no more than 3 min and build your own version of a fast-and-frugal tree, before comparing it with the solution provided below. Remember, the order of the cues in the short text above is not necessarily the order they should be analyzed in. Try to order the cues from important and easy to assess to less important and hard to assess. Of course, there is no single solution to this problem, but here is my own take on the matter:

What can I easily assess during a 5-min pitch? The easiest cue is whether there is a single founder or a team. If there is a team, I will continue considering the other factors. If there is a single founder, I would advise the founder to find a co-founder before returning. Then, I can probably say, within the first minute, whether I can have a beer with the founders. Then, if they are beer material, even before hearing about their product, I would mentally assess the market they address and the scalability of their business. After that, I would consider the existence of the MVP, and only then would I consider the slide with a business plan.

I would then draw the tree depicted in Fig. 7.4, in which the exits are marked in red. Please note that we have analyzed five factors and offered six exits.

5. *Simple rules.* Managers and companies learn mostly from failure. Famous CEOs have shown that learning from failure is often done by distilling their experience into several principles: simple decision rules that prevent them from making the same mistake again and again. Jeff Bezos, the founder of Amazon, distilled some of his experience into simple rules. Aside from his decision-making simple rules, quoted earlier in this chapter, Bezos coined a proverb-like simple rule that guides the internal structure of the company, the famous two-pizza rule: "every internal team in Amazon must be small enough so that it can be fed with two pizzas" (Hern, 2018). These kinds of principles are studied as intentional heuristics (to be distinguished from the unintentional heuristics such as availability or anchoring,

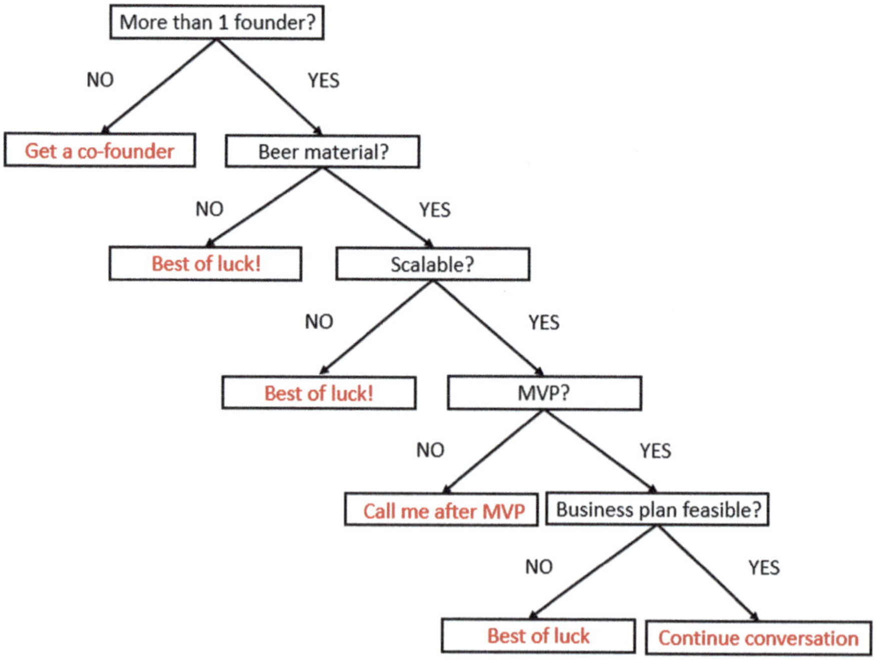

Fig. 7.4 Fast-and-frugal tree to help angel investors decide when to continue discussions with a startup

associated with cognitive biases) or simple rules (Bingham & Eisenhardt, 2011, 2014; Bingham & Haleblian, 2012; Bingham et al., 2007; Eisenhardt & Sull, 2001).

Management and organization science has paid special attention over the last decade to simple rules as decision tools. Bingham and Eisenhardt (2011) showed that what managers and organizations learn are, in fact, portfolios of simple rules. Other studies have shown the positive connection between simple managerial rules and strategy (Eisenhardt & Sull, 2001), capturing opportunities (Bingham et al., 2007), and even the survival of family businesses (Pieper et al., 2015). This is also the main topic of my research. I have interviewed a few dozen CEOs to learn how they create and employ their simple rules.

One interesting thing I discovered during these interviews is that the managers had a personal set of simple rules, which they considered crucial to their roles. Through my research (Atanasiu et al., 2021), I have compiled a long list of such rules. Some of them manage the relationship with clients, others the strategy, but most of them are related to managing people. Below is a selection of simple rules extracted during my research:

The leading position is one of support, not authority.
Don't make decisions for someone else.
Those who come to me with a problem must also come up with three possible alternative solutions.
A high performer with a high salary is worth three mediocre employees paid half that sum.
I hire people who complete my skill set.
The shareholder role shouldn't be mixed with the manager role.
I hire together with my team.
There must be a continuous alignment process for the top management team.
My managers need to share their knowledge with their teams; if they don't do it naturally, I create the context.
All those affected by a decision must take part in the discussion.
For a good work relationship, the ratio between praise and criticism must be 3 to 1.
When something goes wrong in my company, I never search for someone to blame because that someone is always me.

In my interviews with the CEOs, I introduced this concept—*simple rules*—through a scenario. I invite you, the readers, to do this exercise as well.

Question Imagine you have won the lottery and decide to take a sabbatical to explore Patagonia, to go walking on El Camino, or to write that book you always dream of writing. You find a capable person to fill your managerial position while you are gone. When you give her the key to the office, you say: "Look, in my *X* years of experience on this job, I have learned these three practical rules that you can't find in any book: ...." How would you continue this sentence? At first, you might say that no such rules exist, but please take 5 min and think deeply. You will certainly find at least three.

I found that all these managerial proverbs were born from experience and mainly from *unexpected problems*. The process of finding a solution to such a problem is usually perceived as a tension, something the manager thinks continuously. Then, the solution comes as an insight, usually catalyzed by a *clarifier*: a later observation, another event, a conversation, or something read in a book. The insight actually consists of three interwoven insights: (a) identifying and *unlearning* a hidden assumption that proved to be false, (b) *learning* a new guiding principle, which itself can be a simple rule, and (c) distilling a simple rule for the *application* of that principle in day-to-day activity.

Below are three examples of the cognitive journey that prompted three top managers to learn valuable lessons from experience and to distill them into simple rules. Can you think of an analogous personal example?

Examples

1. The CEO of a large marketing company cannot figure out why strategic projects, set at the beginning of the year and communicated to the entire organization, are far behind schedule *(the unexpected problem)*. She observes *(clarifier)* that employees were working on these projects only at the end of the day, and only after they had completed their daily tasks. She realizes that people are not motivated to work on projects just because they are called *strategic (unlearning)*, that it is more important to have strategic projects addressed daily *(new learning)*. How? By applying the simple rule *"For daily attention, strategic projects must be integrated into processes" (application)*.
2. The CEO and main shareholder of a fast-internationalizing tech company admits that the turning point in the growth of his business was when he distilled such a simple rule. Initially, keen on keeping costs low, he hired, for small salaries, people with little experience and did most of the work himself. After a while, he realized that important departments, including sales, are performing badly *(the unexpected problem)*. The "aha" moment happens when he hears a quote from Gandhi *(clarifier)*: "I must follow my people, for I am their leader." He is amazed by how well it suits his situation. He understands that he cannot be good at absolutely everything (*unlearning*). He understands that he needs to hire experts, even if the experts have a higher salary *(new learning)*, and follow their lead. He distills a simple rule that sounds like a proverb: *"A high performer with a high salary is worth three mediocre employees paid half that sum" (application)*. The first contract of the new sales director—hired after this insight—was 30 times larger than the largest one they had until then.
3. While hiring exclusively based on skills, without evaluating personality, the young founder of a technology company faced a conundrum: a well-skilled professional did not get along with the team and created tensions *(the*

> *unexpected problem)*, so she had to be fired. For the manager, the insight came when he struggled to explain his decision *(clarifier)*. That is when he realized that skills are not everything (*unlearning*) and that attitude and team integration are more important *(new learning)*. How did he operationalize this into a simple rule? *"I hire together with my team" (application)*.

After a manager has this kind of insight, the simple rule usually goes through testing, articulating, and refining. One of the main methods of refining is proverbialization. Managers find concise, memorable forms for their rules that they can easily remember and share. The rules are then shared within the organization. As one of the respondents confessed, "the role of a CEO is to create systems that work and to find the metaphor that helps the team vibrate, understand it, and apply it every day." Another executive found a simple rule for sharing simple rules: Never share the rule without telling the story behind it as well. The story of the original mistake makes the rule easier to remember and adopt.

Often, lessons-learned processes are absent or do not work properly (McClory et al., 2017), failing to document, communicate, and archive what has been learned during a project (Love et al., 2016). I believe that if—at the end of a lessons-learned meeting—the team is led by the project manager to refine these lessons into proverb-like simple rules, the information would be better documented and easier to remember and communicate, especially if these new proverbs are the result of a team effort.

7.5 How to Evaluate Decisions

I suggest starting this section with an exercise:

> **Exercise** What was the best decision you made during the last 12 months? What about the worst? How did each of them turn out? Please do not read further before answering these questions. I am willing to bet two things: One is that your good decision turned out well and your bad decision poorly; second, that you may think my question about their outcome a little silly. How can a good decision end up other than well, and vice versa? Well, they can. Nobel laureate Richard Thaler said in an interview: "You can imagine all kinds of good decisions taken in 2005 were evaluated five years later as stupid. They were not stupid. They were unlucky. So, any company that can learn to distinguish between bad decisions and bad outcomes has a leg up" (Javetski & Koller, 2020)

Herbert Simon likened decision-making to a pair of scissors. One of the blades is represented by the quality of the decision-making process and the other by the context in which the decision is made, a context that we cannot control, and that also includes important doses of chance (good or bad luck). In her book *Thinking in Bets*, psychologist and poker champion Annie Duke baptizes the ineffective inclination to judge decisions solely by their outcome as *resulting* (Duke, 2019). Poker is a perfect environment to study decision-making, as hundreds of decisions are made in a night of friendly or competitive playing. A clear case of *resulting* is when a player makes a decision on a move, loses the hand, and then—based on this sole event—thinks that the decision was bad and therefore avoids it in similar situations. *Resulting* is ineffective because the player did not consider the possibility that the decision might have been a good one (its average outcome after multiple plays might have been positive), but perhaps the adversary happened to have a very good hand. We tend to judge decisions only by their outcome, but chance should be considered as well.

Inspired by the book above, I usually ask the same questions in my MBA course (MBA students are top managers, entrepreneurs, etc.—people experienced in making important decisions). I ask each participant to tell me what were the best and worst decisions they made in the previous year. Then, I ask how each decision turned out. Everybody usually says that good decisions had excellent outcomes and bad decisions ended disastrously, representing a good cue to introduce the concept of *resulting*. There is clearly a correlation between the quality of a decision and its outcome, but given the second blade of the scissors (the context), the correlation cannot be perfect. Some good decisions can turn out badly. The opposite may also be true. Because of *resulting,* when everything ends well, we may not realize that perhaps we in fact made a bad decision and were simply lucky. We thereby learn nothing from it. It would, therefore, be a good habit to have lessons-learned sessions not only after failures but also after successes. Conversely, due to *resulting*, a negative result might convince us of the poor quality of our decision, even if context played a greater role, and we will fall into the mind trap described above by Richard Thaler. The key to avoiding *resulting* is—aside from looking at the outcome—to also evaluate decisions by looking at the quality of the decision-making process. The best way to do so is to have a personal or team-based decision journal that can provide a structured sample of choices and data to be analyzed. A template of such a journal will be offered in a next chapter. Another way we can improve our decision-making process is to have somebody hold us accountable for the process. Let us consider another exercise:

> **Exercise** Scenario 1: Imagine that there are parliamentary elections tomorrow. Who would you vote for? How did you reach that decision? If you have an answer to these questions, please consider Scenario 2: there are parliamentary elections tomorrow, and this time, you are invited to speak the Monday after the elections in front of some high school students about civic participation, democracy, and elections—specifically about how we choose our representatives. To illustrate that, you will need to describe in detail the process you undertook to decide for whom to vote. In this second scenario, for whom would you vote tomorrow, and what would be your decision process? Isn't the decision-making process different this time? Isn't it true that, knowing you will have to explain your decision, you will avoid voting negatively, you will closely analyze lists, you will investigate all candidates, you will read the programs, and you will be up to date with topics of interest?

Why is this relevant for improving our business decision-making process? An article published in "Psychological Bulletin" (1999) by Jennifer S. Lerner and Philip E. Tetlock states that we make better decisions when we know that third parties (the public, a jury, even high school students) will hold us accountable for our decisions. It functions when their opinions are unknown to us, when their interest is legitimate, when they are more interested in the decision-making process than in the outcome, and when we were informed of the existence of this third party before we formed any opinion. This research validates two things: It is very useful to have a decision board and it is useful, in general, to have someone to talk to. If you do not have a board, create one! A knowledgeable interlocutor (mentor, business coach, partner, friend, or in the absence of anything else, our own diary) makes us verbalize assumptions, use cognitive dissonance properly, and identify biases or flawed arguments. In short, having someone to talk to and to observe our decision-making process increases the quality of our choices.

7.6 Mindsets

Our decision-making is heavily influenced by our mindset, both individually and collectively. This section provides two frameworks to look at the mindset we employ while making strategic decisions.

1. *Prevention focus and promotion focus.* Let us assume we are facing an economic crisis. We have the old plan in front of us, and we realize that it is science fiction, so we open a new spreadsheet and start from scratch. The danger, in times of crisis, is to think about the new strategy with an exclusive focus on disaster prevention. The psychology professor E. T. Higgins from Columbia University explains (Higgins, 1996) how people are differently motivated in their actions by a *prevention focus* (focused on safety, avoiding negative results, and fulfilling obligations) or by a *promotion focus* (focused on growth, ambition, and achieving the desired goals). Higgins' *regulatory focus theory* has generated many subsequent studies that have shown the connection between motivational focus and effectiveness, innovation, risk inclination, well-being, and so on. Two important conclusions of this body of research should be mentioned here: First, the motivational focus (*promotion/prevention*) also works in groups (team, board) and organizations. The second conclusion is that this type of attitude is not a characteristic of the person, group, company, or even project; it changes depending on context and it can even be changed on purpose. In normal times, the best path is somewhere in the middle, where we combine—alternatively or simultaneously—the preventive attitude with the one focused on growth. In times of crisis, though, with the old plan inoperable and the new spreadsheet pending, the danger is to exclusively adopt a *prevention* focus and to think uniquely about keeping the company alive by cutting costs and optimizing cash flow. It would be helpful, though, after we have taken pragmatic

measures to avoid the catastrophe, to take some time to deliberately reflect on how we can grow in the next period, perhaps by approaching clients differently, by accelerating a secondary activity that better matches the current situation, by concentrating on what we do best, or even by starting a new project. If you are in a meeting where you notice that the overall focus is on *prevention*, take the discussion to a constructive area through a well-placed question or a change in tone. Even if you do not immediately identify potential ways for growth, the simple discussion of this possibility will boost everyone's motivation. The reflex in crises is to try to stick as closely as possible to the original plan. However, the probability of sticking to the pre-crisis plan is zero; either we end up well below the forecast, or we end up surprisingly better. The second alternative needs, though, someone to identify the harmful exclusive presence of an exclusive *prevention* focus and to steer the whole discussion toward *promotion* and possibilities of growth.

2. *Adapters and shapers*. Uncertainty is not inherently good or bad. It has always been a feature of the business environment, but it has recently been growing significantly, and—on top of that—it sometimes comes in tsunami waves, as exemplified by the 2020 pandemic. In recent research by Rindova and Courtney, published by the Academy of Management Review in 2020, the authors differentiate two strategic postures in the face of uncertainty: *adapting* and *shaping*. Managers and firms who *adapt* view uncertainty and the unknown as a constraint and slowly push the limits of knowledge by experimenting, before moving in the safer (known) space they just illuminated. Managers and firms who *shape* view uncertainty as an opportunity, make large bets about the future, and then work to *shape* the future in their favor. Violina Rindova and Hugh Courtney illustrated these two postures with the attitudes of two car manufacturers—Ford and Tesla—toward the trends of the automotive industry (electric motors, self-driving cars, connected vehicles, etc.). While Ford adapts to the new reality as it deciphers it, Tesla has bet on a certain future and has already begun to build its new reality in that direction.

Adapters. The common tendency is to consider what we do not know as an obstacle we need to overcome or as a threat we need to face and to try to gradually adapt to the situation as we decipher it. This attitude comes to us naturally because we innately dislike uncertainty and we reflexively look for ways to combat it, reduce it, or deceive ourselves that it does not exist. Thus, most managers faced the total lack of predictability during the first months of the COVID-19 pandemic like captains who are sailing through a storm: They rolled up their sleeves, alerted the crew, and prepared the company for impact, continuing to sail through the night, rain, and lightning as well as they could. All in all, the *adapter* attitude makes us squint our eyes, hold the steering wheel tightly in our hands, and carefully examine the road ahead (or as much as we see), so we can avoid any obstacles and reach our destination safely.

Shapers. The other type of attitude is crazier, more entrepreneurial, with a greater risk tolerance, and it means perceiving uncertainty as an opportunity to bet on imagined possibilities and then investing in these imagined possibilities. In short, it means building our own reality beyond the fog. Companies that have such an attitude usually have a visionary leader, a clear, high, hard-to-reach goal, and an aligned organization. An example of the *shaper* attitude is to imagine how the trends born during the pandemic (working from home, virtual meetings, social distancing, online courses, cashless payments, wearing a mask) will continue in the following years, to identify what opportunities may arise due to those trends, and then to start implementing today what others will discover the day after tomorrow.

We have discussed two theories in this section that differentiate between two types of attitudes. Treating a strategic situation with a *prevention focus* and an *adapting* posture yields a less risky, less rewarding pathway. Going in with a *promotion focus* and a *shaping* posture is a recipe for a roller coaster ride. However, in reality, these attitudes are just the two extremes of a slider. Both require strategic foresight techniques. Scenario planning, for example, is imagining in detail a series of different (and sometimes extreme) scenarios for the future (over 5 or 10 years), then identifying strategies that the company can implement today to fit the imagined future. Backcasting is a technique that can help us plan the reverse path from a desired future (e.g., one in which we dominate the market or in which a certain merger is successful) to the present. Horizon scanning is an exercise for detecting today various weak signals that may develop tomorrow into trends with major impact.

Research and practice have shown that, for good results, we must alternate the two attitudes and make sure that we do not get stuck in one extreme. The reactive attitude, however, comes naturally to us. That is why we need to consciously add a touch of *shaper* and *promotion focus* to our business strategy and to start dancing with uncertainty. We can create context for innovation to emerge, we can encourage our colleagues to look up from the ground and scrutinize the future with curiosity and calm, we can regularly use strategic foresight techniques, and we can build the courage to bet on our own imagination.

Exercise Now that, hopefully, these attitudes are clear, have a minute of introspection, and do a self-diagnosis on what attitude you adopt most often (prevention or promotion focus? adapter or shaper posture?) and what attitude characterizes the strategy of your company. Then think of methods to add-in some flavor of the opposite attitude to both micro- and macro-levels.

References

Amazon.com. (2016). Letter to shareholders. Retrieved from https://www.sec.gov/Archives/edgar/data/1018724/000119312516530910/d168744dex991.htm

Åstebro, T., & Elhedhli, S. (2006). the effectiveness of simple decision heuristics: Forecasting commercial success for early-stage ventures. *Management Science, 52*(3), 395–409. https://doi.org/10.1287/mnsc.1050.0468.

Atanasiu, R., Ruotsalainen, R., & Khapova, S. (2021). A simple rule is born: How CEOs distill heuristics (under review).

Bauer, J. C., Schmitt, P., Morwitz, V. G., & Winer, R. S. (2012). Managerial decision making in customer management: Adaptive, fast and frugal? *Journal of the Academy of Marketing Science, 41*(4), 436–455. https://doi.org/10.1007/s11747-012-0320-7.

Bingham, C. B., & Eisenhardt, K. M. (2011). Rational heuristics: The 'simple rules' that strategists learn from process experience. *Strategic Management Journal, 32*(13), 1437–1464. https://doi.org/10.1002/smj.965.

Bingham, C. B., & Eisenhardt, K. M. (2014). Response to Vuori and Vuori's commentary on "Heuristics in the strategy context." *Strategic Management Journal, 35*(11), 1698–1702. https://doi.org/10.1002/smj.2257.

Bingham, C. B., & Haleblian, J. J. (2012). How firms learn heuristics: Uncovering missing components of organizational learning. *Strategic Entrepreneurship Journal, 6*(2), 152–177. https://doi.org/10.1002/sej.1132.

Bingham, C. B., Eisenhardt, K. M., & Furr, N. R. (2007). What makes a process a capability? Heuristics, strategy, and effective capture of opportunities. *Strategic Entrepreneurship Journal, 1*(1–2), 27–47. https://doi.org/10.1002/sej.1.

Cohen, M. D., March, J. G., & Olsen, J. P. (1972). A Garbage Can Model of Organizational Choice. *Administrative Science Quarterly, 17*(1), 1. https://doi.org/10.2307/2392088.

Duke, A. (2019). *Thinking in bets: Making smarter decisions when you don't have all THE facts* (Illustrated ed.): Portfolio.

Eisenhardt, K. M., & Sull, D. N. (2001). Strategy as simple rules. *Harvard Business Review, 79*(1), 100–116.

Etzioni, A. (1967). Mixed-scanning: A "third" approach to decision-making. *Public Administration Review, 27*(5), 385. https://doi.org/10.2307/973394.

Fischer, J. E., Steiner, F., Zucol, F., Berger, C., Martignon, L., Bossart, W., Altwegg, M., & Nadal, D. (2002). Use of simple heuristics to target macrolide prescription in children with community-acquired pneumonia. *Archives of Pediatrics & Adolescent Medicine, 156*(10), 1005. https://doi.org/10.1001/archpedi.156.10.1005.

Heath, C., & Heath, D. (2013). *Decisive: How to make better choices in life and work* (1st ed.). Crown Business.

Hein, P. (1969). *Grooks* (1st ed.). Doubleday & Co.

Hern, A. (2018, April 26). The two-pizza rule and the secret of Amazon's success. *The Guardian*. Retrieved from https://www.theguardian.com

Higgins, E. T. (1996). The "self digest": Self-knowledge serving self-regulatory functions. *Journal of Personality and Social Psychology, 71*(6), 1062–1083. https://doi.org/10.1037/0022-3514.71.6.1062.

Javetski, B., & Koller, T. (2020, January 24). Debiasing the corporation: An interview with Nobel laureate Richard Thaler. Retrieved from https://www.mckinsey.com/business-functions/strategy-and-corporate-finance/our-insights/debiasing-the-corporation-an-interview-with-nobel-laureate-richard-thaler

Langley, A., Mintzberg, H., Pitcher, P., Posada, E., & Saint-Macary, J. (1995). Opening up decision making: The view from the black stool. *Organization Science, 6*(3), 260–279. https://doi.org/10.1287/orsc.6.3.260.

Lerner, J. S., & Tetlock, P. E. (1999). Accounting for the effects of accountability. *Psychological Bulletin, 125*(2), 255–275.

Love, P. E. D., Teo, P., Davidson, M., Cumming, S., & Morrison, J. (2016). Building absorptive capacity in an alliance: Process improvement through lessons learned. *International Journal of Project Management, 34*(7), 1123–1137. https://doi.org/10.1016/j.ijproman.2016.05.010.

McClory, S., Read, M., & Labib, A. (2017). Conceptualising the lessons-learned process in project management: Toward a triple-loop learning framework. *International Journal of Project Management, 35*(7), 1322–1335. https://doi.org/10.1016/j.ijproman.2017.05.006.

Mintzberg, H., Raisinghani, D., & Theoret, A. (1976). The structure of "unstructured" decision processes. *Administrative Science Quarterly, 21*(2), 246. https://doi.org/10.2307/2392045.

Nutt, P. C. (1993). The identification of solution ideas during organizational decision making. *Management Science, 39*(9), 1071–1085.

Nutt, P. C. (2002). *Why decisions fail*. Berrett-Koehler.

Pieper, T. M., Smith, A. D., Kudlats, J., & Astrachan, J. H. (2015). The Persistence of multifamily firms: founder imprinting, simple rules, and monitoring processes. *Entrepreneurship Theory and Practice, 39*(6), 1313–1337. https://doi.org/10.1111/etap.12179.

Reisinger, D. (2020, July 9). All Companies Should Live by the Jeff Bezos 70% Rule. *Inc.Com*. Retrieved from https://www.inc.com

Rindova, V., & Courtney, H. (2020). To shape or adapt: Knowledge problems, epistemologies, and strategic postures under Knightian uncertainty. *Academy of Management Review, 45*(4), 787–807. https://doi.org/10.5465/amr.2018.0291.

Schwenk, C. R. (1984). Cognitive simplification processes in strategic decision-making. *Strategic Management Journal, 5*(2), 111–128. https://doi.org/10.1002/smj.4250050203.

Simon, H. A. (1987). Making management decisions: The role of intuition and emotion. *Academy of Management Perspectives, 1*(1), 57–64. https://doi.org/10.5465/ame.1987.4275905.

Simon, H. A. (1960). *The new science of managerial decision*. Harper and Row.

Sutherland, R. (2019). *Alchemy: The surprising power of ideas that don't make sense*. W H Allen, an imprint of Ebury Publishing.

Decision-Making in Groups 8

It is said that two heads are better than one, meaning that a group thinks better and makes wiser decisions than each member taken individually. For instance, the *wisdom of the crowd* phenomenon describes how large crowds can estimate something (the weight of an ox, in the most famous example) astonishingly close to reality, as revealed by averaging all individual responses. Boards and juries are examples of groups especially assembled for making decisions. Many organizations have understood the power of collective decisions. Group decisions have the capacity to generate commitment, motivation, and individual responsibility. However, in many companies, group decisions are difficult to make and sometimes even harder to implement. Why might that be? It is perhaps because in business, two heads are better than one only if there is a well-established group decision-making system in place. This chapter emphasizes the importance of clear assignment of roles and of delegating, discusses pitfalls in group decision-making, and ends by offering tools for collective decisions when the team works remotely.

8.1 Roles

One of the key elements of any good group decision system is the clarity of the roles in each decision. The consulting firm Bain & Company has patented a simple role clarification model under the acronym RAPID, and two of Bain's senior partners—Paul Rogers and Marcia W. Blenko—detailed the framework in a Harvard Business Review article (Rogers & Blenko, 2006). The letters in RAPID stand for Recommend, Agree, Input, Decide, and Perform. The order is not necessarily the one we encounter in reality, but IRADP would not have made for a good acronym. It is important to note that the roles detailed below may change, in the same team, continuously, depending on the decision that is to be made. Let us see how all these functions make up a complete decision-making system:

R. Atanasiu, *Critical Thinking for Managers*, Management for Professionals,
https://doi.org/10.1007/978-3-030-73600-2_8

Recommend The person in this role is the project manager of the decision-making process, the driver of the decision. They need to investigate the context, gather and analyze data, and offer alternative solutions and their recommended course of action. They need to look for input from people with experience in the respective field and from the team that will implement the decision, as well as incorporate that input into the proposal. They also need to get the proposal signed off by people who have veto power. Finally, they need to prepare the decision-making meeting. For this, consultants at McKinsey (De Smet et al., 2017) propose the following routine: have just one person prepare the meeting (a driver/recommender) by sending in advance a short document that includes the problem statement, alternatives, data about these alternatives, one recommendation, and risks associated with it. In my experience, this person also needs to deliver the initial presentation during the meeting. After observing a series of decisions about new projects, a manager in a large technological company shared with me his conclusion that the communication skills of the one who delivers the presentation may make or break a project. A firm attitude can build confidence in the recommendation, whereas a meek voice or a stutter can induce unwanted doubt. People in the recommending role must, therefore, work on their presentation skills, rehearse, and master the data behind the proposal in order to provide satisfying answers when questioned.

Agree This role is for those who have veto power on the proposal and on the final solution. Departments or positions usually associated with this role are regulatory, legal, or purchasing. Heads of departments that are impacted by the proposed solution may also share this role. People in the *Recommend* role must consult and convince the people in the *Agree* role before proposing a course of action. This may lead to a conflict, especially when the protagonists stand on different hierarchical levels. Many organizations have adopted the "function trumps hierarchy" principle in order to overtly allow employees on lower hierarchical levels to play their roles, even in conflict with superiors. The solution to a difference in views between people who *Recommend* and people who must *Agree* may be a negotiated alternative. If this is not achieved, the final decision-maker may intervene early and settle the dispute.

Perform This role is filled by a production team or even by an external partner. In smaller companies, the people in the *Recommend* roles are also those who will implement the solution. However, if this overlapping does not occur, it is advisable to have the input of the *Perform* team before a proposal is made. Often, in silo organizations where white collars and blue collars do not communicate or in multinationals where the headquarters make decisions about periphery markets, precious ground-level data are not considered in evaluating alternatives and proposing a course of action.

Input As also noted above, this role is for people who can provide valuable information on the decision, and it is not limited to the implementing team. While decision roles are usually for members of the same organization, input may be also sought from external production partners, advertising agencies, or market research firms. The difference between *Input* and *Agreement* is that *Input* is not binding. A very useful tool to decide on how to involve your team in a decision was developed by researchers Vroom and Yetton (1973). The tool is a decision tree based on several criteria such as problem characteristics, availability of information, team commitment, and support and can yield a recommendation in approximately one minute. The Vroom–Yetton decision model can be easily found online.

Decide Although made for group decisions, the RAPID model recommends that the final decision is made by a single person, usually the leader of the team. This person needs to fulfill three functions: to decide and to assume the responsibility for the decision, to mediate possible disputes, and to ensure organizational commitment for implementing what has been decided. In their HBR article, Paul Rogers and Marcia W. Blenko stress that two types of problems appear in relation to the decide role. The most common one—in organizations based on power—is that more than one person believes they must have the ultimate say. The other appears in complex, sensitive decisions and is the opposite of the first: Nobody thinks that the decision belongs to them. A clear assignment of roles that is well communicated, understood, and accepted by the whole team can easily avoid these situations.

Aside from RAPID, there are other role-assigning frameworks that a manager can use, such as Responsible, Accountable, Consulted, Informed (RACI) and Driver, Approver, Contributor, Informed (DACI). Whichever framework we may choose, there are some simple principles we must observe. It is important to assign roles to persons and not to departments. Roles may overlap (the same person can hold multiple roles) but must not be fuzzy: I may have two roles, but not one and a half. In similar decisions, people can maintain their roles from one decision to the other. When a new type of choice appears, however, precise assignment and common understanding of roles are necessary, and this is usually done by the leader —the person who has the final say.

Perceived theoretically, the clarity of roles seems like a common-sense idea, something that we surely almost always do. I will end this section on roles in group decision-making with a double exercise:

Exercise 1 Think of a recent group decision in which you were the final decision-maker. Make the list of the roles, according to the RAPID model, as they happened in reality, even if roles were fuzzy. Keep in mind that the same person, including the decision-maker, can have more than one role. Then, make the list of the RAPID roles as they would have been if such a decision-making system were implemented in your organization. Make sure the positions are clear. What difference would this make? What will you change for the next group decision?

Exercise 2 Think of a recent group decision in which you were NOT the final decision-maker. Write down exactly what your roles were, and then make a list of all the roles as you perceived them during the decision-making process, even if they were fuzzy. Write down, afterward, a list of clear roles as they would have been if such a decision-making system were implemented in your organization. What difference would this make? How could you influence your team or organization to adopt a clear decision-making system? What would be the first step in doing so?

8.2 Delegating

Speaking of decision roles, how should managers involve their teams in decision-making for better productivity and commitment? Well, the first thing they can do is to stop making decisions that are below their pay grade. The second is to proactively delegate more. Micromanagement, the tendency of many managers to make decisions that belong to their subordinates and then to control every step of their implementation, is an often-underestimated illness in organizations. A study by Harry E. Chambers and cited in his book *My Way or the Highway: The Micromanagement Survival Guide* discovered that 79% of the employees in the sample have been micromanaged at some point during their career (Chambers, 2004). Even more damaging, the same study showed that micromanagers do not realize what they do. The researchers interviewed employees who confessed to leaving their jobs on account of being micromanaged, then traced the culprits and asked them why they think employee *X* left their job. Amazingly, 91% of micromanagers had no idea that they ever did something wrong. Upon reading this, I thought that perhaps there should be an easy-to-use tool that can show managers whether they might be too involved in their team's decision-making. Inspired by an HBR article (Wilkins, 2014), then, I put together a self-diagnosis kit. If your answer to at least five questions below is yes, you might be a micromanager:

Are you always dissatisfied with your team's work, thinking that you could have done things better?
Do you want to be CCed in all emails?
Do you always need to know where your employees are and what they do exactly?
Do you want to countersign all documents?
Do you require daily status meetings?
Are you the last to leave the office or end your working hours in the evening?
Does your team avoid you?

Well, how did you do? The first step is, then, to stop micromanaging. The second would be to try to delegate even more. Daniel Dines, the founder and CEO of Romania's unicorn UiPath, mentioned at a *How to Web* conference (Bucharest, 2018) that the key to UiPath's success is "pushing decisions as low as possible in the organization." But if we haven't delegated before, how should we start? A McKinsey Quarterly article (De Smet et al., 2017) mentions three conditions: We should start with reversible decisions, we should assess whether the colleagues we delegate the decision to are able to decide by themselves, and we should make sure that there are mechanisms that hold those persons responsible for what they decide. These can be soft mechanisms such as having the person take public ownership of the decision. I would add a fourth condition: to set clear limits to delegation—at least at first—such as contract value, a certain level of estimated risk, or number of stakeholders affected.

One more tool for good decision-making in groups is to limit the size of the group. Marcia W. Blenko, Michael C. Mankins, and Paul Rogers from Bain & Company (two of them are the same partners who wrote about RAPID) have published in their book—*Decide and Deliver: Five Steps to Breakthrough Performance in Your Organization*—research showing that, once the group has reached seven members, each new member reduces decision effectiveness by 10% (Blenko et al., 2010). In my personal experience, a group of seven is already too large for a good decision-making dynamic. Another tool for increasing the effectiveness of group talks and for smoothening meetings is to create the meeting agenda around decisions. Agendas are usually set around topics, which usually are single words or short, verbless expressions such as *merger* or *internationalization*. A better version mentions problems, like "sales did not increase as predicted." But all these meetings are actually organized to make decisions, so—for a smooth and effective meeting—the person responsible for preparing each decision should send before the meeting, as mentioned above, a short document to include the problem statement, alternatives, data about these alternatives, one recommendation, and risks associated with it. And then we should set the agenda of the meeting around decisions to be made, such as "deciding how to increase B2B sales; recommendation: to hire an extra B2B salesperson," not around topics or problems. When set around 3–5 decision points like this, many unfruitful preliminary discussions can be avoided.

8.3 Pitfalls

How can group decision-making go awry? Described below are a few ways in which the lack of a system can lead to wrong, delayed, or poorly implemented decisions. Some of the decision traps described below are caused by group dynamics and culture and others by the way our minds work.

Groupthink is the tendency to make the wrong decisions in groups where conformity is more important than the need to listen to opposing views. It works as follows: Everyone seems to agree with the proposal; I do not, but I will not voice my disagreement because I do not want to be the only one who has a different opinion. Multiply this by 3 or 4 and you can get a group in which, although many would object, no one speaks first because no one else does: absurd, but sadly very frequent. Groupthink and methods to overcome it will be detailed in another chapter of this book.

Forced consensus occurs when a group decision-making process (e.g., any kind of vote) divides the debate between two opposing positions. Let us say that in a board some members support project *A* and others project *B*. And only one project must be chosen. The tendency is to try and convince those who had a different opinion to agree with the solution chosen after the vote: "Now that we voted, you have to accept our solution." In such cases, if obtained, the agreement is made only declaratively, and the greatest danger is that those in the defeated camp will not participate later in the implementation or, worse, will try to sabotage it. Therefore, in those situations, instead of *agreement*, it is preferable to ask for (and obtain) *commitment* from those who disagreed in the first place. This is done with smoothness and diplomacy—in one-on-one discussions—with the final goal being to *disagree and commit*, a much more productive attitude than the declarative agreement.

Forced compromise occurs when the debate between two opposing points of view does not seem to come to an end. Let us say the board needs to choose between two valuable projects, *A* and *B*, and that the two camps do not seem to abandon the fight for their preference. In such situations, a proposal sometimes appears (a well-intentioned, but disastrous proposal) for a third project, or an unfortunate combination of the first two, leading to suboptimal solutions. Compromise is often the best solution for debates, but not always: not when the compromise solution is worse than any of the initial solutions. In his bestseller, *Never Split the Difference*, Chris Voss illustrates the forced compromise with an example: Let us say I would like to wear black shoes tonight at the theater, while my wife prefers me to wear the brown ones. The worst thing would be to try to reconcile both points of view by wearing a black shoe and a brown one (Voss & Raz, 2016).

Several systems. The existence of several isolated decision-making systems in an organization often leads to conflict. If, in my department, we have together established an intelligent and open way of making decisions in which we have clear roles and there is a feedback mechanism not only for implementation but also for the process itself, internal decisions will continuously improve. However, problems will arise when the decision involves actors from other departments in which they decide differently. If, for example, the decision involves a higher budget—which is approved only by the GM—and he is used to making decisions alone, without consultation and without explanation, the foundation of trust on which my department's decision-making system is based will suffer a serious blow. That is why organizations should design coherent and unitary decision-making systems, involving in the designing process all those who will employ them. Clashes between several isolated systems can happen not only between a department and the

GM or the HQ. Other possible clashes could happen in global versus local decision-making, where local knowledge and experience might favor different criteria than the global perspective, or in function versus function decision-making, for example when marketing and product development have entirely different priorities. In these conflicts, the forced compromise described above is the most likely final outcome, and decision-makers should make sure that the quality of the solution is not worse than the first proposals.

The forgotten board. Another problem, unfortunately very common, occurs in organizations that have implemented a unitary, coherent, and open system for decision-making but forgot to apply it to the management team because it is assumed that those at the C level do well without guidance. When decisions are made intelligently and efficiently at all other levels, but any discussion in the board is approached unclearly, incoherently, disorderly, and late, the clash between the hectic system of the board and the coherent system in all other levels usually leads the good system to fail because—as everyone knows—the board can never make a mistake.

8.4 Remote Decision-Making

The COVID-19 pandemic has only accelerated the natural trend toward remote work, and while group decision-making was already cumbersome when everybody was at the office, complexity only increased with distance. Certain professionals, such as software developers, were already accustomed to remote and asynchronous decision-making tools, but most managers are used to decide only in a setting inherited from the Ancient Greeks: the meeting. However, meetings do not function perfectly, do they? Many organizations have tried to replicate the same old ways with new online tools, namely online meetings. I talked, at the end of 2020, with a number of top managers about the advantages and disadvantages of remote decision-making, and most remarks were about meetings. The fact that they mentioned more disadvantages and spoke largely about each one shows that this setting is not optimal.

+ All advantages they mentioned have to do with meetings becoming more efficient. Remote sessions "*are shorter, you have them one after the other, you need to start and finish on time*." Plus, "*there is no more time wasted with jokes*," the information is better communicated because "*people are briefer and more structured, making us decide faster*" and "*we learned to take turns speaking and to really listen*."
− The most mentioned disadvantage is the lack of informal encounters, which means that "*a certain type of information (things heard by chance, which were previously disseminated informally, during breaks) is now disseminated less or at all*." Plus, "*at the office, many decisions are made during coffee breaks, when people feel each other's position*

> *and search for a compromise.*" Some managers have tried to solve this by "*adding 15 min at the end of each online meeting, for small talk.*" Another disadvantage is "*the lack of engagement: face to face, you may realize that the person wants to say something and you can encourage her involvement, but often during online meetings people turn off their cameras and hide.*"

As I said, in most organizations the decision meeting just moved online, with its mix of advantages and disadvantages. However, in some companies, the new and abrupt reality has led to a (long overdue) reassessment of their decision-making procedures, which, in turn, led to better preparation of the decision, shorter (or no) meetings, increased clarity, and better-assigned roles, resulting in better and more efficient decision-making. What can we learn from these pioneers?

Efficient remote decision-making differs from the classical setting in two key aspects: It is predominantly *asynchronous*, and it is mostly done *in writing*. This book tries, over the course of several chapters, to build the case for writing things down. This is one of those chapters. In the case of remote decision-making, writing is necessary. Writing things down allows asynchronous collaboration, good preparation—both in terms of the decision per se and in deciding how to decide—increases transparency, and allows all steps to be documented and communicated. Last but definitely not least, writing, as compared to speaking, encourages better thinking.

Group decisions can be made in many ways. In certain situations, depending on the decision, and, sadly, in certain organizations, depending on the leadership style, decisions are made by one decision-maker who seldom asks the team for their opinions. In other types of situations and in other, more progressive types of organization, decisions are made by building consensus within the team and—if needed—with other stakeholders across the organization. However, it is clearly better to choose how to involve the team depending on the decision to be made and not depending on the personality of the manager or on the progressiveness of the organization. Some decisions are better made alone, and some decisions are better made unanimously. The never-outdated Vroom–Yetton decision model, mentioned recently in this chapter, can help a manager choose in less than a minute, by answering a series of yes-or-no questions, between five ways of involving the team in the decision-making process. Then, a driver for the decision is designated. The driver takes the *Recommending* role (described a bit earlier as part of the RAPID model) and first, she needs to set a channel for the process. This book will not mention any tech platforms that allow collaborative decision-making, but there are plenty, and they offer various features. Irrespective of the channel, the driver opens up discussions with a clear setting on both what and how to decide. How to decide includes a timeline, roles, communication, and the final procedure for deciding.

A timeline is set between the driver and the main decision-maker as a function of the importance of the matter. Things of small importance should not take too much time, and important matters should allow a period for gathering and analyzing data and for reflection and discussion—depending, of course, on the urgency of the matter. Another criterion for allocating more time is whether this is a recurring issue. In this case, more time would be appropriate, as one decision solves an entire series of similar situations. Usually, the timeframe is communicated in detail to all from the beginning of the process (including the final deadline and smaller intervals allocated to different steps).

The roles must be clear, and the assignment of roles should be communicated to all stakeholders, even outside the decision-making circle. The RAPID model described at the beginning of this chapter is a good framework, along with similar ones like RACI and DACI. As mentioned before, the final decision-maker has the most important role. The most encountered advice is to have for this role a single person (or two, such as the two cofounders of a company or the heads of the two departments involved) that can:

- decide on the decision-making procedure
- be responsible for the decision
- be able to promote the decision in the organization
- establish a timeline
- mitigate disagreement, and
- have the final say on the decision or—in collective decisions—on how to proceed further, especially when there is disagreement.

As mentioned above, after consulting with the key factors, the person in the Recommend (RAPID), Driver (DACI), or Responsible (RACI) role (it is the same role with different names; we will use "driver" for brevity) chooses a channel (a productivity platform, a shared document, or just an email thread) for the process and uploads the opening document, the first proposal. Amazon uses a standard format for opening the decision process: a written document of 6 pages, informally known as *the six-pager*. A written document is considered to be a better foundation than a presentation with slides, as the written format allows for more detail and for more complex argumentation. Whatever form it takes, this initial proposal needs to address some key points: problem statement, 2–3 best alternatives, data about these alternatives (for instance, financials), one recommendation, the risks associated with it, roles, timeline, and decision procedure (voting? consensus? default agreement if no veto?). An example better illustrates how such a document could be structured:

Case:

To: all concerned

From: Herbert Pavelich, Head of Sales

As I did not stop mentioning since I took over this position, six months ago, the reward system used in our sales department is overly complex, outdated (it was implemented 14 years ago when the sale process was entirely different), does not reflect the productivity of our salespeople, does not incentivize for going the extra mile, and does not encourage collaboration within the department. As an example: the bonuses given at the end of last year to top performers did not differ significantly from those given to the rest of the team. Also, we reward a multitude of individual indicators but none measuring team effort or team performance, so the current system may be the single main culprit behind the individualistic culture of the department identified in our organizational culture diagnosis this spring. I will not even mention the effect an improvement of the current system may have on the sales figures (actually I do, please find attached). Our target for this decision is therefore to find the best way to restructure this system.

To have all of us on the same page, please find attached the current reward system (salary, commission, bonus) and the sales figures per agent for the last 5 years. I also present in an attachment three different systems that are extensively used in our industry. Based on these existing systems that our competitors use and on our analyses (attached), we propose two options:

Option A. A mild restructuring (*details*) and
Option B. A drastic rewriting of the system (*details*).

Analysis: Option A has the following advantages:

- it is easier to implement, and it can be implemented swiftly during the next trimester
- it will not rock the boat (too much)
- it is better from an operations point of view
- (…)

and disadvantages:

- it does not address the collaborative aspect
- (…)

Option B has the following advantages:

- it addresses all objectives
- it will be fairer, rewarding people directly proportional to their contribution
- it will increase sales
- (…)

and disadvantages:

- in the short term, it may lead to some salespeople being dissatisfied
- (…)

Financial projections for what would be the effect of the two options for next year are also attached.

Based on these analyses, I recommend Option B, in its proposed form or with any adjustments this group process might suggest. Either way, both proposed systems are open for collaborative work in a shared document.

The decision-making timeline is tight: We need to decide which system to implement by Friday next week and set the final implementation details by October 1. The implementation timeline varies depending on which option will be selected.

The decision team is made of four members: I, Herbert Pavelich, Head of Sales, will drive this process, helped by the (already) valuable input of Ms. Pauline J. Jones, our CEO, of M. Steven Marcus, COO, and of Ms. Marjoleine Van Zante, Head of HR. This kind of decision must be also approved by the Board, but early individual consultations between Ms. Jones and the board members reveal no obstacles in that direction. All of my sales team has been consulted in this process. During my analysis, I had several one-on-ones with all of them. For the next five days, each salesperson is kindly invited to participate in drafting the option(s) and to comment and share (in the shared document) their opinions on which option seems better for them personally and for the company. The choice between the two options will be taken by the decision team after all suggestions and especially all objections have been discussed. It will happen on Friday next week, during an online meeting, and the aim is to build consensus, despite different members of this team having now different preferences. If a consensus is not reached, we will vote—with the CEO holding two votes—and the solution can be adopted with a minimum of 4 votes to 1.

Thank you for your valuable input!

Herbert

The process then takes place asynchronously, on any choice of collaborative document or platform, with each member of the decision team and each salesperson being able to comment on, suggest, and object to aspects of the proposed plans. In less complex or important decisions, even the final decision may be taken without a formal meeting, if no more objections are documented in the collaborative system.

Aside from such written proposals (which are hugely useful in non-remote decisions as well) and collaborative drafting of options (idem), other tools that can be used in remote decision-making are decision polls, which may indicate early the position of key stakeholders. Most platforms offer this feature. Alternatively, such polls can be done with online tools or even using email. A good decision poll describes the situation in 2–3 sentences, then asks 1–3 open questions that do not anchor the respondents. Instead of "Would you agree with these changes in the reward system?," a better question would be "What would you change in the current reward system?" Even for at-the-office decision-making, such decision polls —conducted using electronic means—may prove efficient, as it is not easy to obtain individual preliminary input from larger teams.

After a decision has been made, it needs to be communicated to all stakeholders in a highly transparent manner, especially to those who were not included in the initial consultation. Transparency, an important trait of the regular decision-making process, has increased tremendously in importance with remote work. People need to be involved in decisions, understand how they are made, and know all aspects of the decision that has been taken. Transparency during decision-making influences the team's commitment to implement. I will reiterate here that, in remote settings as well, dissenters need not be convinced that they are wrong but rather be persuaded to disagree and commit. This, by the way, usually requires some synchronous and delicate discussions. Most of the principles of remote decision-making apply to the traditional meeting-based process, as well, from the careful preparation of the decision meeting by the *driver* of the decision to the need for transparency.

If your organization adopts a decision-making system in which roles are clear, decision power is pushed down, and groupthink is avoided, then two heads are, indeed, better than one and the system is able to yield better decisions that are easier accepted and implemented.

References

Blenko, M., Mankins, M. C., & Rogers, P. (2010). *Decide and deliver: Five steps to breakthrough performance in your organization.* Harvard Business Review Press.

Chambers, H. (2004). *My way or the highway: the micromanagement survival guide* (1st ed.). Berrett-Koehler.

De Smet, A., Lackey, G., & Weiss, L. M. (2017). Untangling your organization's decision making. *McKinsey Quarterly, 2017*(3), 68–80.

Rogers, P., & Blenko, M. (2006). Who has the d? How clear decision roles enhance organizational performance. *Harvard Business Review, 84*(1), 52–61.

Voss, C., & Raz, T. (2016). *Never split the difference: Negotiating as if your life depended on it* (1st ed.). Harper Business.

Vroom, V. H., & Yetton, P. W. (1973). *Leadership and decision-making.* University of Pittsburgh Press.

Wilkins, M. M. (2014). Signs that you're a micromanager. *Harvard Business Review, 84*(1). Retrieved from https://hbr.org.

Problem Solving

9

Articulating (and writing things down) is a valuable critical thinking tool. This chapter details its use in problem solving. Among other aspects, we will discuss how to clearly define (and write down) the problem, how to discover (pen in hand) its root cause, how to set (on paper) a clear objective for our problem-solving effort, how to gather (and write) a good set of alternative solutions, how to establish (and write) clear criteria, and how to select (and document) a course of action.

Words have power. I am not writing here about their obvious power in communication, but about the underestimated effect of articulating our own thoughts in decision-making and problem-solving efforts. We believe that the fluid, natural way in which we investigate situations and then decide on a course of action is good enough, but I argue here that by simply verbalizing our thoughts and putting them in writing we can be more effective. In *Principles. Life and Work*, Ray Dalio describes the key to his success: "Experience has taught me how valuable it is to reflect on the criteria on which I make a decision and write everything down on paper" (Dalio, 2017). In both our business and our day-to-day lives, when we need to solve problems and to make choices, writing things down helps structure our thoughts better. I am sure you have felt this often: The moment you need to explain something in writing, you have more clarity, as if the pen and the keyboard contain extra neurons. Any problem solving and decision-making sub-process can benefit from verbalization. In the following section, we will discuss a step-by-step approach to problem solving that focuses on clearly articulating (and writing down) each step of the way.

Question: Think of a complex problem that you need to solve at the office. What are the steps that you need to pass through? If the first is understanding and defining the problem and the last is implementing the solution and gathering feedback, what steps should be in between?

R. Atanasiu, *Critical Thinking for Managers*, Management for Professionals,
https://doi.org/10.1007/978-3-030-73600-2_9

This chapter will go through a classical model of problem solving: defining the problem, root cause analysis, alternative generation, analysis, decision, and implementation, with a focus on clearly articulating (verbalizing, but—better yet—writing) every step of the way. The model is depicted in Fig. 9.1.

While different cases will be used to illustrate different steps of the problem-solving approach, one of them, presented below, will be the red thread throughout the whole process:

> **Case** Alex and George have worked together in IT project implementation as freelancers, with consultancy contracts. At some point, they started developing a testing tool in their spare time. After a year, they successfully assembled a testing platform that can translate code into normal language, thus allowing for testers that do not have coding skills. They then gave up their freelance careers, put together 50,000 euros of their own money and founded a company to develop a complete product and launch it. They named it Testing123 Ltd. to illustrate the ease of use and also in honor of their passion for live rock music. They also pledged to have no salaries for themselves for 6 months.

To launch the platform on a busy market, the two founders relied on the quality of their work, on personal connections with testing departments of multinationals, on keeping the price—for the first year—50% lower (200 euros per license per year) than relevant competition, and on Alex's graduating several online marketing courses.

Their previous freelance careers generated good relationships with testing department managers from large software developers in Bulgaria and France, so they will use these as first leads. The plan is to have as clients three or four local branches of large multinational enterprises (MNEs) that are happy with the product and then to have these branches promote the platform to their headquarters. Until sales will take off, they will also rely on implementation fees, as this is what they know they are good at. Implementation will be done by the two founders and will be monetized as consultancy: 100 euros/hour.

While performing a premortem exercise, the two founders identified the poor quality of the platform as the main cause of failure in 12 months.

***

Six months after launch, Testing123 Ltd. has only one customer, X-Coding Bulgaria. David, the GM of the Sofia branch, is a good friend of George's: They were student roommates. X-Coding Bulgaria has acquired 40 licenses (the maximum needed) and 30 h of implementation assistance. Alex and George were not able to convince any other client. Their time is fully spent between assisting implementation

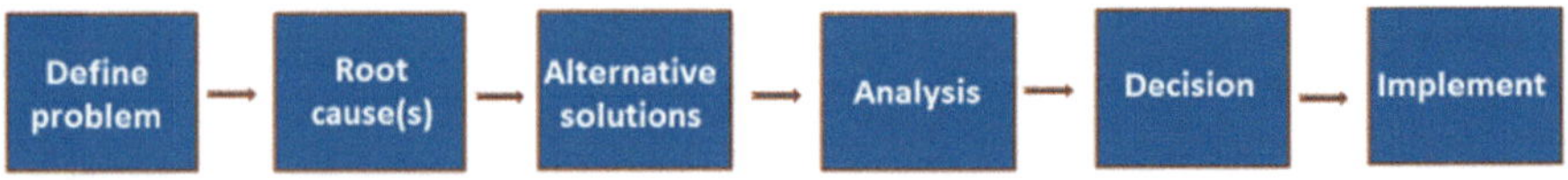

Fig. 9.1 Sequential model of the problem-solving process

at X-Coding, meeting prospective clients (testing department managers) in Bulgaria and France, and coding add-ons suggested by these potential customers.

The original 50 k and the revenue from X-Coding will be spent completely in the next 2 months, and Alex and George consider firing the two developers they have just hired. The only joy is given by the testers and developers at X-Coding who already use the platform. They consistently mention that the product is exceptionally good. However, David has not succeeded in promoting the platform to X-Coding International. He says that Bulgaria is too small in the big picture and that he has no power at all at the international level.

It is not unusual to finish reading this case with an inquisitive frown: "So? What is the question?" No real-life problem, be that in business or not, comes with a pre-defined question, and there is an art (that can be perfected) to identify the right questions to be asked in order to solve it.

9.1 Defining and Articulating the Problem

The first step in solving a problem is to define it correctly. And this is best done in writing. The founders of a startup who see the forecasted cash flows going into the red can define the problem like this: "Soon we will run out of money." This is a difficult starting point for understanding the causes and finding a solution. With a more precise formulation, such as "In August, we will need 12,000 euros to pay the X bill, and, in September, we can recover by collecting what we sold over the summer," the vague problem turns into a precise need of cash for a precise period of time, which is easier to manage. Similarly, a problem first identified vaguely as "Sales are low" must be reformulated in an operational-friendly way as "Sales for product X did not maintain on market Y last year's growth, as forecasted" and then written down. In our Testing123 case, the problem, at first sight, is "The company is running out of money." A better formulation would be "The company will be running out of money in 2 months." As we will see below, this is just the immediate problem, and the whole multi-faceted situation can be unveiled by causal analysis. One easy-to-avoid trap in defining the problem is framing it as "lack of *X*," which points out to *X* as the obvious and only solution. In our case, defining the problem as "we don't have a salesperson" limits the exploration for alternative solution. Try to frame the problem to allow multiple solutions.

9.2 Identifying the Causes

In Western culture, there is a bias toward a simplistic perspective: seeing a problem as having one cause and one solution. This Western bias was cleverly illustrated by the late Hans Rosling and his co-authors Ola Rosling and Anna Rosling Rönnlund in their (highly recommended) bestseller *Factfulness*: "The simple and beautiful idea of the free market can lead to the simplistic idea that all problems have a single cause—government interference—which we must always oppose; and that the solution to all problems is to liberate market forces by reducing taxes and removing regulations, which we must always support. Alternatively, the simple and beautiful idea of equality can lead to the simplistic idea that all problems are caused by inequality, which we should always oppose; and that the solution to all problems is redistribution of resources, which we should always support" (Rosling et al., 2018). The Buddhist philosophy, on the other hand, sees situations as having a multitude of causes, a multitude of effects, and, if we consider these situations as problems, a multitude of possible solutions, and I believe that businesspeople would be better off adopting the Eastern, more complex perspective.

Ray Dalio makes the case for dedicating time to diagnosis: "Diagnose problems to get at their root causes. Focus on the *what-is* before deciding *what-to-do-about-it*. It is a common mistake to move in a nanosecond from identifying a tough problem to proposing a solution for it. Strategic thinking requires both diagnosis and design. *A good diagnosis typically takes between 15 min and an hour*, depending on how well it is done and how complex the issue is. It involves speaking with the relevant people and looking at the evidence together to determine the root causes" (Dalio, 2017). After understanding, defining, and articulating the problem, we need, therefore, to identify its cause(s). Establishing the root cause(s) is crucial in two ways: for defining and articulating the right objective, which should address both the immediate cause and the root cause, and for preventing the problem from reoccurring. When there is a fire, the firefighters need to put out the fire (the immediate problem), to identify and act against the gas leak (the immediate cause), and then to recommend redoing the whole gas pipe system (the root cause). Business problems are not always similar to fires, and we need wisdom, experience, analysis, and reflection in order to prioritize our actions toward the effect and the causes. This is done in two steps: identifying the causes and then integrating them into the objective of our problem solving.

Identifying the immediate cause is often very simple. In our Testing123 case, the main cause of the business running out of money is that they only have one client. There may be other causes—we will do a thorough analysis soon. Solving only their apparent problem (the need for money—the fire) and the immediate cause (the lack of clients—the leak) can easily be done. For instance, by finding a second client. But this will not provide a lasting solution; it will only postpone the problem. We (in fact "they") need to perform a root cause analysis to get to the bottom of the situation.

The most popular methods to find root causes are the *five-whys* technique and the *Ishikawa* (fishbone) analysis. We will illustrate the *five whys* with short cases and then we will do both a *five-whys* analysis and an *Ishikawa* analysis on the Testing123 situation.

Five whys is the most popular root cause analysis method, so it gives—like other popular techniques—a false sense of familiarity. This, in turn, leads some managers to think that they know how to apply it, although they often do not. For instance, I have seen cases where the *whys* were all applied to the same, initial statement.

The *five-whys* method goes deep in search for the root cause by applying a cascade of *why* questions, starting with the initial problem definition, and with each additional *why* applied to the previous answer. A simple example can illustrate the method:

> **Problem**: The client did not pay for the service we provided.
> **Why?** Because we did not send them the invoice.
> **Why?** Because the sales agent who signed the contract and the client service employee who managed the service delivery both thought that the other should send the invoice.
> **Why?** Because there are gaps and overlaps in task allocation.
> **Why?** Because there is a lack of clarity on what each department and each employee needs to do.
> **Why?** Because we do not have clear job descriptions and clear procedures.

Please observe how, each time, the next *why* addresses the answer immediate above ("Why are there gaps and overlaps in task allocation? Because there is a lack of clarity…"). An important point is the following: the number 5 here is just a rule of thumb and we do not need to take it literally. We should stop when we feel we have discovered the root cause and this can be done after four *whys* or seven *whys*. Aside from feeling that "we have finally got to the bottom of this," the signal that we have reached the root cause is that, by eventually solving it, we can make sure that the problem will not reappear in the future. In our example, solving the last statement by adopting clear job descriptions and clear procedures will do that. Let us try our hand at another case:

> **Case** You manage the small and medium enterprises (SMEs) department in a large bank, and you have clear targets on the number, size, and conditions of loans given to SMEs nationwide each month. To reach these targets, you mainly count on your "army" of SME loan representatives: one in each branch. Your philosophy is to spend at least 50% of your time outside of the office, visiting branches, having meetings with members of your team and with clients, and generally trying to understand first-hand the reality in the field. Today's schedule includes a visit to one of the most important and successful branches of the bank, situated in the center of the second-largest city. It is the end of the year, and this year—despite delivering very well in most indicators—the branch has been behind in the number of new SME clients. Your meetings with the SMEs representative (a very serious and experienced employee, a lady in her 40s that has been with the bank for almost 10 years and has always received the best evaluations) and with the branch manager (an experienced banker, with a very strong personality, good in dealing both with people and with numbers) unveils the immediate cause: there is a personnel shortage, two other employees are on maternity leave, and the branch manager has given the SMEs representative duties in other areas, duties that fill up more than half of her daily schedule.

On your drive back, you try to take a step-by-step approach to problem solving, one that begins with clearly articulating the problem, the immediate cause, the root cause, and the objective to be reached by the proposed solution. You define the problem in clear terms: "This year, branch *X* only reached 80% of its target of new sales to SMEs," you identify the immediate cause and a subsequent one: "The SMEs representative only works on SMEs for less than half her working hours, because the branch manager has given her duties in other areas, duties that fill up more than half her daily schedule," and then you ponder on the root cause. You follow a mental *five-whys* approach, with the first two being already solved:

Problem: This year, branch *X* only reached 80% of its target of new sales to SMEs.
Why #1? Because the SMEs representative works on SMEs for less than half her working hours.
Why #2? Because the branch manager has given her duties to other areas, duties that fill more than half her daily schedule.
Why #3? Because the branch manager has different business targets from you, and his requests are more likely to be implemented than yours.
Why #4? Because the SME representative has two bosses who give her conflicting directions, and she tends to favor her branch manager, with whom she works directly and who she sees daily.
Why #5? Because this is how the organization is structured: as a matrix, with most branch employees reporting to two managers.

Thus, you realize that the root cause is the matrix structure of the organization, with most branch employees having two bosses who oversee their activity: the branch manager and the department manager, bosses who often give different and even conflicting directions. The employee shares the same office with the branch manager, so any conflicting directions tend to resolve in favor of the local manager. You realize that this is a general problem of the bank and identify several other branches where the lack of performance can be at least partially explained by this matrix structure. You articulate the root cause as "The matrix structure of the organization allows for conflicting directions to employees" and you realize that, if solved, this root cause would prevent future occurrence of this kind of situation.

Let us return to our red-thread case. If we were consultants hired to solve the problem(s) of Testing123 Ltd., we should perform a thorough root cause analysis way before even thinking about solutions. Let us start with doing the *five whys* and the Ishikawa analyses. Before seeing my take, below, I encourage you to draft your five-whys (3 minutes) and Ishikawa (10 minutes) analyses on a piece of paper.

Five whys

Problem: The company will be running out of money in 2 months.
Why #1? Because they do not have any new clients in the anticipated time frame.
Why #2? Because of many marketing, sales, and strategic miscalculations.
Why #3? Because the two founders have no business skills and experience and are unaware of that.

Observe that, perhaps because the answer to *Why* #2 is so general, I have used just three *whys* and managed to identify the founders' lack of business skills as the root cause. The *five-whys* method explores a single path and goes deep until a root cause is identified. This may leave some aspects of the problem unexplored. In order to search wide and then to go deep, we can use an *Ishikawa*/fishbone analysis.

Ishikawa root cause analysis (fishbone diagram). This type of analysis is done by identifying the main factors that could be involved, drawing them as branches of a common body (like a fishbone), and then exploring on each branch possible causes associated with those factors, on as many levels as possible (causes of causes of causes). *Ishikawa* is like a tree of multiple *five whys*. Obviously, this analysis is subjective: different eyes can see different main aspects, different causes, and a different number of levels. In my take on Testing123, I have set five domains: cash, sales and marketing, strategy, product, and founders. For each, I have identified 2–5 causes and for some of them a deeper cause, which proved to be the same in all cases: a good sign that the analysis identified the right root cause. When second- or third-level causes are not identical on different branches, the person or team doing the analysis needs to look at every cause on all branches and to identify a good, actionable root cause.

The main issues of the Testing123 situations are discussed below and presented, along with their respective deeper causes, in Fig. 9.2.

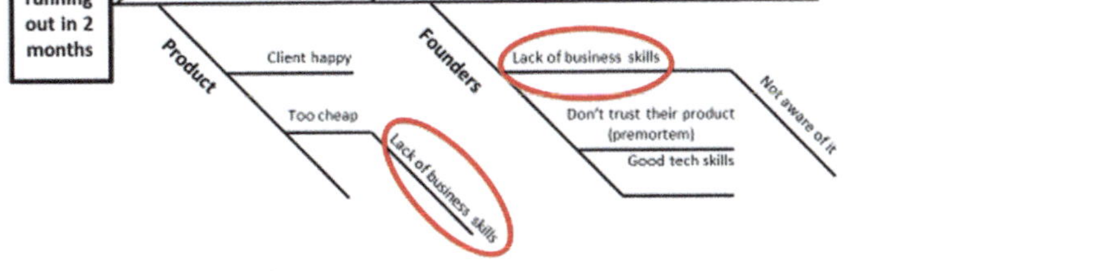

Fig. 9.2 Ishikawa root cause analysis of the Testing123 situation

Cash. The company is running out of cash because they have made no new sales and the initial funding plus the revenues from the only existing client are being depleted. Another reason for the cash flow problem is the fact that they only allocated 50 k as initial investment, probably planning for a shorter sale cycle than what they found in reality. Yet another reason is the small price they decided to start with. Bad planning and bad pricing are clear signs of a lack of business skills in the company.

Sales and marketing. Despite one of the partners having done many online marketing courses (this may have given a false sense of competence and confidence), the sales and marketing skills in the company are dangerously low. The main problem is their sales strategy. Trying to convince a local branch of an MNE might be doable (although they did that with only one client), but it would surely take more time than they planned. The real mistake is to assume that a branch will promote the service to its headquarters. This is rarely achieved, both because the acquisition channel is different at the HQ level and because heads of national branches may see their involvement in promoting a product as a conflict of interest. The whole sales strategy of Testing123 relies on this false assumption: that a satisfied branch manager will help promote their product internationally. Another issue lies with the price. Their assumption was that setting a price well below the market would give them a boost in sales (which was proven wrong). In fact, for novel products and services, both corporate clients and individual consumers rely on the price as a good indicator of the quality of the product. In this case, an acquisitions department may see their 50%-off price as a sign that there might be something wrong with the service.

Strategy. One of the main strategic issues is the poor sales strategy, as mentioned before, with a much longer cycle than anticipated and with slim chances of internationalization through local branches promoting to their HQ. Another issue would be how the founders occupy and plan to occupy their time. First, they have many consultancy hours to deliver. While this is indeed paid work, it is certainly not scalable. If the founders' schedule is already busy with implementation consultancy for one client, what would they do if they had more than one? The reason they set their business model to include one-on-one implementation hours is probably their past successful careers as consultants; however, this now constitutes a bottleneck. Another issue with how they occupy their time concerns coding add-ons that prospective clients mentioned as nice-to-haves. When trying to sell a tech product or service, it is ineffective to add features that a) are requested by non-committing clients and b) only benefit individual clients. It is better to resist such requests and to code add-ons (in our case) only if accompanied by a written agreement and only if the respective add-on improves the platform for current or future users. Another error is actually a future one: the plan to keep the price low for the first year and then to double it abruptly. This is not an option; clients would not understand the sudden increase and would want it reflected in increased quality or supplementary features. Both existing and potential clients, when presented with an invoice or an offer with a suddenly doubled price, will feel they were treated unfairly and will walk away.

Product. The product is good, and the clients are happy, but as mentioned above, it is much too cheap to create value and to induce trust in potential buyers.

Founders. The founders are good tech people but lack business skills. Although the clients are happy, the founders suspect that their product has poor quality. When I write a case study, I take reality-inspired bits and pieces and assemble them. This part—with tech specialists identifying the poor quality of their work as a potential cause of failure—is inspired by many discussions with startups. In an interesting illustration of the Dunning-Kruger effect (see the chapter on changing our mind), I observed that—when asked about weak points of their business or about the most likely causes of failure—startup founders automatically think of areas they usually focus upon—the tech part—and almost never identify the weak business model. If they lack business skills, they do not realize it, because to realize that you lack business skills you need a certain level of business skills. This is the Dunning–Kruger effect in a nutshell, more on it in a future chapter.

Both diagnosis methods point to this common root cause: There is a lack of strategy, planning, and sales and marketing skills in this company. In fewer words, there is a lack of business skills. The *Ishikawa* analysis has identified the same root cause as the *five whys*: the lack of business skills of the founders. If, in your business problem diagnosis, you decide to perform both techniques, make sure that the result of the first one does not anchor you when you do the second. If this is a team effort, a good idea is to divide the team into two and have each subgroup perform one technique, before comparing results. It is not unusual to obtain different root causes after the two analyses; in this case, make sure that you take some time to discuss, negotiate, and synthesize one root cause. If this is not possible, it may be the case that the problem has two root causes and they both need to be addressed.

9.3 Articulating the Objective

Whether it is a negotiation, embarking on a new career, starting a company, or managing our lives, the clear articulation of the objective (the goal) of your endeavor is very important. And writing helps. Chris Voss ran the FBI's hostage negotiation department and then specialized in teaching business negotiation techniques. At the end of the book, *Never Split the Difference*, he offers a *cheat sheet* to prepare for any negotiation, and the most important point on the cheat sheet is to write in advance the large purpose of the meeting ("Why am I going to see this man?") and the immediate objective, with a good and a bad scenario ("What is the best result I expect? But the worst?") (Voss & Raz, 2016). This triple articulation provides tools for the discussion, but just as importantly, it prepares the mindset for negotiation.

When it comes to starting a new project or even setting up a company, especially if there are several partners involved, articulating and writing down the goal is the most important preparation step: one that can prevent many further problems. If my goal for the startup is to sell it after 5 years, become a serial entrepreneur, and retire at 40, while my partner's goal is to leave it to his future grandchildren, then it is better to clarify things before going to the trade register.

The exercise of writing down our goals on paper not only helps in setting them clearly, but also increases our chances of achieving them. Many studies confirm this; for example, Milne et al. (2002) found that writing down your goals doubles the chances of meeting them. Will you try it?

Question(s). What about a purpose in life? Do you have one? Can you write it on paper? What are your goals for this year? And for the next 10 years?

After we articulate the problem and identify immediate causes and root causes, we may run into a conundrum while we try to articulate the goal. How do we articulate an objective that involves both putting out the fire, stopping the leak, and preventing a future one? When solving the root cause automatically solves not only future problems but also the current one, defining the goal is simple. Most often, though, this is not the case. The key, then, is to set multiple goals and to prioritize them, or to set a complex goal (made up by multiple goals) and try to shoot two rabbits with one cleverly constructed silver bullet.

Let us articulate goals for the two cases we have discussed in this section. In the Testing123 case, we have identified the current problem: "money will run out in 2 months" and the root cause: "there are no business skills in the company." If we solve the root cause (by somehow bringing in business skills) we will not necessarily have the time to solve the immediate problem (the fire—the cash flow problem). The solution, therefore, is to combine the two in a complex objective and to try to find complex solutions for it. Articulating a complex objective is not complicated, it just makes good use of the conjunction *and*. In our case, a well-articulated objective would solve the need for cash (let us say 50 k for 3 months) and the root cause:

Objective: To get 50 k in 3 months and to bring in business skills.

For the bank matrix organization case, three things need solving: the fire (the KPI), the immediate cause or the gas leak (the conflicting directions given to that particular employee), and the root cause, the old gas pipes (the matrix structure). These cannot be all assembled into a common goal, as they need different timelines and completely different solutions. The first two, however, *can* be combined:

Immediate objective: To fully restore the employee's focus on SMEs so that she can meet the target.

leaving the more strategic objective to be tackled later:

Strategic objective: To minimize the effects of the matrix organization on field jobs.

After articulating objectives, the next step is to generate and articulate a set of options.

9.4 Articulating a Set of Options

When faced with a complex problem, the first thing some hasty managers do is rush in with the solution. If, however, the problem is approached systematically, after defining it, finding the root cause, and articulating the objective, we must find a consideration set: a shortlist of alternative solutions. I argue in one of the previous chapters that having at least two options considerably improves the quality of the chosen solution. So, why not three?

Finding a solid set of at least three possible solutions requires creativity and is best done as a team. The classic method, brainstorming, can lead to premature invalidation of potentially good and ingenious proposals that are insufficiently well formulated and can prevent shy people from speaking. An alternative to brainstorming is brainwriting, a method that generates a large set of alternatives by combining writing (each individual writing his own ideas) with reading (each individual reading some of their teammates' ideas for inspiration) and with speaking (the session ends with the group debating on the list of options). Brainwriting avoids some of the pitfalls of brainstorming, and it can be used successfully in smaller or bigger teams. There are several variants: I describe here a short version that I use both in class and with the companies I work with. After a clear objective is articulated and understood, each member of the team takes a sheet of paper and writes down three possible solutions. The scenario is as follows: "You are a consultant for this problem, please propose three solutions." Then, they pass their sheet of paper to the neighbor on the left and receive the one from the neighbor on the right (assuming a circle). Now, everybody has in front of them a set of three fresh alternatives they are seeing for the first time. After reading them, participants are requested to write on the sheet they currently hold, below the three existing ones, a set of two new alternatives under the scenario "You are a consultant for this problem, please propose two solutions." These solutions can be:

- two of their three original ones, or
- two of the ones received from their right-hand neighbor, or
- solutions that combine elements, or
- fresh ideas sparked by the process.

This second sheet of paper then moves the same way—to the left—while a new one arrives from the right. Now, in the last writing stage, each participant has a new paper in front, with five new solutions from their two neighbors on the right. After reading these as well, each participant finally writes down their final recommended alternative according to this scenario: "You are a consultant for this problem, what would be your *best* proposal?".

This first part, which involves writing, has two advantages over brainstorming: first, everybody offers their suggestions (even the quiet members), and second, the chances of ideas being dismissed too early are slim. The outcome of this first part is a list of options: one per member. Obtaining this consideration set is the main purpose of the exercise. The second part involves speaking (finally!). Each member reads their proposal and then comments on the best ideas they came upon in the process. The decision-making process continues by analyzing the alternatives and choosing the best solution, as will be detailed further in this chapter. Brainwriting provides a set of interesting and diverse alternatives that have already passed through a primary selection. Every time I conducted such an exercise, all participants agreed that the final set contains much more interesting potential solutions than their first ideas. If a larger set is needed, other variants of the technique involve keeping the number of alternatives proposed each time at three and performing up to six rounds. The original format is called *the 6–3–5 method*, as it involves six rounds of 5 min in which each of 6 participants produces three ideas each time, thus yielding 108 ideas. Originally, brainwriting needs everybody to be in the same room, but online variants have been offered as well (for instance at https://635.tecmark.co.uk/). Still, people need to be online at the same time. I have also successfully conducted brainwriting sessions using the features offered by online group communication tools such as Zoom or Teams.

If we have more than one goal (for instance, in the Testing123 case, we have the immediate goal of obtaining 50 k euros and the strategic goal of bringing business skills into the company), then the set of options that we build should contain potential solutions to all goals. That can be achieved by silver bullet solutions that address two matters with one shot or with complex solutions linked with an "and." In our case, brainwriting may lead to the following results:

> *Silver bullet solution:* Find an angel investor to invest 50 k as working capital (for, say, 10% of the business) and to dedicate part of her time as sweat equity (working for shares) in order to draft a strategy, set a marketing plan, and conduct sales (for, say, a supplementary 10% of the shares).

> *Silver bullet solution:* Sell the company or part of the company to X-Coding.

> *Complex solution*: Try to get state or European grant funds for startups to fulfill the cash need. In the meantime, contract a reseller as an exclusive channel to sell and implement the service, to allow the founders to concentrate on the platform.

> *Complex solution:* Get access to a crowd-investing platform such as AngelList or Seedblink for the 50 k, and hire a CEO with industry knowledge and strategy, marketing, and sales skills.

Complex solution: Get a bank loan for 50 k, and hire a sales manager.

Sometimes, brainwriting yields out-of-the-box solutions such as this one:

Complex solution: Have Alex sell his apartment (for the cash need) and move in with George, then go to a business school and offer their master students internships at Testing123 (for business skills).

After generating and writing down a set of 2–4 potential solutions, we need to choose the best one. We do that by first identifying and analyzing the assumptions behind each option and then by running each alternative against a set of criteria.

9.5 Articulating Assumptions

This book has an entire previous chapter on identifying assumptions, and my critical message there is that false assumptions are the main cause of projects that fail. The problem is not that we cannot assess the assumptions as false, but that *we do not even realize we make them.* Major business decisions can lead to surprisingly bad results because we unconsciously rely on a hidden wrong assumption. It is hard to identify hidden assumptions, hence the reason they are called *hidden*. We can try to spot them by asking a simple question: "What should be true for this plan to work?" A few techniques for identifying hidden assumptions (true or false) are described in the dedicated chapter: performing a premortem analysis, speaking to someone and making a list, and thinking of what a skeptical and influencing person would say (an investor, the CEO, the manager of the purchasing department).

If we use any of these methods to think about the key assumptions hidden behind the alternative solutions proposed for Testing123, we may identify some of the following:

- We can find an angel investor who is interested in Testing123.
- We can find an angel investor who is able (has the time and the skills) and willing to get involved in running the company.
- We can find an angel investor and the deal can be negotiated, signed, and paid for within 3 months.
- An angel who seems to have business skills, really has them.
- X-Coding is interested, strategically, in scaling horizontally by acquiring service suppliers.
- An international deal with X-Coding will take less than 3 months.
- A crowd-investing platform is interested in Testing 123.
- We can find a CEO.
- A bank loan is available for a 6-month-old startup with a negative cash flow.

… and so on.

Once identified, some assumptions can be assessed on the spot as false (the one about the bank loan, for instance, is a good candidate), allowing us to remove that option from the consideration set. Other assumptions can be tested (such as the one about finding angels who are interested in this business), for instance by talking to one or two investors or by participating in a pitching session. Yet other assumptions can offer a higher or lower score for feasibility in the decision phase.

9.6 Articulating Criteria and the Decision-Making Process

Although rarely adopted, the habit of writing down criteria before making a decision can yield many benefits. If we have to choose a new apartment, we can start searching without a plan, in which case we will probably choose one of the first apartments we visited because we liked the view from the balcony. We often live happily with the resulting decision. For a better result, however, we should write down a plan for our decision-making process. This written plan should mention at least two elements: the criteria we consider and the way we will decide. For instance, when looking to buy an apartment, we may consider criteria such as price, location, number of rooms, which floor, the general aspect of the building, neighbors, proximity to transport or shops, and so on. The decision process may have a first phase called elimination-by-aspects, in which options that do not fulfill certain threshold criteria ("within my budget," "less than 10 min by foot from a metro station" or "not the ground floor") are eliminated from the consideration set, leaving a shorter set of 2–4 options to be considered against all (weighted) criteria. The final step, in such a personal choice, would perhaps be consulting our gut feeling for the final verdict between two finalists. Even if it seems complicated (although the written plan should not be longer than this paragraph), some plan is better than no plan: We thereby at least know what we are deviating from.

Applying these steps to our Testing123 case, we may first employ an elimination-by-aspects phase in order to make the short list of options smaller. One of the criteria, feasibility, may help us eliminate the bank loan. If we set a threshold at 3 months, we can also safely eliminate selling to X-Coding. In other situations, we may also employ a fast-and-frugal decision tree (described in the chapter on individual decision-making) to help navigate a series of clear-cut criteria. After the consideration set gets shorter, we should make sure we do not fall into the trap of considering the options as mutually exclusive. Think *and* instead of *or*. One example is considering investments by an angel *and* a crowd-investing platform. But we should think *and* instead of *or* not only in terms of the final solution, but also in terms of possibilities to pursue. One such example is looking simultaneously for both investment and grant funds, at least as long as resources (time, costs, bandwidth) allow pursuing both paths. Another example of combining two options would be to find an angel who can invest the 50 k but is unwilling to be involved in running the business. Nevertheless, the investor may mentor the founders for a month and, afterward, the funds allow them to hire a CEO, hire a sales manager, or choose a reseller.

The next step would be to consider all remaining options against all criteria. For instance, we may consider criteria such as the outcome (the amount of funding provided, for example), timeline (this may actually be the crucial criterion, as—in this case—reaching the immediate objective too late is useless), risks (losing the collateral in case of a bank loan, navigating bureaucracy and complicate legislation in case of grant funds, partial loss of control in case of securing an investment), stakeholders (the impact of different options on parties other than the business and its founders; for example, the possible conflict of interest in David's case if an offer is made to X-Coding). Another important criterion is the alignment with long-term goals. If, for instance, the founders set up this company with the long-term plan of leaving it to their offspring, looking for investment is not an option because seed investors do not rely on long-term dividends, but on subsequent financing rounds and a clear plan for exit in a few years.

A useful tool for deciding among several options based on several criteria is the weighted matrix described in a previous chapter. Clearly, the matrix is just an indicator, and the two founders may very well rediscuss its outcome and perhaps apply their instinct to validate the chosen path ahead.

This case study analysis will not end with firmly selecting a solution; but let us see what the two founders might do after analyzing their options based on these criteria. After careful consideration, the two founders may choose to look for either investment or grant funds for the cash need and solve the business skills issue by searching for a CEO or for a good reseller. Strategy, especially for startups, involves carefully allocating (scarce) resources for the best effect toward growth. In our case, for example, they may pursue in parallel the three financing options (including, why not?, the crowd-investing platform) as long as the possibility is there and the resources needed (time, effort, attention, money) do not exceed the team's capacity.

9.7 Articulating the Implementation Plan

Clear deadlines and clear milestones set in advance help us to monitor the implementation of a chosen solution. In our case, for instance, Alex and George might choose to pursue three financing options for 1 month, then to re-analyze and put all firepower behind the solution found to be most likely to succeed. Clearly set milestones also help us correct the course, if the results are not as expected, or even fall back on a Plan B.

Make sure to use a double feedback loop in order to question, adjust, and learn from the implementation of our chosen solutions. A simple feedback loop means correcting course as a function of what we observe as consequences of our actions. A second loop looks at (and challenges) the objectives, how we make decisions,

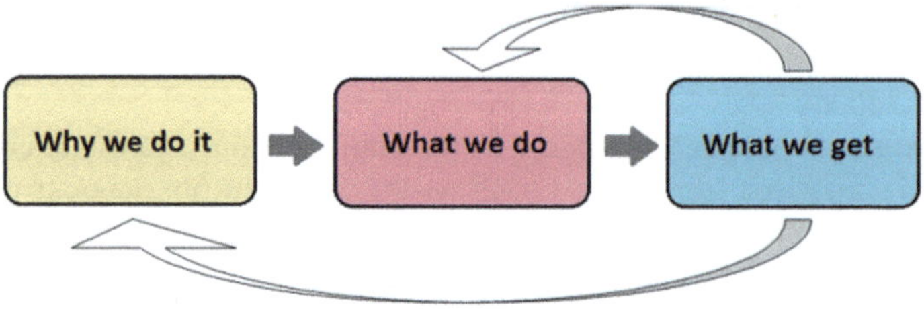

Fig. 9.3 Double-loop learning

and what indicators we set for controlling the course (and why those are chosen), as depicted in Fig. 9.3.

Chris Argyris, the father of organizational learning, speaks in an HBR article (Argyris, 1991) about the importance of double-loop learning: “I have coined the terms *single-loop* and *double-loop* learning to capture this crucial distinction. To give a simple analogy: a thermostat that automatically turns on the heat whenever the temperature in a room drops below 68° is a good example of single-loop learning. A thermostat that could ask “Why am I set at 68°?” and then explore whether or not some other temperature might more economically achieve the goal of heating the room would be engaging in double-loop learning. Highly skilled professionals are frequently very good at single-loop learning. After all, they have spent much of their lives acquiring academic credentials, mastering one or a number of intellectual disciplines, and applying those disciplines to solve real-world problems. Ironically, though, this very fact helps explain why professionals are often so bad at double-loop learning.” A double feedback loop needs intellectual humility from the manager and an organizational environment that encourages experimentation and personal growth.

9.8 Debriefing

At the conclusion of a project, the whole process should be carefully analyzed while looking for lessons worth learning. After a project failure, most teams set a debriefing meeting. In healthy organizations, that meeting is a lessons-learned one; in not-so-healthy organizations, the words used are *responsibility* (read *blame*) and *consequences* (read *punishment*). Nevertheless, failed projects are analyzed, one way or another. The danger lies with successes, where often the team only gets together to open the champagne. Successful projects deserve a debriefing meeting as well. Of course, managers and firms mainly learn from negative outcomes (Bingham & Haleblian, 2012) and mistakes (Eisenhardt & Sull, 2001), and learning from negative situations lasts longer (Madsen & Desai, 2010), but success can also be a good source of learning. Also, without analysis, we may take credit for success and ignore the role of context and luck.

Finally, we should employ a meta-analysis in which we look at our decision-making process per se. This usually requires a third party to help identify our blind spots and a good documentation of our decision-making and problem-solving processes. I chose to frame this chapter on complex problem solving on the benefits of clear articulation and of writing things down. While immediate benefits are clear (writing gives our ideas more structure, we can revisit, we can share the knowledge), this long-term benefit of being able to later analyze our decision-making process is rarely used. Documenting our decisions in a decision journal is perhaps the most useful tool in bettering our decision-making skills. As mentioned before, research by Lerner and Tetlock (1999) shows that we make better decisions when we know we will be held accountable to a third party (the public, a jury, the board, the boss, the spouse). If we do not have a third party to help us with our decision, the decision journal will also take this role and will help us make better choices.

Unlike the decision journals available online, which usually look at decision-making from a personal disposition perspective, my recommended format has a more pragmatical and rational perspective. It prompts the decision-maker to go through part of the process described in this chapter: to write down the objective of the decision, the timeline (for deciding and for implementing), the alternatives (this prompts the decision-maker to *have* some), the identified stakeholders and how are they affected by each alternative, the criteria, what would be a good decision-making process, and how irrationality may affect us while deciding (biases, intuition, etc.). The next rubric is the decision itself, the expected outcome, the associated assumptions (as stated before, a good method to identify hidden assumptions is to write down what should be true in order to attain the expected outcome), as well as the associated risks. Then, the final rubric should be filled in after the outcome is known. This journal is suited for business decisions—both individually and team-made—but works perfectly for life choices as well. Table 9.1 presents an example of a journal entry written by the CEO of a company about the choice of how to finance the internationalization process.

If we articulate and write down the problem, its causes, assumptions, alternatives, criteria, and decision-making process, we will likely reach better solutions for our challenges, although I am sure you knew that already. The hard part is not convincing yourself that this is better, just as the hard part in quitting smoking is not convincing yourself that smoking is bad; instead, the hardest part is implementation. In our case, an initial and very easy plan for gaining the habit of following such a process is to apply it once, soon after reading this chapter. Just choose a present challenge and go through the steps. It might take an hour or two, but it is worth it. Then, when we do it a second time, we might just create a new and productive habit. Good luck!

Table 9.1 Example: Hypothetical entry in a decision journal

Objective	To finance internationalization (*details*)
Deadline of decision	April
Deadline of implementation	End of year
Alternatives	List on the local stock exchange List on a regional stock exchange Get a bank loan Raise a round of financing from VC funds EU money
Criteria	Amount obtained Reimbursing conditions (if the case) Collateral Co-investment required Prerequisites Cost Speed Our experience in financing What others did
Decision-making process	Elimination-by-aspects until a shortlist, then looking at combinations of options and at options that can be tried on simultaneously, then a weighted criteria matrix for choosing one option to propose to the board along with two other alternatives, then discussion on the board to reach agreement (consensus needed), then validation by shareholders vote
Irrational influence	Bad previous experience with banks Inclination not to work with the authorities (for EU money) Probably loss aversion for the collateral guarantee
Final decision	List on the local stock exchange
Expected outcome	List in November or December and obtain 2.5 million euros at 20 million euros valuation
Assumptions/risks	The valuation proposed by the IPO consultant will hold Our numbers for this year will be good, as budgeted No major event to disrupt the market
Expected effect on stakeholders	Team—pride, but also defocus from current business Board—pressure during process, possibly conflict CEO—possibility for another mandate if successful, possibility of early termination if not Shareholders—liquidity, gain, but also possible decrease in share value Clients—increased presence in media Partners—trust
Outcome	(to be written in January)

References

Argyris, C. (1991). Teaching smart people how to learn. *Harvard Business Review, 69*(3), 99–109

Bingham, C. B., & Haleblian, J. J. (2012). How firms learn heuristics: Uncovering missing components of organizational learning. *Strategic Entrepreneurship Journal, 6*(2), 152–177. https://doi.org/10.1002/sej.1132

Dalio, R. (2017). *Principles: life and work* (Illustrated ed.). Simon and Schuster.

Eisenhardt, K. M., & Sull, D. N. (2001). Strategy as simple rules. *Harvard Business Review, 79*(1), 100–116

Lerner, J. S., & Tetlock, P. E. (1999). Accounting for the effects of accountability. *Psychological Bulletin, 125*(2), 255–275

Madsen, P. M., & Desai, V. (2010). Failing to learn? The effects of failure and success on organizational learning in the global orbital launch vehicle industry. *Academy of Management Journal, 53*(3), 451–476. https://doi.org/10.5465/amj.2010.51467631

Milne, S., Orbell, S., & Sheeran, P. (2002). Combining motivational and volitional interventions to promote exercise participation: Protection motivation theory and implementation intentions. *British Journal of Health Psychology, 7*(2), 163–184. https://doi.org/10.1348/135910702169420

Rosling, H., Rönnlund, A. R., & Rosling, O. (2018). *Factfulness: Ten reasons we're wrong about the world–and why things are better than you think* (Reprint ed.). Flatiron Books.

Voss, C., & Raz, T. (2016). *Never split the difference: Negotiating as if your life depended on it* (1st ed.). Harper Business.

Part III
Critical Thinking in Persuasion

One-on-One Persuasion

10

When trying to convince a client to buy your service, the boss to fund your project, or a peer to change a procedure, most people rely on a false assumption: if we ourselves are convinced of something, then we can easily convince others. We therefore rarely prepare for such a meeting and often fail to achieve our goal. This chapter provides a step-by-step recipe for preparing for a persuasion effort, recipe that includes, among others, crucial steps such as getting the other to care, identifying *pro* arguments customized for the other, and—most importantly—finding out beforehand why they might say *no* (a kind of persuasion premortem).

10.1 Verbal Persuasion

This section is better read with a personal example in mind, so think of someone you need to persuade of something in the coming days. It could be a client, a supplier, your boss, someone else you work with—anyone. And the topic could also be anything related to work. Have you thought of such an upcoming situation? Is such a meeting already set for next Wednesday? Let's make that meeting work better!

The first problem with our persuasion efforts is that we put too much trust in our natural ability to convince, and we therefore usually turn up for the meeting totally unprepared. We expect the meeting to go smoothly: we think we will waltz into the room, open our mouth, and that the wisdom and charm that we are hiding somewhere inside will just flow out, articulated into the perfect pitch, leaving the other no choice but to beg us to sell him our service or whatever we are trying to sell. Unfortunately, it usually does not happen this way, despite our natural talent. I will therefore make a case here for preparing thoroughly for such a meeting. Jot down your ideas on a piece of paper, try to think what the other will say, and even try to rehearse with a friend or in front of a mirror. You need to prepare for all possibilities. I reiterate here Chriss Voss' advice to write down, before such a meeting,

R. Atanasiu, *Critical Thinking for Managers*, Management for Professionals,
https://doi.org/10.1007/978-3-030-73600-2_10

three things: the clear purpose of the meeting, the best result we expect, and also the worst.

Let me use an exercise as an example that opens up the next topic:

Exercise Step 1: Please pretend you sell beverages in a park and you see me running. Try to convince me with a short sentence to buy a bottle of Coca Cola from you. Before you continue reading, please write down 2–3 such sentences.

Step 2: Please imagine that *you* run through the park and you see *me* trying to sell a bottle of Coca Cola to you. And you say no. Why would you say no? Think in practical terms and write down 2–3 reasons why you did not buy the beverage.

If you are like most people, in Step 1 you wrote things like "it's cold and refreshing", "it will give you a boost of energy", or "most athletes drink Coca Cola during long runs". Generally, you offer me reasons to say "yes". If you are like most people, in Step 2, where the situation is flipped, you wrote practical things like "I don't like to stop while running", "I don't carry a wallet", "I already had a Coca Cola five minutes ago", or "I only drink Pepsi". Please observe now that the reasons to say "no" have *nothing* to do with the reasons to say "yes." And that reasons to say "no" take precedence. If you don't carry money while running, the fact that the beverage is cold and refreshing is irrelevant. All those *pro* arguments are powerless in the face of my lack of money. However, our natural choice is to offer only arguments that would get the other to say "yes". This should not be our first approach. Before offering arguments in favor of our claim, we need to deal with the reasons for which the other would say "no", in a particular case of persuasion premortem. Premortem (described elsewhere in this book as a tool for risk assessment and for identifying false assumptions in projects) could be a valuable tool for persuasion.

So, how can you prepare to tackle my reasons to say "no"? If you cannot ask me directly, you need to use your imagination, to put yourself in my shoes, and to identify a few likely candidates. An efficient method is to perform a persuasion premortem before the interaction. You could imagine that it already happened and that I said "no" to your offer. Why did I say "no"? Why didn't I buy the Coke? Perhaps I don't have money. Perhaps I only drink Pepsi. Perhaps I just drank four bottles of Coke and I don't need another one. Thinking of three potential obstacles and of ways to present them to me ("Hey! I know that perhaps you don't carry a wallet while you run") will make you much more prepared for our interaction, will show your empathy for my perspective, and—more importantly—can give you an edge for persuasion: "I know that perhaps you don't carry a wallet while you run, but that is not a problem. I see you running every day. Have the Coke now, while you are thirsty, and you can bring me the money tomorrow."

Let me illustrate with another example. Imagine that next Wednesday you have a meeting with a salesperson who will try to sell you their newest service. Your company does need that service, and you do not have a clear opinion on this: you expect the meeting to help you make up your mind. If, at the meeting, the other starts by emphasizing why their offer is great, your mind will reflexively search for reasons you might say "no". Only if and after our mind deals with these reasons to say "no" will it pay attention to whatever reasons there may be to say "yes". If we do not discard these obstacles, the answer will be "no", regardless of how many reasons you hear in favor of a "yes". Still, unfortunately, when it is our turn to persuade, we ignore the other person's reasons to say "no". We usually stick to offering as many reasons as possible to say "yes", which rarely works. Going back to that sales pitch you will receive on Wednesday, I bet you would be pleasantly surprised if the other started by saying "I know that, for this kind of service, you have a traditional supplier and you have no reason to change them." That will show you that he has tried to put himself in your shoes. He may then continue by dislodging the obstacle: "... but you don't have to give up the other supplier entirely, you can buy from us only the service elements they do not offer."

This principle to first dismantle the obstacles, along with others, is embedded in a five-step process designed to maximize our chances to persuade. I will use a short case inspired from reality to illustrate this process. As with most techniques described in this book, the purpose of this process is to be applied only if you feel it will benefit your effort.

Case A young entrepreneur wants to launch a platform that showcases bad B2B debtors in the courier service industry. This particular sector is chronically affected by bad debts, and his idea is to help courier service providers put all these debtors in a single public place. The problem with such a platform is that—while it may work when fully populated—it is hard to launch, as most courier companies are reluctant to be the first to provide a list of debtors. That is why the young entrepreneur has chosen to convince an open-minded CEO of a courier business, a famous and charismatic character on the Romanian business scene. After having a meeting confirmed for next week, he uses his time to prepare the persuasion effort by addressing and rehearsing the steps described below. As we proceed through this example, please have in mind your personal situation.

Step 1. State the problem, and get the other to care. This is a composite step, and often the second part—getting the other to care—is the crucial part of the whole process. The key to this, and the key to the whole process, is empathy. While we think we know what makes other people tick, upon closer inspection we often discover that we believe the others to be simpler versions of ourselves, moved by the same interests and reasons as we are. They are not, and putting ourselves in other people's shoes is a skill that requires constant exercise.

What is important to us is often much less important to the other, and the first thing we need to do is to create a connection between our claim and the interlocutor's needs. If, for instance, I go to the boss's office saying that I want to be promoted as the new area manager, this topic will be low on his priority list (mainly because it is about me, not about him or about the company), so my persuasion efforts will be met with a yawn, and the boss will likely send some emails while pretending to listen to me. You can anticipate the verdict, and the verdict comes back the way it does because the boss does not know how I—from the position of area manager—can influence the smooth running of the company and its annual performance. By the time I tell him, he is already bored. If, however, I ask him for a meeting to tell him that I have found the cause of the miscommunication with our customers in the respective area and that I know how to overcome it, he will be eager to listen to me. The first thing in such a pitch, then, is to show why we deserve the other's attention, turning the discussion to their area of interest. I will quote here the bestselling author, scholar, and Zen Buddhist monk Thich Nhat Hanh, who says that "the truth must be presented in ways that others can accept."

The natural way to understand what moves the other is to stop assuming and ask. If we calibrate through kind inquiry our image of the other's perspective and mindset, we will be in a much better position to influence them.

Each of these steps will be illustrated with what our young entrepreneur might have said to the CEO of the courier company.

> ***Example*** We know—not as well as you do—but we know that a major problem for courier companies is the existence of customers who do not pay. What proportion of your clients pay late or never? We can reduce this by *X%* if you make your bad-debtors database available.

Step 2. Give your solution to the problem (the objective of your persuasion attempt) by emphasizing the implication for the other (the benefit, but also the action required). A clear (but short) description of what you propose can give the other a sense of clarity that helps a quick decision process (hopefully in your favor). Full transparency of what is required from them will also make you score points. Empathy is also required for this step, as for all other steps. We need to present things from the perspective of the other.

If, for instance, the software solution you propose to a bank solves problems that the bank does not even know it has, it is unlikely to sign the contract. If, for instance, your solution provides a series of benefits and they are related to the customer, you can make the effort to translate those benefits as benefits for the bank: "If online payment is easier, your customers will be happier" can be replaced with "If online payment is easier, your customers will be happier and will migrate all their banking operations to your bank, increasing both revenues and market share."

> ***Example*** We have prepared and plan to launch a public list of bad debtors in your business sector *(be as detailed about this as possible)*. We need a first partner, someone who can understand and trust that this will work, someone who has the courage to be the first mover. This is why I came to kindly ask you to be our first customer and to give us access to your bad-debtors database.

Step 3. Acknowledge the obstacles and deal with them. We usually go to the meeting prepared with a series of pro arguments, and then the other brings just one argument against, and everything is lost: "Your software may be the best for online

payments, but our bank never signs contracts with startups," "We would like to increase your salary, but we have no money," "The only criterion for approving investments is ROI, and your research project doesn't guarantee any profit," "You would be perfect for the area manager position, but unfortunately the job requires 5 years of experience in the company, and you only have 4." I admit, I chose counterarguments that are difficult to dismantle. But this is not always the case; a little documentation and prior preparation can work wonders.
After running a premortem on the meeting, you are able to acknowledge and deal with some of the potential obstacles, the other's reasons to say "no". If you cannot calibrate your assumptions by asking the person what would prevent them from saying "yes", you need to put yourself (mentally) in their shoes, use your empathy, do a little research, and then try to imagine what could be their reasons for saying "no". Clearly, it might be the case that the reasons you identified do not overlap with the real ones. But, in the absence of anything better, bringing them up will increase your credibility. If, however, you can calibrate, or your intuition is right, after acknowledging the reasons (which is useful in itself) you can build on them by using the word "but": "I know that your bank never signs contracts with startups, *but* we are ready to implement our service in collaboration with X-Soft, the company you have worked with in recent years. We have delivered joint projects before and they are happy to collaborate on this one."

> ***Example*** (1) I know that fiscal authorities attempted to publish a similar list for individual tax-payers and there were many errors. In our case, … *(explanation).* (2) I also know that a lot of invoices are in fact contested. We have a mechanism that checks … *(explanation).* (3) I am very aware of the danger of being sued. Our lawyers … *(explanation).*

Step 4. Bring arguments to your offer/claim. Only now, as a fourth step, is it time to bring in reasons in favor of our position. These reasons are not the opposite of the reasons against our claim (treated earlier); they usually refer to totally different aspects. Now that the obstacles are removed, these pro reasons have more persuasive power. We may be tempted to win by brute force and to present a long series of advantages. This is not a good tactic. We want to convince the other, not to puzzle them. A better choice would be to try and find the best three pro arguments and to start with the most important—allocating the most time and depth to describing and defending it—to continue with the second—with a bit less emphasis —and then to only offer one more, the third, in less detail.
Just like some entrepreneurs build products for copies of themselves on the (false) assumption that all customers are like them, we often have the tendency to use on others the reasons that convinced us in the first place. Reasons in favor, as with reasons against, must be adapted to our audience. Think of what would be important for the other; what would make them tick. During a workshop in a large company, I facilitated an exercise in which two managers, heads of their divisions, applied the process described here to persuade one other. One of them, the head of Division *X*, confessed that for the past 6 months he had tried in vain to persuade the

head of Division *Y* (also participating in the exercise) to adopt a certain procedure. When asked to put forward his arguments, we all realized that they all concerned his own division. "If *you* adopt this protocol, *we* will be more productive." It did not work out. I then asked him to find three reasons why the other division, Division *Y*, would benefit from the procedure. He had not thought about that before. After about five minutes, however, he came up with three valid reasons, put them forward, and the procedure was accepted on the spot.

Finally, if you are asking for a raise, do not explain why is it that you need more money, but explain the benefits you can bring to the company if you get that raise. It is more complicated, but 10 times more effective.

Find below an example of how we can add reasons in favor of our claim, adapted for our case. The discourse here is presented schematically. In real life, you should not number your reasons, but you should nonetheless have a fluent argumentation.

> ***Example*** I have three reasons to believe that this would work out for you: (1) Clients on the list will pay their debt, (2) Clients will pay on time in order to avoid getting on the list, (3) When all courier companies are on the platform, you can verify the track record of new customers.

Step 5. Call to action. Often, such a meeting apparently ends well, with the other giving clear signs of being won over by your perspective. And yet, all your effort can be lost if you do not convey a clear image of what exactly you expect from the other party. Thinking that everything is understood is a mistake. When you feel that the process went well, you need to describe in a clear and pragmatic way what the other needs to do, step by step. There is a difference between "I believe you" and "I will do as you say," and while many people are happy when hearing the first and they then relax, your purpose is to get the other party to commit to the second sentence, not the first.

> ***Example*** If you agree, please put us in contact with the person who is responsible for non-paying customers in order to take over the database. We also need to sign this contract, so we brought a draft for you to read before next time.

10.2 Persuasion in Writing

What if we need to persuade a person or a group not during a meeting, but through an email to be sent or a *six-pager* that documents a decision to be drafted? All these are argumentative essays, so we will discuss next the principles of persuasion applied to writing an argumentative essay. First of all, what is such an essay? Few of us ever said: "I have to write an argumentative essay." But we did write one! An executive emailing the members of the board, a citizen writing a petition, a journalist writing an opinion article, a real-estate salesperson emphasizing in a pamphlet the advantages of buying this house or that apartment: all of them are in fact writing argumentative essays. An argumentative essay is a piece of writing that tries to convince the target audience.

Persuasion can be achieved in many ways, sometimes in dubious ways. People can be persuaded by poor arguments and doubtful claims, by appeals to emotion, by often-repeated nonsense, or even by lying. But persuasion-no-matter-what is not the purpose of this book. We aim here to construct rational, well-structured arguments. The following section is about constructing powerful arguments in writing.

Case Imagine you need to write an opinion article for a business magazine *(the principles apply,* mutatis mutandis, *to writing an email or a memo).* You are the CEO of a large company, and you have a monthly column in a prestigious practitioners' magazine. This month you choose to write about micromanagement, the phenomenon in which a manager controls too closely the work of subordinates.

How should we start? I would propose to start, before writing anything, with planning. The best structure starts with a preliminary step, in which to perform a Socratic questioning. The next step is to actually write the article (we will discuss its structure below). The last step is to revise it. Let's take these steps one by one:

Socratic questioning is a form of disciplined questioning used to explore ideas in depth. It was used by Socrates as a method of teaching, as documented by his disciples. We will use it to clarify our own position, before starting to write the article. I recommend using this powerful tool for other circumstances as well; its use is not limited to persuasion in writing; in any case, I believe that the power to extrapolate is a characteristic of any critical thinker.

Although it was originally designed as a dialog, we will try Socratic questioning through a soliloquy (a dialog with ourselves). Planning to write about micromanagement can be done by asking yourself, and answering, some of the following questions.

- *What exactly am I saying?* I am saying that micromanagement is a very common and damaging phenomenon.
- *Is this always the case?* Well, although micromanaging sometimes brings results in the short run, it is not productive in the long run.

- *Based on what?* Here, we should list the reasons that support our claim as well as the sources we might quote or the examples we might use. Let us think of the main reasons supporting my claim: micromanagement kills motivation and is therefore counterproductive for the team; micromanagement keeps the manager from doing his own job and is therefore counterproductive for the manager himself; and last but not least, micromanagement prevents everybody from growing. All these should be supported with examples, analogies, studies, or articles.
- *What are the assumptions?* Remember the importance of hidden premises? This is where you should list the relevant ones. In our case, I think an important assumption that we must treat in our essay is whether micromanagement is indeed an important phenomenon for our audience and how often they encounter it in their professional lives.
- *What are the alternative or opposing viewpoints? What counterarguments could there be?* Well, one might argue that—on a day-to-day basis—subordinates make mistakes and the company cannot afford to wait for their learning curve, so it is better for the manager to get involved and to closely control his team's actions. We definitely need to address this in our essay! Another counterargument is that micromanagement should be acceptable in the case of novices. It should, but for a limited period, until they learn.
- *What exactly should be done?* The most dangerous thing about micromanagement is that micromanagers do not realize they are doing something wrong. The first thing to be done, then, would be to encourage people to self-diagnose their management style.
- *What would the consequences be* if things continue in the same manner? Low productivity and managers who do not have the time to think strategically. And if we fight this phenomenon? Higher productivity and higher motivation for the team and more success for the managers in the long run, admittedly after an initial period of struggle.
- *Why is this important?* This is when you answer the reader's question "Why should I bother reading this?" You should involve the reader personally. One way would be to make him wonder whether he is not a micromanager himself.

Now that you have answered these questions (better done in writing), you have a clearer picture of what you are going to say. It is time to start writing the main piece.

Writing. The structure of an argumentative essay should follow these general points:

1. *Intro*
2. *State the issue and your position on the issue*
3. *List and develop the arguments that support your position*
4. *List and rebut counterarguments*
5. *State what exactly should be done*
6. *End in style.*

You noticed that this structure somewhat resembles the structure used for planning meetings, discussed at the beginning of this chapter. Being a persuasion effort, it is normal to have the same principles. I have presented them here in a slightly different order, but I emphasize again that this framework is not set in stone; as any other tool described in this book, it should be adapted to your needs and personal style.

We will go through all these steps by using the micromanagement article example:

1. *Intro*. This is where you persuade the reader to care about your topic and to continue reading. The first chance to do that is in choosing the title. Try to think like a journalist: the title sells. We can think up something like "Micromanagement: Does Everybody Do It But You?", or "How to Manage a Micromanager," or "The Micromanagement Disease: Symptoms, Diagnosis, and Cure". (actually, the last two are real article titles). Even if you are not writing an article but an email, and if you are not a CEO but a consultant to the CEO and you just email your findings and your opinion to the CEO, do not write in the subject line "The Micromanagement Problem," or "Re: Micromanagement," or just "Re:." Try to engage the CEO from the start, even before her opening the email, by using a strong, newspaper-style title.

   After the title comes the first phrase. Do not waste it. It usually makes the difference between people reading on or not. Do not start by saying "In this text, I will assess the dangers of micromanagement." Start with something that can capture the reader's interest.

   Here are some options:

   - Open with an analogy: *"If, instead of letting your children do their homework alone, you help them with every assignment, they will never learn. And, even worse, they will not become independent, responsible adults. Moreover, you will not have time for your adult activities. In the exact same way, managers ..."* ... you get the picture.
   - Open with facts and statistics: *"A study mentioned in Forbes discovered that 79% of all employees say they have been micromanaged at some point in their career. Also, in a survey from 2003, employees singled out micromanagement as the most significant barrier to productivity they ever faced."* By the way, this approach would also clarify our assumption and prove that micromanagement is indeed frequently encountered.
   - Open with a personal question in order to engage the reader: *"When I mention the word "micromanagement," who comes to mind? Your boss? Or yourself?"*
   - Open with a quote: *President Theodore Roosevelt once said, "The best executive is the one who has sense enough to pick good men to do what he*

wants done." He continued, "... and self-restraint to keep from meddling with them while they do it."

2. *State the issue or problem and your position on the issue.* You can say that

> In many companies, including my own, teams work intensively under the close observation of their dedicated managers, managers spend long hours to check their subordinates' activity, and yet their combined productivity is low.

Then, state your position on the issue:

> Micromanagement, the phenomenon in which a manager controls too closely the work of his or her subordinates, is a serious affliction of the corporate world: one that undermines productivity, dissolves trust, and wipes out autonomy from the delicate motivation mix. Micromanaged teams have a high staff turnover, low levels of job satisfaction, and great resistance to innovation. We all should screen our management style and see whether we can give our employees more autonomy and literally mind our own business.

3. *List the arguments that support your position.* Do not list all your reasons! There *is* such a thing as argument inflation. If you present 100 reasons, the reader will be baffled, not persuaded. You should decide on three to a maximum of five strong arguments. The first reason usually influences the most, so you should begin with your strongest argument. If you choose to support your point with three arguments, for instance, the best strategy is to elaborate on the first one for a larger paragraph or two—with plenty of facts, expert opinion, examples, and analogies—then treat the second in a short paragraph and the third in a longer phrase. In our case, as we established during the Socratic questioning stage, I would proceed in the following three main directions:

   - Micromanagement is counterproductive for the team. I would explain (and illustrate with examples) that micromanagement kills motivation by affecting autonomy and job satisfaction. I would also quote data that speak to the fact that in micromanaged organizations, the employee churn rate and absenteeism run high. Low motivation, high turnover and high absenteeism will surely cripple productivity. Micromanagement is therefore killing productivity, and until identified, it is killing it in silence.
   - Micromanagement is counterproductive for managers themselves. In this second line of argumentation, I would concentrate on the benefits for the manager if he stops micromanaging. Giving up control over others shows greater control over one's self. Also, delegating and trusting the team will allow him to actually perform his real duties: to construct a strategy, to innovate, to identify and seize opportunities, which—in turn—will lead to greater success for all.
   - Micromanagement stops everybody's growth. The micromanaged team will not have the liberty or the courage to explore new perspectives. The manager will not have the time to look at the horizon because he is stuck with today. Nobody can grow in a micromanaged environment.

4. *List and rebut counterarguments.* Bringing forward a contrary position tremendously increases our credibility. It shows that we are not partisan ideologists but free thinkers who have considered all possible courses before choosing this one. We can repeat the premortem exercise with our reader(s) in mind in order to imagine these possible obstacles. Assume they have already read the article and were not convinced. Why weren't they? What kept them from being persuaded? We also identified counterarguments in our Socratic questioning. We should frame them wisely and then find effective ways to rebut them. Or, if they are valid, we need to adjust the conclusion.
   Below is an example of stating a possible counterargument and then rebutting it:

   > Of course, a micromanager might give me example after example of how he always saves the day. He may say, for instance, "Yesterday I intervened just in time to prevent a member of my team from losing an important contract. I took over the negotiations, solved the issue and closed the deal. What is wrong with that?" Well, nothing is wrong if it happened once. If it is frequent behavior, on the other hand, I would say that the job of a manager is not to solve the daily crisis, but to analyze and improve the performance of his employees. A good manager does not manage tasks and situations; he or she mainly manages people.

   An example of how a good counterargument can help shape the conclusion is this one:

   > A manager once asked me, "What if the member of my team that I am allegedly micromanaging is not purely incompetent but is a novice? Shouldn't I spend extra time to repeatedly show him or her how things should be done?" And I answered: "By all means! But that is not called micromanagement; it is called mentoring. You should continue the process, but not forever. Remember to gradually hand over the wheel when the employee is prepared!"

5. *What exactly should be done?* In our micromanagement article, a call to action can describe a solution and—in the meantime—involve the reader a bit more. We can, for instance, add a self-diagnosis tool for managers, a questionnaire that we have also mentioned in another chapter, in which five positive answers might reveal a tendency for micromanaging:

   Are you always dissatisfied with your team's work and you think you could have done things better?
   Do you want to be CCed in all emails?
   Do you always need to know where your employees are and what they do exactly?
   Do you want to countersign all documents?
   Do you require daily status meetings?
   Are you the last to leave the office in the evening?
   Does your team avoid you?

6. *End in style.* Here, as with the title, you need to be an artist again. The ending should be catchy and energizing. You could perhaps return to the opening statement, but with a twist. Or maybe you can end with a call to action. For

instance, in this case, I would come up with a 10-day self-treatment plan for the readers who just found out—through the questionnaire—that they micromanage. *Revise.* After writing the essay (the article, the email, the memo), we are under the impression that it is perfect and that our job is done. Far from it. In the next step, we need to revise. We read what we have written and then make some changes. And then? Revise again. It helps to trim our text on purpose: see what phrase does not bring anything new and delete it. We then could ask for feedback from someone we trust and then revise once more following (or not) the advice. If we have the time, it is wise to sleep on it. Usually, the next day we lose part of the author's bias so it is easier to *kill our darlings*, to eliminate or dramatically change entire paragraphs that, a day prior, seemed heavenly. The text does not seem to be *ours* to the same extent, so the mind is freed to identify flaws.

As a conclusion, empathy is the main ingredient in effective persuasion. Understanding the preferences of the other, their past experiences, and their present obstacles against saying *yes* will help us better cater and convey our message. In the end, I reiterate the same advice: these formal steps must not limit you. Develop your own structure, your own voice, and your personal style, because authenticity is very, very persuasive.

11 Debating

This chapter focuses on situations when we disagree with the other(s) and we need to convince them to abandon their point of view and to adopt ours. In our professional lives, we often need to discuss things with people who do not share our point of view: a supplier who interprets a provision of the contract in their favor, a client who has unreasonable expectations, a colleague who did a poor job, or even the boss who thinks that things need to be done his way. We need to persuade them into understanding and adopting our point of view. This kind of informal debate is the topic of this unit. Preparing for a debate is quite similar to preparing to persuade verbally or in writing, the principles are similar. Some aspects should be emphasized, though: in a debate, you must take extra care to think of all possible counterarguments, of clever ways to bring them up yourself, and of smart ways to rebut them.

This chapter begins with three quotes that I think relevant. First, Charlie Munger's advice on how to prepare for a debate:

> I never allow myself to have an opinion on anything that I don't know the other side's argument better than they do.

Then, Rapoport's rules, rephrased by Daniel Dennett (2014) on how to compose a successful critical commentary:

> You should attempt to re-express your target's position so clearly, vividly, and fairly that your target says, 'Thanks, I wish I'd thought of putting it that way.' You should list any points of agreement (especially if they are not matters of widespread agreement). You should mention anything you have learned from your target. Only then are you permitted to say so much as a word of rebuttal or criticism.

Also, in a dispute, it is important to be kind because, for the other, losing a debate is painful. I quote here the bestselling author Haruki Murakami, who wisely said that we should

> always remember that to argue, and win, is to break down the reality of the person you are arguing against. It is painful to lose your reality, so be kind, even if you are right.

R. Atanasiu, *Critical Thinking for Managers*, Management for Professionals,
https://doi.org/10.1007/978-3-030-73600-2_11

I organized this chapter as tips and tricks, and because I believe there is a fine line between tips and tricks in debating, they will be discussed together:

Define. Many heated discussions are in fact pointless because people give different meanings to the same word. Here is an example:

> **Case** I own a small business together with my partner, Jim. An investor, seeing what we have achieved so far, is offering to invest 100,000 euros for 10% of the shares. I very much want the investment, so I tell my partner
>
> > We need this kind of money in our company if we want to finance its growth. This is the only way to achieve success!
>
> To which Jim replies:
>
> > But having an external investment is not the path to success; it is the path to *diluting* our success. We can achieve great success on our own!

We can argue for hours—we may even lose our temper if we do not stop and define what success *means* for each of us, because we may have very different meanings for it. I may see success as accelerated growth, scaling to new markets, and a fat exit in 5 years. Jim may see success as linear growth and steady profits from satisfied customers turning into regular dividends, just like his father conducted their family business. This might be why Jim does not intend to sell: not now and definitely not the whole business in 5 years. These are two different, almost opposing definitions of business success. If we do not stop and define the word, our dispute is a dialog of the deaf. If we do stop and define, then we can discuss and negotiate to reach a common vision and a relevant business strategy: a very useful discussion. The investor issue will be resolved accordingly. So do not get angry, define!

Pause and recap. Sometimes discussions have the tendency to derail. This can be caused by bringing up an older disagreement, by using a red herring (digressing, see more in the chapter on fallacies), by using a straw man (distorting the other's argument to make it easier to attack, see more in the chapter on fallacies), or by insisting on a small issue, unimportant in the big picture of a complex argument. The solution is to pause and recap. You can recap either side. If your opponent is derailing the conversation, like in a red herring, or their point is not clearly expressed, it is useful to recap his or her position before countering it:

> "So, basically what you are saying is that Scotland should be independent because smaller countries can be better managed in times of economic crisis, right? Well, …," and now you counterargue more efficiently.

If you feel that your point is misunderstood or that your opponent is altering your words in a straw man fallacy, you can recap your own position. Here is an example from another imaginary discussion:

> Wait a minute! I wasn't saying that corporations should dictate the social conversation! What I was in fact saying is that corporations should be allowed to be more involved in the social conversation; they should be allowed to have a say on how society functions. It is an entirely different thing.

Put yourself in their shoes! I will not stop repeating that empathy is crucial to persuading the other. People are different: their interests are different, their life experience is different, and their education is different, so they will be receptive to some arguments and indifferent to others. If you are in a sales pitch, you should not describe why your service is good in general; you should focus on why it is perfect for the one you are pitching to. Think like this: "If I were them, why would I need my service?" In debates, too, you need to always adapt your arguments to what makes the other person tick. Empathy is even more important when there are opposing views, especially when some root beliefs go unstated. Understanding what keeps the other anchored is a necessary step for unlocking a dispute.

Synonyms. Use a synonym that is appropriate for the point you are making. A famous example of good use of synonyms involves an NGO trying to set a global awareness campaign about the deforestation of the Amazonian jungle, a few decades ago. They kept saying that the jungle was dying, and no one seemed to care. The problem was that people associated the word *jungle* with darkness and vicious animals, so the general public was not very sympathetic. This continued until a clever PR person came up with the solution to replace the word *jungle* with a term he invented for this purpose, *rainforest*. And that really did the trick! People cared much more that the Amazonian *rainforest* was dying and joined the efforts to save it.

Assuring. Sometimes people introduce a premise with expressions such as "It's common knowledge that…," or "Everybody knows that …." This is not a sign that the premise is undisputable; more often than not, it is a sign that the person has no more solid arguments for their position. When you encounter such an expression, instead of feeling assured, do not hesitate to ask for explanations. Especially when the bluff is introduced by a more extreme expression like "Any fool knows that …."

Softening. A smaller, less aggressive conclusion makes the argument stronger and harder to attack. You can therefore build stronger arguments by softening your claim. Instead of "Everybody does that" say "Most people do that." In this case, your statement is not vulnerable to a single counterexample. Instead of "He did it on purpose" say "Maybe he did it on purpose," because an assumption is harder to challenge than a certitude.

Adjectives. This is a simple trick that often gets unnoticed. It involves using adjectives in order to support your point. For example, instead of "Yesterday, the board took the decision to cancel my project…" one may say "Yesterday, the board took the *reckless* decision to cancel my project…," or instead of "We have an offer for you…" one can say "We have an *interesting* offer for you." The use of such adjectives, if unnoticed, may sway the listener.

Concession. As mentioned in the chapter on persuasion, be the first to bring forward opposing arguments to your claim or to emphasize possible weak points in your reasoning. This way, your gain will be threefold: first, your trustworthiness will increase significantly. Second, you can choose to phrase those opposing arguments however you like, before your opponent can use them. Third, you will have the tranquility to pace your response the way you like. An efficient persuasion technique is to follow the acknowledgment of a weakness with a twist: a "however" or a "but." Robert Cialdini gives the perfect example in his latest book, *Pre-suasion*: "In 1588, British troops, massed against a sea invasion from Spain at Tilbury, were deeply concerned that their leader, Queen Elizabeth I, as a woman, would not be up to the rigors of battle. In addressing the men, she dispelled their fears (…): 'I know,' she asserted, 'I have the body of a weak and feeble woman. *But,* I have the heart of a king, and a king of England, too.' It's reported that so long and loud were the cheers after this pronouncement that officers had to ride among the men ordering them to restrain themselves so the queen could continue" (Cialdini, 2018).

SEXI. The final tip involves a technique used in formal debating. Its name sounds sexy in order to be well remembered and applied in battle, but it is merely an acronym. Although it was designed for debating, we can successfully apply this structure of an argument not only in our informal debates but also in our less confrontational persuading attempts, as illustrated with the case below. *SEXI* stands for

- Statement
- Explanation
- eXample
- Impact.

In formal logic, a simple argument is made of a conclusion and at least two premises that offer support for that conclusion. These elements are in fact the *Explanation* and the *Statement*. Unfortunately, in real life, a simple abstract explanation does not succeed in convincing the other without an *eXample* (I know, please do not inform the acronym police) and without emphasizing the *Impact* your claim may have (mainly on the other). The *Impact* can be alternatively placed at the beginning if the interlocutor does not see your claim as important. The SEXI structure offers completeness to our argument, but clearly, the audience should not be able to make out the four parts as distinct. The argument should flow nicely, as illustrated in the example below.

Case Imagine you are a C-level manager in a large company, and the CEO is addressing the board of directors, arguing for the adoption of a fleet sharing system. Can you distinguish the *Statement*, the *Explanations*, the *eXample*, and the *Impact*?

All our employees that do fieldwork have personally assigned cars. I believe we should replace that with a fleet sharing system, a smart way to manage our fleet that allows employees to use an app to book any available car and their badge or mobile phone to access and drive it. This will reduce the number of cars we use and the down-time for each car, dramatically lowering our transportation costs. The system has other benefits, like theft protection, information about accidents in real time, and even a car wash service. I have seen this system adopted by our branch in Austria and this move reduced their travel and fleet operation costs by 45%. I have also spoken to some of our Austrian colleagues, and they are thrilled with the system: they love the app and the fact that they can always get a clean, fresh-smelling car. Also, as we heard earlier a proposal to offer our employees gym memberships as a benefit in kind, we can use the savings from transport to fund this new program right away.

Business disputes are rarely won solely by offering good arguments and by using clever debating tools, and winning a dispute rarely leads to constructive action and future cooperation. We should be prepared for battle, but should always have a clear idea of what we want to achieve and what relationship we prefer to have with our opponent after the discussion. Although fights are sometimes unavoidable and even beneficial, adopting an emphatic attitude and a long-term perspective might occasionally yield better results.

References

Dennett, D. C. (2014). *Intuition pumps and other tools for thinking* (1st ed.). W. W. Norton & Company.

Cialdini, R. (2018). *Pre-suasion: A revolutionary way to influence and persuade* (Reprint ed.). Simon & Schuster.

Fallacies

12

Fallacies are bad arguments that seem good and can therefore trick us. After a critical thinking course, students usually remember the fallacies. Could it be the pompous, Latin names? Could it be the anecdote-like structure and the fun they had during class exercises? Could it be that everybody has numerous examples for each and every fallacy? Perhaps it is that after the course they start encountering and recognizing fallacies everywhere they look? Fallacies can be spotted anywhere, from political discourse to advertising, from the office to the kitchen table. This chapter goes through a list of fallacies we may encounter both in business and in our day-to-day lives, with examples, a description of their mechanisms, and advice on ways to counteract them. Let me start with an example:

> *Are you going to fall asleep while you read this chapter, like you always do when you read things related to management?*

What is the problem with this kind of question? It is a tricky, dishonest one: a trap. The chance is that many of you answered with a firm *no*, which—upon careful reading—means that you will not fall asleep now, but you do fall asleep when you read work-related stuff. Both answering "yes" and "no" means that you admit dozing off when you read about management, which I am sure you did not intend to admit, even if it is true (it is for most of us, don't worry!).

This is an example of a ***loaded question***, a fallacy that works as follows:

Mechanism: You are forced to give a straight answer to a question that contains an unpleasant assumption (about you, usually). Any straight answer would validate that assumption.

It is called a loaded question because the question is loaded with the assumption. The question is always built so that it prompts a straight answer, but not always "yes" or "no." Please find below some examples:

R. Atanasiu, *Critical Thinking for Managers*, Management for Professionals,
https://doi.org/10.1007/978-3-030-73600-2_12

Other examples

How did you manage to deceive your clients for so long?

Is it true that your sales increased considerably after you broadcasted those misleading commercials?

Besides not paying tax, what is your company's main competitive advantage?

How to counteract. By directly answering a loaded question, you admit that you did deceive your clients, that the commercials were indeed misleading, and that indeed you do not pay taxes. The way out is to refrain from answering straight and —instead—to answer and clarify the malevolent assumption: "Those ads were not at all misleading." But sometimes you can get caught in the heat of discussion and give such a self-incriminatory answer. Often, people who spot the loaded question tend to respond with another question: "What makes you say we don't pay taxes?" My advice is to counter with a statement, not with a question, as it is much more powerful: "We have always paid our taxes."

Journalists and politicians often corner their opponents with loaded questions. After falling into this trap and giving a straight answer to a loaded question asked by a journalist, former Secretary of State Madeleine Albright wrote in her memoirs: "I must have been crazy; I should have answered the question by reframing it and pointing out the inherent flaws in the premise behind it. (…) As soon as I had spoken, I wished for the power to freeze time and take back those words. My reply had been a terrible mistake, hasty, clumsy, and wrong.… I had fallen into a trap and said something that I simply did not mean. That is no one's fault but my own." (Albright, 2003)

This brings in two general aspects of fallacies: intent and skill. Most of the time, people use fallacies because they do not know better. From now on, you will be able to recognize when someone argues with a fallacy. Please don't automatically infer intent; be kind and try to gently educate the other, without hurting their feelings. However, some earn a living from influencing what others think. Are they trained to do it? Did they attend a special fallacy school? Or is it just a weird talent? Is it nature or nurture? I don't know the answer to these questions. I do, however, know what needs to be done to avoid falling in fallacious traps. The feature I love about fallacies is that once you learn about them you can never be fooled again. They are like riddles, or jokes, or police novels, they have power only if you don't know them yet. So let's get to know them, in order to start developing immunity!

This chapter continues with two short texts full of fallacies, in which you are invited to recognize any logical flaws. The two pieces of text will be revisited at the end of the chapter, where all their fallacies will be analyzed. After the two cases, we will go through a series of most common fallacies, each described like we did with the loaded question: examples, mechanism, and countermeasures. Let's begin!

Case 1 Mr. Peter Josef is the leader of the PPP (Power to the People Party) in a small Central European republic. He led his party to an unexpected win in the recent election (32%—too little to rule alone, but enough to appoint the prime minister). The PPP's main promise during the campaign was the introduction of the universal basic income system, a social security system that simplifies welfare by giving all citizens an unconditioned sum of money.

Today, the newly elected Parliament is in session for the first time. In a surprising move, Mr. Josef is trying to use this very first session to convince the assembly to pass his basic income law this very day. You are a journalist for The Economist, writing an article on Mr. Josef. The local media portray his discourse as "looking reasonable and well-argued at first sight, but revealing argumentation flaws upon more careful analysis." Do you see any argumentation flaws in his speech below?

"Dear colleagues,

UBI, the universal basic income, or the unconditional basic income, is a novel and wise social security system that protects against poverty and unemployment by regularly giving all our citizens an unconditional fixed sum of money. My plea to you is to vote for implementing this system as soon as possible, and today I will offer supplementary reasons for this position. I will first remind you of the many reasons we have emphasized throughout the campaign: it is a very simple system, very easy to implement, replacing complicated, unjust, and overlapping processes; it is transparent, very easy to control; and it protects everybody against poverty or unemployment, even the citizens that are not covered today. But aside from these things that you already know, please consider the following series of arguments:

Some of the oldest democracies in the world have implemented forms of basic income (the US in Alaska, Canada in Ontario) or discussed implementing it on a wide scale (the Swiss held a referendum in 2014 to introduce a 2500 CHF income for all adults and a 650 CHF income for all children). Moreover, countries such as Namibia, India, and Brazil have started pilot programs, proving that basic income is a valid policy irrespective of how wealthy a country is. Rich democracies and developing countries are doing it; our country cannot fall behind. We must follow this trend at once.

Moreover, the introduction of the basic income does not only protect the unemployed; it also helps lower the number of unemployed people. In oil-rich Alaska, for example, the Alaska Permanent Fund distributes some of the oil money as a subsidy to all its citizens (1000 USD per capita per year). The fund started in 1976 and continues today. As a result, unemployment in Alaska has dropped from 11% at the beginning of 1977 to 5.9% in 2020!

But let us not focus on the past! Have you considered the future of jobs? We live in a world that changes at an unprecedented pace. Let me tell you a story: my next-door neighbor—Linda—is a bank teller. She is 31, very bright, and does a great job at the bank. But her bank is planning to introduce a self-banking service this year, and Linda will soon end up without a job and without the possibility to land one, as all other banks will make the same shift. Linda's case shows that all our jobs are going to be made obsolete by automation. What will we live on, then? Who will contribute to the social security system, with everybody unemployed?

As I said, ATMs, computers, and robots have already replaced bank tellers: they are about to throw tens of thousands of professional car drivers into unemployment;

soon enough, lawyers and general practitioners are going to be replaced by Watson; and—if we don't act now—automation will make us all unemployed within a few years, with nobody to support the current welfare system. That is why we should establish a guaranteed income to all: income supported not by contribution but by taxation. We know we can!

We are at a crossroads. We have to choose now. We will either be brave and start introducing this novel and smart security system today or otherwise watch helplessly as the current system fails to protect large categories of citizens.

I have been accused of ignoring criticism. In order to prove that wrong, let me now address your objections to the basic income! Economists, politicians, and moralists have objected. I will take them on one by one:

Economists. How can anyone with an economic degree oppose the basic income? A social system that offers no protection against poverty and unemployment is clearly a social system destined for failure.

Politicians. A lot of politicians have argued against this idea. But they drive through the poor neighborhoods in their luxurious limousines without ever noticing the starving people on the street. How can they even dare to have an opinion on poverty prevention while wearing Armani and Gucci and Rolex? One more question, this time directly for our colleagues here who oppose this bill: What will you do when voters will eventually realize that, by opposing this system, you are merely trying to preserve privilege?

And finally, moralists. Many have doubted this idea on moral grounds, saying that it would encourage laziness. But this is fallacious. I am glad to end on a high note. The guaranteed basic income is undoubtedly moral because a system that provides all citizens with unconditioned means to lead a decent life cannot be anything but ethical.

Thank you for your attention and support! And please vote for the basic income: it is the only logical choice!

(Disclaimer: Basic Income is a complex issue and I have no strong opinion on it. I have chosen this topic randomly for this case study and decided on which side to build the speech only after sketching faulty arguments for both sides.)

What do you think about the discourse? Convincing? Sound and logical? Did you spot any flaws?

How about in the following quarrel (on a lighter note):

> **Case 2** Imagine it is June 2020, in the midst of the COVID-19 pandemic. You witness a heated discussion between the compliance manager and the chief of transportation about the implementation of certain anti-COVID measures for truck drivers.

Compliance manager: All drivers must carry boxes of disposable gloves and use them whenever they leave the truck cabin, especially at gas stations and restrooms.

Transportation manager: This is insane! I am on the roads every day. All other drivers keep themselves clean and safe, but without using such drastic measures.

They don't wear gloves; they just wash their hands or use disinfectant gel. I don't want my drivers to be the laughingstock of other drivers.

Compliance manager: Are you talking about the drivers at Eurotransport? Their CEO was the most ardent advocate against strong anti-COVID measures and now—I don't know if you know—he has just been diagnosed with COVID-19.

Transportation manager: If my drivers are forced to wear gloves every time they leave the cabin, tomorrow you will ask them to wear full hazmat suits, and the next thing you know they will have to have portable toilets in the cabin. This is unacceptable. Listen, do you drive?

Compliance manager: No, I don't have a driver's license.

Transportation manager: Well, someone who hasn't spent hundreds of hours behind the wheel shouldn't draft rules for truck drivers.

Compliance manager: Listen, my department has really thought this through. Either we implement these rules now and every driver abides fully, or we must close the transportation department for 3 months, put the drivers on leave, and use a third party.

Transportation manager: The guys in your department, do they do anything else all day aside from imagining how to mess up the lives of people who actually work?

Compliance manager: Don't tell me about my boys; keep a sharp eye on yours! I know how truck drivers are. My brother in law is a trucker and he always brags about the way he skips work and fools the system to get paid more than he deserves.

Transportation manager: That must be because he is related to your wife.

Compliance manager: What?! Don't ever say anything bad about her, she is a saint! And, besides, he is actually her half-brother. They were raised separately.

What about this heated dialog? Did they correctly address the matter? We will return to discuss both these cases at the end of the chapter. Until then, the best way to describe fallacies is through examples, so let's start down the list of most common fallacies, each with its fancy name, its mechanism, examples, and the best ways to be refuted.

Slippery slope. Imagine you negotiate a deal. You and the other party analyze the draft contract (their proposal) and, with diplomacy and kindness, you point out that there is asymmetry as early as the first page. Your negotiation partner replies:

> *I notice you start by objecting to things on the very first page. I propose that we leave this article as it is for now and we move to the important parts. If we start like this, nothing will stop us from arguing for hours about every article, and then we will spend the night here or, even worse, we will not sign until noon tomorrow and miss the deadline!*

Has something like this ever happened to you, aside from—years ago—your parents describing your disastrous future if you didn't do your homework? What is wrong with this line of reasoning?

Mechanism. In a slippery slope argument, the arguer argues against an undesired event *A* by saying that this event will have a cascade of increasingly improbable, increasingly disastrous consequences, culminating with a preposterous one, *B*. We do not want *B* to happen: therefore, we should not let *A* happen in the first place. The slippery slope works with the escalation of exaggeration. It is called a slippery slope because the one arguing seems to slip further down on a slippery slope of bad logic.

Other examples

Maintaining a 9-to-5 schedule while working from home is absurd! I have researched the origin of the fixed-working-hours program. It comes from the industrial revolution 200 years ago, when workers pushed the levers of power looms. You could not do it remotely, so if a worker were late when the whistle was blown, the whole loom was inoperable. But now we have the Internet, we are not in the textile industry, and we are no longer in the 1800s! If we keep this strict 9-to-5 schedule today, tomorrow we may want to re-introduce the 12-h-a-day shift, as was the case in the steel industry in the nineteenth century. And next year we might allow child labor again!

I know it's repetitive and tedious, but we shouldn't externalize this task to that RPA (robotic process automation) company. This is how it all starts. First just a single task, then everything that concerns production, and the next thing you know they fire us all and replace us with robots.

How to counteract. The way to refute a slippery slope would be to pinpoint to the interlocutor where exactly the argument goes berserk and why: how can maintaining a 9-to-5 schedule in our company lead to child labor? It is immoral to use a fallacy with the intent to fool the audience. However, when you wink at your audience and you use humor, the effect is very funny. This is exactly what a company called DirecTV did, a few years ago. They produced a series of commercials based on slippery slopes. You can find them online by searching "DirecTV slippery slope commercials." Enjoy!

Ad hominem. Were your suggestions ever silenced with remarks like these, below?

> *I will not take advice from someone who hasn't been with this company for more than 2 years!*

or

> *Oh, please! I will not take suggestions from a junior.*

What is wrong with this line of arguing? In general, should we factor in the characteristics of the person making a claim when we assess the claim itself? We should, clearly, consider the big picture, look at the person's traits and past behavior, but these should only be of secondary importance when looking at a statement. The statement itself deserves our full consideration, no matter who made it.

Mechanism. Instead of discussing the point, an *ad hominem* discusses the person who makes the point, following the scheme.

You are so-and-so or you did so-and-so; therefore, you are wrong or — even worse — you are not entitled to an opinion.

This is not a personal attack, as some label it. A personal attack consists in offending remarks like "You're a liar!" Fallacies are arguments, not insults. They are bad arguments, but still arguments, with premises and conclusion. The name "ad hominem" is short for "*argumentum ad hominem*" (Latin for "argument against the person)," and it can sometimes be completely void of offense, such as in this example:

You cannot offer your opinion on dictatorship unless you lived through one!

In this case, not living through a dictatorship is far from being offensive. Still, instead of considering the message, the example above only addresses the person delivering the message.

Other examples

"A study done in the Nordic countries has shown that the iPhone has the lowest antenna signal among its peers."

"You would *say that! You work for Samsung!"*

and a special kind of ad hominem, called ***tu quoque***, which in Latin means "So do you!":

You should hire a proper accountant to do your taxes!

Nonsense! I know for a fact that you also used to do your own taxes when you started, 25 years ago.

Please observe that, in all these cases, the matter was not addressed at all. The suggestion offered by the junior, the opinion about dictatorship, whether the iPhone has an antenna problem, and employing an accountant—all these were never discussed. Instead, the authors were discussed: being junior, not living through a dictatorship, working for Samsung, also doing their own taxes. However, the statement and the statement's author are two very different entities. Assessing the author instead of her claim is offensive to logic and common sense. This is sadly a very common fallacy and it sometimes occurs in absurd settings, where no one would ever expect it. For instance, the London School of Economics is one of the most prestigious schools in the world. Its academics used to be asked to advise the UK government on Brexit. However, according to a 2016 article in The Guardian (Henley, 2016), at some point, the government said that it refuses to receive further advice from LSE academics who do not hold a British passport.

Another absurd example that really happened in a company went something like this:

The third issue for today was discussing Anna's proposal to shorten the recruitment process. However, as Anna does not work here anymore, I say we move to the next point on the agenda.

How to counteract. How do we get out of this? With diplomacy, we stress that the message and its bearer are two different entities, and we propose to focus on the former. "It doesn't matter if I did the same thing 25 years ago, that does not mean that I am not right to suggest a proper accountant!"

If, for remarks like "I will not take suggestions from a junior," this approach does not help, and you are still keen to pass on the suggestion, there is a trick. You can extract yourself from the context and say, "But it's not my idea, I heard the CEO saying it" or "I read that in the Harvard Business Review." Then, hopefully, the person will concentrate less on the messenger and more on the message.

False dilemma. In case you were ever puzzled or even convinced by a statement like this one:

Either we vote for my investment project, or we just sit back and watch the competition eating us alive!

then you must learn about false dilemmas. They are the appanage of strong-willed, no-nonsense persons who never doubt their opinions.

Mechanism. Also known as a false dichotomy or black-or-white thinking, this is a fallacy where one tries to claim that a situation admits of only two options: the one they propose and another, disastrous one. It is fallacious when, in fact, other options may be possible, such as—in our example—another investment project or any other profitable endeavor.

Other examples

False dilemmas can be found everywhere, from political discourse:

Vote for me or throw your vote away for another four years!

to commercial communication:

You can manage your clients manually, like a hundred years ago, or you can buy our CRM.

to domestic arguments. For instance, I mischievously used false dilemmas with my daughters when they were little:

Girls, do you want to go to bed now, or in 5 min?

or

Would you like tomato salad or cucumber salad as a side?

My girls are grownups now and, in the meantime, they have both won debating championships, so persuading them is not so easy anymore.

How to counteract. The obvious way out of a false dilemma is not just to acknowledge that there may be other possibilities but to simply point out a third plausible alternative.

Ad populum. Did you ever do something just because you saw it done by people around you whose opinion you value? For instance, did you buy a new device just because all your friends had one? I admit I have. When a company employs a new management fad just because everybody else in the industry has done the same, without analyzing advantages and costs, the deciding manager falls prey to the *ad populum* fallacy.

Of course, paying attention to and allowing ourselves to be influenced by the behavior of our peers is a valuable adaptive trait. What the others do serves as a good indicator for what we should do. The problem arises when we follow the behavior of others without passing it through the filter of our own thinking. Unfortunately, this also happens at an organizational level, especially in adopting management fads. Management fads have been documented extensively. A Google search reveals a multitude of articles on management fads, written in trustworthy outlets such as the Financial Times, the Harvard Business Review, businessinsider.com, and Inc.com. I will not name any such management approaches, but all these articles describe the same usual suspects. None of them are fads per se; many companies have successfully adopted such techniques. What makes them a fad is when companies adopt them mindlessly, without considering the fit, the costs, the timing, and the risks.

Mechanism. "Ad populum" is short for "argumentum ad populum," and is also called the bandwagon fallacy, the democracy fallacy, appeal to popularity, herd mentality, or even appeal to the mob. It implies that because many people believe a certain thing, it is automatically true, or because many people do a certain act, it is automatically right (with the corollary: because many people buy a certain product, the product is automatically good).

The word *automatically* is what turns a healthy social criterion into a fallacy. Even without the word *automatically*, the arguments above may be true often, but definitely not always. On the contrary, Mark Twain used to say, "whenever you find yourself on the side of the majority, it is time to pause and reflect."

Other examples

Ad populum can be very easily enacted without being articulated. We see people around us doing something, and we follow without thinking, in a wordless fallacy we play on ourselves. However, it can also appear as means of persuading the other, from trifle matters:

Everybody shows up late. Why should I be on time?

to important, strategic choices like internationalization

All our competitors have expanded to Hungary first, then to Poland, and only after that have they tackled Western Europe. Are you suggesting we go straight for the German market? Nonsense!

or lobbying for tax cuts:

We, in the fashion industry, should lobby to have tax cuts for both haute couture and pret-a-porter. All the other industries are lobbying—some successfully—for tax cuts. The alternative energy industry, the IT sector, agriculture: they all do it. So why shouldn't we give it a try?

Some theories explain the cyclic evolution of the markets by the herd behavior of most investors who, instead of being influenced mainly by the fundamentals of the respective stocks, are influenced mainly by the aggregate behavior of the others. In short, these theories say that investors buy mainly because other investors buy and investors sell mainly because other investors sell, in a feedback loop that reinforces either behavior.

How to counteract. Whether a wordless fallacy we play on ourselves or an argument offered by somebody else, the way out is to make sure we don't do something *automatically*, just by imitating other people. While allowing the behavior of others to have its influence on us, we must always find solid intrinsic arguments for our own behavior.

Post hoc ergo propter hoc. This is a mouthful. It is Latin for "after this therefore because of this" and its proper English translation would be "correlation does not imply causation" or "false cause." While many times things that happen simultaneously have a causal relationship (observing such patterns is the basis of the scientific method), automatically inferring causation is a fallacy. This way of thinking leads to superstition and can be a sign of an external locus of control. Individuals characterized by an internal locus of control believe that the events in their lives are mainly the consequences of their own actions. In contrast to this, individuals with an external locus of control believe that the events in their lives are mainly the consequence of luck, fate, or the interests of other people or groups, such as in this example:

The plunge in sales started last April, immediately after we redecorated the offices. I want them redone this instant!

where the redecoration is found responsible for the plunge in sales.

Mechanism. Post hoc *ergo propter hoc*, in short, *post hoc*, is a fallacy based on inferring automatically that event A is the cause of event B if A and B happen simultaneously or if B follows shortly after A. It may often be so, but not always and not automatically. It is a fallacy, for instance, when in fact another factor, C, causes both A and B. But most often it is a fallacy when it is merely a coincidence. The Internet is filled with such coincidences, called spurious correlations, that show amazing similarities between—for example—plotted graphs of murders in the USA and the rate of Internet Explorer usage. A famous such theory is the skirt length theory, coined in the 1920s, which asserts that the length of the skirt is a good predictor of where the markets are going. The higher the skirt, the more the market will rise.

Other examples

Adapted from a real commercial lawsuit, this is a good illustration of a post hoc:

The repair works in the main hall of the shopping mall have drastically affected our sales. The scaffolding partially blocked our entrance for 6 months, from October 10th. Our ice-cream parlor suffered a sharp decrease in profit and we request from the operator of the mall a compensation equal to our decrease in profit compared to the previous 6 months.

The judge recognized (*mutatis mutandis*) that the scaffolding could explain just partially the drop in sales, stated that the cold season was a more likely cause, and ordered compensations based on year-on-year differences in sales.

How to counteract. A way to refute this fallacy is to prove that there is no logic behind the causation (what would be the chain of events that leads from redecorating the offices to clients no longer buying?) or, even better, to find the true cause of the effect.

Red Herring. Imagine you are on the street, overhearing the following dialog:

> Her: *"Speaking about dangers to the environment, I cannot praise enough the nuclear power phase-out that is going on in Germany."*
>
> Him: *"But Germany is led by a woman, and everybody knows that women can never be good political leaders!"*
>
> Her: *"Wait a minute, women can be as good politicians as any man, and even better ones! Think of ..."*

What happened here? The man was perhaps losing the nuclear plants argument, so he threw in another topic, a controversial one, a hot one, and the woman fell into this trap. This fallacy gets its name from dog trainers who drag a very smelly red herring across the fainter smell trail of a fox. Experienced dogs follow the original fox trail, but inexperienced dogs forget about it and follow the new, more poignant one.

Mechanism. A red herring works like this: when caught in a losing argument, some people may throw in a new, more controversial topic, and inexperienced opponents may forget the original argument and follow the new one. The new topic must be controversial: that is, highly disputable. The sexist remark in our example is clearly a red herring, thrown in just to take the discussion elsewhere.

I don't believe that we need more examples to understand how the original argument can often be derailed. Just think of the last dispute you had: at the office, at home, wherever. The chances are that it did not follow the same exact topic from beginning to end.

How to counteract. This is a tricky discussion. I used to recommend that an experienced critical thinker should always spot a red herring and insist on staying on the original point, or the original trail. But then I realized that this can be interpreted as fear to engage on the second topic, so in order to show that I am not avoiding the second topic, a good answer here would be "These are two different debates. And I believe I have good arguments to win both of them. Let's talk about each topic for 5 min, in whichever order you prefer."

Hasty generalization. Generalization is a powerful tool to infer new truth from existing truth. There are two rules of decency for generalizing: we should do it from a sample that is *large enough* (readers more familiar with statistics can calculate the size of a good sample, but for us laypersons, generalization should ideally not be done from a sample of one) and from a sample that is *representative* (that resembles the characteristics of the population we generalize to). When these rules are broken, we deal with a fallacy called hasty generalization, when usually people generalize from just one case:

> *We have one client from Bulgaria and that company always pays on time. I wish we had more Bulgarians as customers! We should hire a local salesperson.*

In this short section on hasty generalization, we will discuss both criteria (size and representativeness), and then I will make an appeal against generalizing in humans.

Mechanism. A bad generalization is one that is made from a sample that is either too small or not representative. In order to cover both issues (size and representativeness), let's discuss a short case study.

> **Case** Imagine that you are the CEO of the company, I am the client service manager, and I argue for shortening the payment terms for all our clients from 60 to 30 days by saying that I have personally discussed this with many clients and nobody objected to the change. In order to make sure that the decision is taken on solid ground, you, as the CEO, need to ask two questions:

1. Is the sample large enough? In our case, what does the client service manager mean by "a lot"? 51%? 75%? 99%? Also, are we OK with not asking all the clients?

and the second question—not so intuitive, but equally important:

2. Is the sample representative? Perhaps the manager spoke with the vast majority of the clients, but not with our largest client.

Other examples

The selling approach I proposed works: I have done the first sale. We should adopt this approach throughout the firm.

This example takes a different perspective on a problem that was also discussed in the chapter on decision-making, when we talked about *resulting*—the tendency to evaluate decisions based solely on their outcome, without looking at the context. We concluded then that we also need to analyze the quality of the decision-making process. This section adds that—in order to evaluate decisions based on their outcomes—we need to look at a series of outcomes, not at a single one. It would be better to evaluate a series of outcomes that followed a decision or a series of similar decisions, and we can do that by employing the decision journal mentioned elsewhere in this book.

An interesting and easily deceiving instance of hasty generalization is when the generalization is done from a sample of one, but where that one is either famous or anecdotic, described with a detailed and vivid story:

Smoking doesn't kill you! My aunt, a famous actress, smoked two packs a day for all her life and she lived to be 102. Moreover, she died in full health, in a skiing accident.

Generalizing from a small sample or from a non-representative sample may be unprofitable in a business context, but it is morally wrong when applied to people who did not choose to belong to a category. Hasty generalization and its converse, the applying of group labels to individuals, is the key ingredient in racism, sexism, homophobia, ethnic hate, and so on. When we talk about persons, and especially about categories that they did not choose, the humane thing is to avoid any generalization and to consider each individual separately and without any bias. It is not easy, but it is worth it if we aim to become better human beings.

How to counteract. I don't have a clear recipe for treating the hasty generalization, apart from asking the two magical questions: "Is the sample large enough?" and "Is the sample representative?" Along with respecting the basic principles of sampling and statistics, one may point—in a simplistic way—to any flaws in logic that may result from a hasty generalization: "What if we had a second client from Bulgaria and they were always late? Would you still draw the same conclusion? The opposite? Would you still look to hire a salesperson?"

The next part of the chapter will go through other few fallacies, in short:

The circular argument, where one brings *A* as a reason for *B* and *B* as a reason for *A*:

Your previous experience and performances seem perfect for this job. But can anyone from your past employer recommend you?

I'm not sure if I can get hold of my ex-boss to write a letter; he's not in the country right now. But my colleague in sales, Mark Johnson, can recommend me.

And can we trust this Mr. Johnson?

Of course, I vouch for him!

or even worse, when *A* and *B* are in fact the same thing, articulated differently:

Encouraging internal competition is beneficial for a company because motivating teammates to outperform each other cannot lead to anything but good results.

Clearly, "encouraging internal competition" is the same as "motivating teammates to outperform each other" and "is beneficial for a company" is synonymous with "cannot lead to anything but good results."

Ad baculum (an appeal to force—it literally means "appeal to the stick") does not imply more than verbal violence, but to win a dispute because you threaten the opponent is enough to make it intellectually unacceptable. *Argumentum ad baculum* can be summarized by the expression "or else!" as in the following example:

> *"This is the project I support," says the CEO, "and any other opinion will be carefully noted ... as ground for reconsidering your status in this company."*

A straw man is done when one person distorts what another has said in order to make their argument easier to attack (it is easier to attack a straw man than an actual man). The key, as in the dialog here, is to recap your own point:

> *Adopting this decision-making protocol might reduce the time we spend arguing over insignificant details and shorten the time to market for our ideas. It also might see fewer and shorter meetings.*
>
> *I believe that throwing a lot of money at consultants to tell us how to decide is the last thing we want right now.*
>
> *I didn't say we need to bring any consultant.*

The fallacy fallacy. Just because someone supports a conclusion with a fallacy does not make the conclusion false, unlike what one of these people think:

> *The Minister of Finance who drafted the fiscal code was caught taking bribe, so the new fiscal code must be rubbish.*
>
> *That is an ad hominem fallacy, my friend! You are wrong: you used a fallacy, and therefore the new fiscal code is brilliant.*

Cherry picking means presenting just the part of the facts that support our point of view and it is best illustrated in our *Universal Basic Income* case below.

This concludes our quick stroll through this list of common fallacies. Of course, there are many more fallacies: you can find many resources, should you be interested. One of them is an interesting book named *76 Fallacies*, by Michael LaBossiere (2013). Another is a website called yourlogicalfallacyis.com, which presents fallacies in a fun, visual form. If, in the heat of a dispute, your discussion partner makes a fallacy and you don't remember its name, you can later send your opponent a link with the fallacy's name, its description and a good example.

Let us now try our new knowledge on the cases that opened this chapter. I propose two ways for doing this. If you have the time, go back to the beginning of the chapter and—pen in hand—try to identify as many fallacies as possible in the two pieces of text. You can then compare your outcome with my take, below. It could be fun! The fastest way, though, is just to read my comments.

> "Dear colleagues,
>
> UBI, the universal basic income, or the unconditional basic income, is a novel and wise social security system that protects against poverty and unemployment by regularly giving all our citizens an unconditional fixed sum of money. My plea to you is to vote for implementing this system as soon as possible, and today I will offer supplementary reasons for this position. I will first remind you of the many reasons we have emphasized

throughout the campaign: it is a very simple system, very easy to implement, replacing complicated, unjust, and overlapping processes; it is transparent, very easy to control; and it protects everybody against poverty or unemployment, even the citizens that are not covered today. But aside from these things that you already know, please consider the following series of arguments:

Some of the oldest democracies in the world have implemented forms of basic income (the US in Alaska, Canada in Ontario) or discussed implementing it on a wide scale (the Swiss held a referendum in 2014 to introduce a 2500 CHF income for all adults and a 650 CHF income for all children). Moreover, countries such as Namibia, India, and Brazil have started pilot programs, proving that basic income is a valid policy irrespective of how wealthy a country is. Rich democracies and developing countries are doing it; our country cannot fall behind. We must follow this trend at once. ***Ad populum****—just because others did it does not automatically make it good.* ***Cherry picking****—presenting just the part of the facts that support our point of view: In fact, in 2014 the Swiss have overwhelmingly voted against this system—77% of the population opposed.*

Moreover, the introduction of the basic income does not only protect the unemployed; it also helps lower the number of unemployed people. In oil-rich Alaska, for example, the Alaska Permanent Fund distributes some of the oil money as a subsidy to all its citizens (1000 USD per capita per year). The fund started in 1976 and continues today. As a result, unemployment in Alaska has dropped from 11% at the beginning of 1977 to 5.9% in 2020! **Post Hoc—*correlation does not imply causality***. *Alaska's unemployment did not decrease* ***because*** *of the fund; it fluctuated based on many factors. Besides, the subsidy itself is so small it cannot have major effects. Also, I have* ***cherry-picked*** *the unemployment data. I chose 1977 with its 11% instead of the very year of the inception of the system, 1976, when the rate was only 7%.*

But let us not focus on the past! Have you considered the future of jobs? We live in a world that changes at an unprecedented pace. Let me tell you a story: my next-door neighbor—Linda—is a bank teller. She is 31, very bright, and does a great job at the bank. But her bank is planning to introduce a self-banking service this year, and Linda will soon end up without a job and without the possibility to land one, as all other banks will make the same shift. Linda's case shows that all our jobs are going to be made obsolete by automation. ***Hasty generalization****, here in its worst version—generalization from just one case. Linda losing her job doesn't imply that "all our jobs are going to be made obsolete by automation." Apart from the generalization, this argument relies on the false assumption that Linda, once fired, can only be hired by another bank and for the exact same job.* What will we live on, then? Who will contribute to the social security system, with everybody unemployed?

As I said, ATMs, computers, and robots have already replaced bank tellers: they are about to throw tens of thousands of professional car drivers into unemployment; soon enough, lawyers and general practitioners are going to be replaced by Watson; and—if we don't act now—automation will make us all unemployed within a few years, with nobody to support the current welfare system. ***Slippery slope***: *self-banking today and self-driving cars tomorrow do not imply all of us becoming unemployed in a few years.* That is why we should establish a guaranteed income to all: income supported not by contribution, but by taxation. We know we can!

We are at a crossroads. We have to choose now. We will either be brave and start introducing this novel and smart security system today or otherwise watch helplessly as the current system fails to protect large categories of citizens. ***False dilemma***. *There are other options.*

I have been accused of ignoring criticism. In order to prove that wrong, let me now address your objections to the basic income! Economists, politicians, and moralists have objected. I will take them on one by one:

Economists. How can anyone with an economic degree oppose the basic income? A social system that offers no protection against poverty and unemployment is clearly a social system destined for failure. ***Straw man***: *Mr. Josef wrongly claims that the basic income would replace "a social system that offers no protection against poverty and unemployment," which is not the case. All European countries have strong systems in place. He made the argument much weaker before attacking it.*

Politicians. A lot of politicians have argued against this idea. But they drive through the poor neighborhoods in their luxurious limousines without ever noticing the starving people on the street. How can they even dare to have an opinion on poverty prevention while wearing Armani and Gucci and Rolex? ***Ad Hominem***: *he attacks the persons (politicians), not their argument.* One more question, this time directly for our colleagues here who oppose this bill: What will you do when voters will eventually realize that, by opposing this system, you are merely trying to preserve privilege? *This is a* ***loaded question***. *The assumption that opposition comes from trying to preserve advantages was hidden inside another question: "What will you do when voters will eventually realize?"*

And finally, moralists. Many have doubted this idea on moral grounds, saying that it would encourage laziness. But this is fallacious. I am glad to end on a high note. The guaranteed basic income is undoubtedly moral because a system that provides all citizens with unconditioned means to lead a decent life cannot be anything but ethical. ***Circular argument***: *It is actually "A" because "A rephrased." "The guaranteed basic income" = "a system that provides all citizens with unconditioned means to lead a decent life" and "is undoubtedly moral" = "cannot be anything but ethical."*

Thank you for your attention and support! And please vote for the basic income: it is the only logical choice!

Well? Was it easy to spot fallacies in this political discourse? What about the following heated discussion?

Case 2 Imagine it is June 2020, in the midst of the COVID-19 pandemic. You witness a heated discussion between the compliance manager and the chief of transportation about the implementation of certain anti-COVID measures for truck drivers.

Compliance manager: All drivers must carry boxes of disposable gloves and use them whenever they leave the truck cabin, especially at gas stations and restrooms.

Transportation manager: This is insane! I am on the roads every day. All other drivers keep themselves clean and safe, but without using such drastic measures. They don't wear gloves; they just wash their hands or use disinfectant gel. I don't want my drivers to be the laughingstock of other drivers. ***Ad populum.*** *The argument brought forward does not address the core of the matter, just the behavior of others.*

Compliance manager: Are you talking about the drivers at Eurotransport? Their CEO was the most ardent advocate against strong anti-COVID measures and now—I don't know if you know—he has just been diagnosed with COVID-19. **Post hoc**. *Being against strong anti-COVID measures for drivers most probably had nothing to do with the poor man getting infected.*

Transportation manager: If my drivers are forced to wear gloves every time they leave the cabin, tomorrow you will ask them to wear full hazmat suits, and the next thing you know they will have to have portable toilets in the cabin. ***Slippery slope***. *This is the classic example.* This is unacceptable. Listen, do you drive?

Compliance manager: No, I don't have a driver's license.

Transportation manager: Well, someone who hasn't spent hundreds of hours behind the wheel shouldn't draft rules for truck drivers. ***Ad populum:*** *it is not a driver's license that gives you the right to an opinion.*

Compliance manager: Listen, my department has really thought this through. Either we implement these rules now and every driver abides fully, or we must close the transportation department for 3 months, put the drivers on leave, and use a third party. ***False dilemma.*** *A well-intentioned manager can easily find other alternatives.*

Transportation manager: The guys in your department, do they do anything else all day aside from imagining how to mess up the lives of people who actually work? ***Loaded question.*** *It implies that they do not actually do anything else.*

Compliance manager: Don't tell me about my boys; keep a sharp eye on yours! I know how truck drivers are. My brother in law is a trucker and he always brags about the way he skips work and fools the system to get paid more than he deserves. ***Hasty generalization,*** *from a sample of one.*

Transportation manager: That must be because he is related to your wife. ***Ad Hominem***, obviously. Also, ***red herring,*** *trap in which the compliance manager readily falls, as we see below:*

Compliance manager: What?! Don't ever say anything bad about her, she is a saint! And, besides, he is actually her half-brother. They were raised separately.

How about this dialog? Are fallacies easy to spot? For you, after reading this chapter, the danger is now to spot many fallacies around you and to believe that there is no more logic, decency, and common sense in this world. Please do not feel this way, it will soon pass. Do not lose your faith in humankind and, if you spot a fallacy, please do not automatically assign intent. Better be kind and try—with diplomacy—to explain and educate.

References

Albright, M. (2003). *Madam secretary*. Miramax Books.

Henley, J. (2016). LSE foreign academics told they will not be asked to advise UK on Brexit. *The Guardian*. Retrieved from https://www.theguardian.com

LaBossiere, M. C. (2013). *76 Fallacies*. CreateSpace Independent Publishing Platform.

Ten Fair-Play Principles in Argumentation

13

What is the purpose of argumentation? To win? Clearly, winning or losing an argument usually has consequences. These consequences can be less important, such as you having to do a small task that should have been done by your teammate, or very important, like your innocent client spending time in prison, if you are a bad lawyer. Whatever the case, the ultimate purpose of a dispute should be the truth and finding the best solution. Not winning. In an ideal world, all disputes would be conducted in a spirit of fair play. In a fair-play conversation, each participant enters with the willingness to convince the other, while allowing the possibility to be convinced herself. If people kept that in mind, the world would be a better place: a little dry, but better. However, in this less-than-ideal but fascinating world we live in, discussions often take wrong turns, so I have put together 10 fair-play rules to be remembered and hopefully followed in debates. Some of them are direct referrals to a specific fallacy (like the straw man, ad hominem, and red herring), others are just rules that follow from common sense:

1. ***Argue for the truth, not for the win!*** A lot of boardroom discussions and disputes fail to reach the best solution for the company because so many managers have an irrational need to win arguments. The fact that we fall in love with our opinion is not even the main engine behind this need; it is our competitive side and the need to dominate others. The next chapter on how to change our minds offers some psychological explanations for this behavior.
2. ***Argue against the point, not the person!*** This is a bilateral ailment. We often mix up, in our argumentation, the message with the messenger. We do it when we argue using ad hominem, saying that our opponent's point is irrelevant because they are this-and-that or they did this-and-that. In a twisted way, though, we also do it when we listen to a valid counterargument to our position and take it personally. The argument and the person are two different entities, and it is fair-play to actively ignore the personal traits of the one making the point, even if that person is clearly subjective on the matter. Sticking to countering the point, and not the person making the point, raises the discussion

R. Atanasiu, *Critical Thinking for Managers*, Management for Professionals,
https://doi.org/10.1007/978-3-030-73600-2_13

to the rarefied air of pure ideas. And, when we ourselves are under attack, follow Margaret Thatcher's example: "I always cheer up immensely if an attack (on me) is particularly wounding because I think, well, if they attack one personally, it means they have not a single political argument left."

3. ***Never distort what the other says!*** As discussed in the chapter on fallacies—more specifically when I described the straw man fallacy—it is unfair to misconstrue the argument of the other just to make it easier to attack. On the contrary, we should follow Daniel Dennett's advice "to re-express your target's position so clearly, vividly, and fairly that your target says, *Thanks, I wish I'd thought of putting it that way.*"
4. ***Stay on the point!*** Do not be the one using a red herring, and also do not be the one falling into that trap. Remember from the fallacy chapter that a good technique is to (a) acknowledge the red herring: "Hey, these are two different topics and I am happy to show you that my views for each of them are correct ones. Please choose one topic to start with and, after I win that argument, we can return to the other." When in business disputes, stick to what is relevant. Some people mistake volume of information for clarity. These two, volume of information and clarity, are not in the same category. Clarity is better achieved with less information, fewer words, and fewer digressions.
   In domestic arguments, do not bring back to life older disagreements. In Internet arguments, do not fight grammar (too much). In complex arguments, discuss simple arguments one by one. Stay on the point and make sure the other does too.
5. ***Don't get mad!*** What do we instinctively do when someone we have a disagreement with raises their voice? We raise our voice as well. How many times has that worked out? Not so many, I imagine. Did we do it again after a while? Yes. What did we reflexively learn? Apparently, nothing. Therefore, I propose that we go against our instincts on this one and develop simple rules to guide our behavior. For instance, every time the other raises their voice and you are inclined to answer in kind, go wash your hands. A short break and some cold water may work magic. And, after the pause, when you are back, you can recap, as discussed in the chapter on persuasion. Buddhists say that when somebody says something bad to you, an unpleasant feeling arises in your body (for instance, rage) and dictates your response. But if you take the time to mindfully analyze this feeling ("Wow! I feel my pulse quickening, my hands sweating, and my temper exploding!"), it goes away in a minute and then you can answer *what that person said*, and not *what it made you feel like*.
6. ***Listen!*** Listening is more than shutting up and waiting impatiently for the other to take a short breath so you can jump in. Really listen, with your full attention to the other's point, not to your next reply, so you are able to rephrase their argument at any point. Jonathan Haidt and Greg Lukianoff (2019) quote the psychologist Adam Grant, who said that—for productive disagreement—you need to "argue as if you are right, but listen as if you are wrong." And, although personal examples are powerful ways to illustrate your argument, some people tend to bring the discussion to themselves, irrespective of the initial topic.

Don't do that! Try to be empathic and use many second-person pronouns in your speech!

7. ***Be ready to admit weaknesses in your argument!*** This will not harm your goal; on the contrary, you will appear more trustworthy. The best option is to acknowledge the weakness yourself before the other person realizes it. If the other observes it first, be ready to admit it. Afterward, you can try to demonstrate that the smaller argument you lost is not crucial for the overall issue. But in the end, if it is the case, do not be afraid to declare yourself defeated and to embrace the other's point of view. Charlie Munger says that "we all are learning, modifying, or destroying ideas all the time. Rapid destruction of your ideas when the time is right is one of the most valuable qualities you can acquire. You must force yourself to consider arguments on the other side."
8. ***Treat your opponents as if they are really good!*** Do not make the mistake to underestimate your audience. If you are about to make a point on a topic you are an expert in (let's say marketing), while you expect the audience to be less informed (say they are accountants), treat the argument with respect and prepare for it like you are about to deliver it to a room of experts. It shows respect for the others and for the argument itself and, also, it may prevent surprises. What if one of the accountants did their MBA and excelled in the marketing class? Prepare well!
9. ***Use logic!*** A well rounded, coherent argument is always a powerful weapon. Although manipulation, appeal to emotion, and irrational influence may seem today to have replaced logic as the persuasion tool of choice, playing fair and being articulate in your argumentation is still the best strategy in the long run. Credibility is critical in almost all jobs and organizations and, once lost, is quite hard to regain.
10. ***Be empathetic!*** Trying to understand the other has a double advantage. First, as discussed in this book, arguments that are tailored to your audience are so much more powerful. Second, while trying to understand the other person's perspective, you might discover or uncover the inner resorts of their rigid position or the root cause of their ill temper. And addressing those roots may be more useful in trying to make their position more flexible than counterarguing. Even if it will not, understanding where their belief comes from may attenuate our fervor and increase our willingness to abandon the fight and build bridges instead.

Reference

Lukianoff, G., & Haidt, J. (2019). *The coddling of the American mind: How good intentions and bad ideas are setting up a generation for failure* (Illustrated ed.). Penguin Books.

14 The Courage to Change Our Mind

We don't like to change our minds, and this often leads to costly outcomes, both for our businesses and for ourselves. This chapter goes through 12 psychological mechanisms that keep us prisoners of wrong beliefs, each with business-case examples and mechanisms to counteract. We will see how *the Dunning–Kruger effect* makes less-skilled managers believe that they are better skilled and how *cognitive dissonance* makes people in the taxi industry think that ridesharing is successful *because* it is illegal.

> **Question** What is an example of a strong opinion that you hold: one that leads your managing style, your business strategy, or your life choices? We all have those, and it is good to acknowledge them. Please identify a strong opinion you have and write it down. We will have a challenge at the end of this chapter.

The common assumption in many organizations is that leaders must be decisive, consistent, and determined. In business, as in war, changing your mind is regarded as a sign of weakness. However, this common assumption needs to be reconsidered, especially as the business environment becomes increasingly unpredictable. As discussed in a previous chapter, most business plans fail because they are based on flawed assumptions. The only way out is identifying the flawed assumption, changing our minds, and deciding on a new course. When the flawed assumption is a deep-rooted belief, however, there are several cognitive and social mechanisms that conspire to keep it. Describing these mechanisms, along with their respective coping methods, is the main goal of this chapter. I chose the third-person perspective, and I mainly describe situations when we try to persuade others to change their mind, but all the lessons from this chapter should be first applied to our own deep-rooted beliefs.

In any project, there is a more dangerous thing than being inefficient: to be efficient in the wrong direction. There is a subtle but very important difference between *efficient* and *effective*. If, for instance, you want to go from Paris to Brussels and take the A11 highway instead of the A1, all your efficiency efforts,

R. Atanasiu, *Critical Thinking for Managers*, Management for Professionals,
https://doi.org/10.1007/978-3-030-73600-2_14

such as waking up early to beat the traffic, will get you away from your goal even faster. *Effective*, on the other hand, is an effort that successfully delivers the end result. And if the A11 is not taking us to Brussels, the sooner we change (our mind), the better. This is why it is very useful to dig up our deep-rooted beliefs from time to time and to re-examine them. It is worth re-analyzing whether our KPIs really take us toward the desired goal or perhaps away from it. But, *nota bene*, my arguing here is not intended to automatically discard old, deep-rooted beliefs. They are not automatically wrong. Rather, I argue for fighting the mechanisms that keep us from examining these beliefs, for analyzing them, and—clearly—for discarding them only if they prove to be wrong. If an old belief is dusted and analyzed only to be proven right, it will be even more useful than before. Listed below are 12 mechanisms that I have found to be involved in our clinging to old beliefs. For each, I will describe how it works, illustrate with examples, and list known methods to escape their effect.

Confirmation bias (because I have evidence that I am right). We think we decide rationally, but more often we make a quick decision based on gut feeling and first impression and then look for information that confirms it. This automatically leads us to confirmation bias, which has two aspects: we look for and consider just the information that confirms our point of view, and we also look the other way or find silly counterarguments for information that contradicts our point of view. Actively ignoring disconfirming evidence is, perhaps, more damaging to the accuracy of our perspective than looking only for confirming information. A famous example of ignoring the evidence if it contradicts your view is recounted by Philip Tetlock and Dan Gardner in their bestseller book *Superforecasting: The Art and Science of Prediction*. The authors mention that, in 2010, while the Federal Reserve implemented a policy of quantitative easing to counteract the financial crisis, a long list of economists and commentators wrote a public letter to Ben Bernanke, then the chairman of the institution, calling for a stop in implementing this policy, as it would lead to inflation. Their advice was ignored and inflation did not rise in the following years. In 2014, Bloomberg reporters (Melby et al., 2014) asked these same experts how they felt about the letter, 4 years after it was published. They all said that they were right in the first place and that they are still right. Either inflation is not measured correctly, or inflation is right around the corner (Tetlock & Gardner, 2016). The USA has not suffered any sharp rise in inflation as of the writing of this book (2021).

One of the most encountered forms of confirmation bias is the self-serving bias: our tendency to attribute our successes to our qualities and good nature and our failures to context and bad luck, and vice versa for everybody else, as described by what psychologists call the fundamental attribution error. If I am late for the meeting, it is because there was a lot of traffic. If you are late for the meeting, it is because you don't respect your co-workers. If you get a raise, it is because the boss prefers you. If I get a raise, it is because I have earned it: just look at all my evening hours spent at the office. Everybody thinks this way, I just hope that now that we know, we will do it less often. Confirmation bias manifests itself in science (*I spent a year studying this: all the other experiments support my hypothesis, this last disconfirming experiment cannot be correct, so I should repeat it*), in management (*after launching a kiwi-scented beer, we will conduct market research asking the consumers a slanted question - what is it that they love best about this new product*), and in every aspect of life (remember, last time you were caught in a dispute, how easily arguments and facts that supported your perspective came to mind? How come we are slower in finding counterarguments?). This last effect—having our mind serve our interests—is called motivated reasoning, and it describes the way we rationalize our preferences. A study by Dan Kahan and his collaborators shows that we are able to spot an error in the design of a scientific experiment when the research is about a hand cream (a neutral topic), but not when the same faulty experiment supports gun control (and we are ardent supporters). And education (in our case, numeracy) does not decrease the politically induced bias; it actually increases it! (Kahan et al., 2013) Sadly, confirmation bias not only affects individuals, but also organizations. Often, early signs of bad managerial decisions are ignored both by the managers who made the decisions and by their colleagues who are closer to the market and better able to spot these signs.

What can we do? Before making an important decision, we must actively look for disconfirming evidence and ask for advice against our point of view. A designated devil's advocate at the decision table is one way of uncovering confirmation bias. Devil's advocate (*advocatus diaboli* in Latin) is an old official position in the Catholic Church employed with finding reasons against the canonization of a saint. While another colleague finds confirming evidence (the candidate's character, the miracles performed), the devil's advocate tries to find flaws in the character and fraud in the miracles. The canonization process continues only if this disconfirming effort is not successful. Similarly, a managerial devil's advocate is a person whose views are known to be opposed to the decision to be taken and who is invited at the decision table to offer their arguments. Even if such a person does not exist, many organizations designate a team member to actively play this role. Another method of fighting confirmation bias is to ask neutral questions. When asking for advice or conducting market research, a slanted question can guide the respondents to give a supporting answer that does not actually reflect their true position, as in the kiwi-scented beer example above. Asking people what is it that they love best about your product may yield positive feedback even when the consumers' actual preference is against it. A good book on how to ask questions that minimize bias is *The Mom Test*, by Rob Fitzpatrick (2013), in which the author describes how to formulate questions about your business plans that even your mother (who loves you and will tell you that any idea you have is great) will answer objectively. A slanted question that will yield slanted answers from most people would be "Isn't my idea to open a nail parlor for cats great?." But even if, for instance, you ask "Should I open a nail parlor for cats?" a less-than-objective respondent might give you false information. A better way would be to extract yourself from the situation and ask, "Would you take your cat to a specialized nail parlor?." When conducting any market research, we need to remember David Ogilvy's famous quote, "People don't think what they feel, don't say what they think and don't do what they say" (Ogilvy and Parker, 2012) and acknowledge that consumer behavior is three times removed from declared preferences.

> **Exercise** Can you think of a strategic belief that you hold dear? Write down the belief. Also, write down which three pieces of evidence, if found, could disconfirm it. Then start looking.

Groupthink (because they all say so). Have you ever belonged to a group in which it felt uncomfortable to challenge a shared view? This is a manifestation of groupthink, the tendency to perpetuate wrong beliefs in groups where conformity is an important norm. In his famous conformity experiments performed in the 1950s, Solomon Asch discovered that groupthink manifests in two ways. The first, softer version, happens when you know that the group is wrong, but because contradicting the group feels very uncomfortable, you decide to keep your dissent for yourself. The second, more dangerous version, happens when you actually convert to the common belief just because there seems to be a consensus, although initially, you had clear arguments against it. The most famous example of groupthink happened to the Kennedy administration, while preparing the Cuban invasion at the Bay of Pigs in 1961. The concept of *groupthink* itself was coined by Yale psychologist Irving Janis (1972) while researching and describing this event. President Kennedy assembled a committee to plan the invasion of Cuba by a small army of Cuban refugees assisted by US military training, ships, and the air force. The committee had the best and brightest minds, and still they all agreed to carry on with the plan despite its many problems. Surprise was initially a key factor, but they went on with the plan even after The New York Times revealed its existence. The support of the local population was initially the most important resource, but when the landing place was changed to an unpopulated area, nobody spoke up. Ultimately, the invasion failed dramatically. Questioned afterward, a number of members of the committee revealed that they had important doubts about the plan but felt reluctant to voice them because each thought he was the sole dissenter. The failed invasion led to a dramatic increase in tension between the two superpowers, the USA and the USSR, in a rapid development that led to the Cuban missile crisis of 1962. Luckily, with the Bay of Pigs disaster, the Kennedy administration learned a valuable lesson. The decision-making dynamic was radically changed, dissent was encouraged, Kennedy himself held his thoughts or even left the room to allow everybody to express their opinions, and the president's brother—Bobby Kennedy—was officially designated as the devil's advocate. This change eliminated groupthink and led to a string of brilliant strategic decisions that prevented a nuclear war.

What can we do? It is the role of leaders to prevent groupthink in their organizations. Sometimes, leaders must follow the example set by President Kennedy (after he learned his valuable lesson) and take a step back to let members of the group freely express their opinions. Encouraging subordinates to express criticism is also a key quality of a leader. Sometimes, though, organizational (or national) culture prevents dissenters from speaking up. A technique employed by Japanese managers counters this obstacle: everybody writes their opinion on a piece of paper before the meeting. After a decision is made, people read out loud their pieces of paper and—if a contrary opinion was not voiced during the meeting—the consensus is attributed to groupthink, and the matter is reopened for discussion.

The organizational psychologist Marla Gottschalk (2015) found groupthink to be responsible, along with blind ambition, for the chain of faulty decisions that led to the Volkswagen emissions scandal. In her article, she proposes that leaders identify groupthink in their teams and organizations by asking whether different viewpoints exist, whether dissent is welcome, whether the group is open toward the exterior, and whether plans are openly discussed with members who might offer a different perspective.

Finally, the abrupt example of the legendary CEO of General Motors, Alfred Sloane, might find analogs in today's business environment. He is quoted as saying, after a meeting, "Gentlemen, I take it we are all in complete agreement on the decision here. Then, I propose we postpone further discussion of this matter until the next meeting to give ourselves time to develop a disagreement, and perhaps gain some understanding of what the decision is all about." (The Economist, 2009)

> **Exercise** Think of a belief that your team or organization holds, but that you disagree with. Write down the belief and the reasons for your disagreement. Then write down the best way to confront the group about it and—if you have done it already—the way the group reacted.

Reluctance to challenge authority (because the boss said so). This mechanism is a subtle variant of groupthink, and it functions on the same basic principles, but in this case, the pressure comes from a figure of authority. It is often caused by fear to challenge the boss and it also happens when the boss is not feared but revered. As this second variant is harder to spot, I have chosen to illustrate the whole mechanism with a single example.

Meg Whitman is one of the most successful businesswomen in the world. During her illustrious career, she has served as an executive or board member for eBay, HP, Procter & Gamble, Walt Disney, DreamWorks, Hasbro, and Dropbox. Her most famous tenure is her 10 years as the CEO of eBay—from 1998 to 2008—taking the company from USD 5.7 million to USD 8 billion in revenue. The main priority during the second half of her time at eBay was international growth and—after being pushed out of Japan—the main target was China. She therefore concentrates on winning the Chinese market, pours a huge budget into this project, and even moves to Shanghai for a summer. But still, despite Whitman personally overseeing this expansion, the expansion to China is a failure. The main reason is the ambition of Jack Ma of Alibaba, who, upon hearing that eBay is moving to his home country, sets up Taobao to fight for that market. And Taobao eventually wins, despite fighting against a giant. Two main mistakes were made by eBay in China. The main one was considering it as just another market, where the methods are the same as everywhere else, where you can lead without employing locals and without adapting to this unique market. A while later, during an event in Shanghai,

Meg Whitman (2012) shares her learnings from the eBay failure: a project in China needs a long-term view, needs Chinese people to implement it, and needs to be uniquely designed for China. The second reason for Whitman's defeat was not changing her approach, despite early signs of failure, but instead pouring more money into the project. Eventually, eBay gives up the expansion to China and, soon after, Meg Whitman leaves the company. One interesting question is how such an experienced executive ignored the signs and pursued a losing project without changing her approach. But this is not the topic of our current section. An even more interesting question, and more appropriate here, is why her executive team did not express concerns to their leader? The answer pinpoints the exact mechanism we are discussing here. Although Meg Whitman is characterized by former employees as a very tough boss, she also values honesty. Still, her team believed their rock star CEO had all the right answers and can never be wrong. As witnessed by eBay, this is a wrong assumption about any leader.

What can we do? This tendency to avoid questioning the decisions made by an authority figure is more prevalent in cultures with a high power distance index. This index is one of Hofstede's famous cultural dimensions and measures the perceived distance between hierarchical levels (Hofstede, 1980). A technique to overcome this cultural obstacle originates from Japan and has been employed in many Western companies: if the goal of a meeting is to make a sensitive decision, participants speak in ascending hierarchical order. This eliminates the possibility of anyone not speaking out of fear to contradict their superior. Kennedy's approach after the Bay of Pigs disaster is also a valuable tool: encourage dissent in your team, encourage people to openly address you in full honesty, and leave the discussion (and the room) from time to time to allow the team to reach their own consensus before sharing their views with you.

> **Exercise** Write down three ways that can encourage the people in your team to express their disagreement with your opinions or decisions. Then write down three methods that you can use to express disagreement to your superiors in such a way that they will not only value the information, but also appreciate the approach.

Backfire effect (because this belief defines me). This bias is, in my opinion, one of the most twisted of the human mind. Described in a study by Nyhan and Ryfler (2010), the backfire effect manifests itself when our deep-rooted beliefs are challenged with contradictory evidence. Instead of changing our minds, we do the opposite: we increase our confidence in our beliefs and defend them even more. While the original research studied political beliefs, I have witnessed the backfire effect in many business situations. It usually happens when the belief that is being challenged is defining for the person's identity or when the person overvalues her status and sees dissent as a personal affront, or both. For instance, I have often participated in pitching sessions, where startups present their businesses to potential investors. One of the most important benefits for any startup that presents in a pitching session is that—even if they do not get an investment—they surely receive valuable feedback from the panel. This feedback usually points out the flaws in the business model and, as it comes from experienced investors, is often terse. I have seen the backfire effect manifest at some startup founders when their fundamental business assumptions were challenged by the sound arguments of an investor. Instead of welcoming the feedback, the founders rushed to defend their assumptions and, afterward, during the networking phase of the evening, they kept telling everybody how they were right and the investor that challenged them was wrong, to catastrophic effect in terms of their prospects of raising money.

What can we do? Recent research by Wood and Porter (2018) has failed to replicate the backfire effect exactly as described by Nyhan and Ryfler (2010); however, in business, contradicting is often perceived as a personal attack, which leads to at least a pathological clinging to the initial opinion, if not to increased adherence to it. An example of the backfire effect that we can work on would be the interaction with customers that have a complaint. A complaining customer is already in a fighting state of mind, and a company should use lots of empathy and diplomacy in its response. Counterarguing, even on solid ground, can lead to unwanted adversity, which customers are inclined to spread afterwards through their social media network. So, what can we do? First of all, when people are contradicted, they automatically build a defense wall. The solution? First, start with empathy. If we use the unhappy customer example, start by saying that you completely understand their reaction and that you would feel the same in their situation. This positioning changes the focus of the conversation from adversity to problem solving. Then, do not contradict, even if your counterarguments are solid. Direct confrontation can—with some diplomacy—be reframed as agreeing and expanding the other's perspective:

> *I agree with you, this measure sounds exaggerated and useless. I would certainly be annoyed if the system made me authenticate so many times every day. We did not design this precaution for customers like you, who understand the risks of online payments and are familiar with the needed precautions, but for less careful clients. Please bear a little longer with the existing system while I propose to our security team to think of alternative authentication systems for different classes of users. And thank you, this is valuable feedback; if we find a solution, many users like you will no longer lose precious time.*

Direct confrontation should be especially avoided in public (and online forums are public spaces) because if there is an audience, the discussion is perceived as an attack on the person's social status. Another key element is to separate the issue from the person and to emphasize that you are discussing the issue. This is especially useful when the opinion under scrutiny is tightly linked to the person's identity, such as political or religious beliefs or—in business—beliefs about one's profession and capabilities. In this case, psychologists advise starting by increasing the other's self-confidence. After an introduction such as the following:

> *Tech employees are not easy to manage, and you are the best team leader in this company. I base my approach to developers on what I learned from you,*

a dissenting remark might be better tolerated.

Further good advice would be to always leave a decent exit for the other. Nobody wants to leave the battle scene defeated, so we should offer the other, toward the end of the discussion, the possibility to acknowledge their change of mind without losing face. For example, this can be achieved by acknowledging that their mindset was appropriate in the prior situation, but that now that the situation has shifted, it is only normal to change their mind. You will score fewer ego points in this setup, but scoring ego points should not be the goal here.

Finally, a very ingenious solution to counter the backfire effect was imagined and successfully tested by a group of Israeli researchers led by Boaz Hameiri (Hameiri et al., 2014). The solution, which they named paradoxical thinking, consists of agreeing with the person's point of view and expressing views and ideas congruent with that view, but more extreme. This counterintuitive approach makes the other express a more conciliatory attitude and embrace a more moderate view.

Exercises

(a) Think of a dispute in which the other's opinion grew even stronger during the discussion. Which of the methods described above would you have used and how?

(b) Think of the same dispute and consider whether you were also, perhaps, a victim of the backfire effect.

Debate as duel (because I need to win). Boardrooms are full of people who viscerally need to win arguments. Once the debate starts heating up, the topic—or the truth, for that matter—no longer counts. Instead, it is a fight to the death. Many people fail to see that an argument is a balanced game in which each participant has the possibility to persuade the other while accepting the possibility to be persuaded himself. When a debate is not conducted through the need to reach a common truth but through a need to win, opinions become pathologically rigid. In his famous TED talk titled "For argument's sake," philosopher Daniel H. Cohen (2013) speaks about the war-like view most people have on argumentation, with military expressions like *killer argument* and *good defense* and, in the end, the necessity of having a winner and a loser. He then explores the cognitive outcome of such a discussion and argues that, in fact, the winner did not gain anything in a cognitive sense. Winners start with opinion *X* and end up with the same opinion *X*. Indeed, they may win some ego points, but ego points are beside the point. More important, Cohen argues that the loser of the argument does not lose anything. On the contrary, from a cognitive point of view, they start with opinion *Y* and, at the end of the discussion, gain a new, presumably better opinion, *X*. The winner, therefore, gains nothing; the loser is in fact the cognitive winner. This interesting perspective might be useful if we share it before discussions reach a certain temperature.

What can we do? When debates get heated and the topic is no longer the key issue—being replaced by participants' egos—the best attitude is calm and empathy. Calm is the antidote of escalation and, employed purposefully, can tone down all those involved. Thich Nhat Hanh, a Zen Buddhist monk, scholar, peace activist, and successful writer, thinks that—when confronted with an offensive remark—people do not respond to the remark but to the way it made them feel. He then advises his readers to inhibit rage, to wait a few seconds, and then to surprise the offender by answering the remark itself. Empathy is the other ingredient of a successful attitude here. This kind of situation requires a special, deeper kind of empathy. Of course, during an argument with people that cannot conceive of losing, we need to understand their perspective. But trying to understand the hidden reasons behind their position can yield even better tools to address the issue.

A very practical tool can be used when a discussion is blocked by the other's need to win the argument. First, I would stop and define fair-play in arguing: *each side must allow and acknowledge the possibility to be persuaded by the other*. If this principle is not respected, then this is not a discussion, but a series of parallel monologues. Then, I would express my willingness to change my opinion, if presented with good arguments. And in the end, I would tell the other: "We have been arguing for 30 min already. If we continue this discussion for another 30 min, is there any possibility of your changing your mind?" This question has two benefits. The indirect outcome is that having the other contemplate the possibility of being wrong creates a small fissure in their concrete wall of certainty. Second, as a direct outcome, the other may answer. If they answer "yes," then the discussion starts again on a much better track. If they answer "no," well, there are better ways to spend 30 min of my life than arguing in vain.

Exercise Remember this technique and employ it, as an exercise, during your next heated debate.

Status quo. Because I don't want to change anything.

That is the way things are done around here.

If it is not broken, why fix it?

Let's not rock the boat!

These and similar lines are often encountered in organizations, mostly when the prospect of a change arises. Managers who make decisions and organizations that must implement these decisions show a strong bias toward alternatives that preserve the status quo (the current state of affairs). But the environment changes at an ever-increasing pace.

Lulled by a successful cash-cow line of business, Xerox was slow to change and, when it finally did, it had to let go half its employees during the transformation (2000–2005) from a tech company into a service company. Kodak did not adapt fast enough to the digital photo world and had to file for bankruptcy in 2012. This kind of situation usually happens when decision-makers are slow to challenge an assumption that was valid during a previous successful period but it no longer is. In her analysis published in Forbes, Andrea Simon (2013) observes that for successful executives, change is literally pain. She describes three reasons for which CEOs that are aware of the need for change are slow to initiate it: they are afraid of the unknown, they are driven by habit, and they have an irrational hope that the good old times will return.

What can we do? Changing our strategy in response to changes in the environment requires first a change in mindset. The resistance to change needs to be acknowledged and we need to allocate special effort to overcome the status quo bias and change from *A* (the current state) to *B*. The effort must be increased if we are not sure which path to choose from the status quo; for example, if we need to abandon our comfortable view *A*, but we are not sure if we should choose *B* or C instead.

At an organizational level, cultures in which sins of commission are punished more than sins of omission are fertile ground for the status quo bias. In many companies, doing something wrong is punished more than not doing what needed to be done, inducing a reluctance to do or change anything. This kind of culture inhibits autonomy, agility, and innovation. If you lead such an organization, you should change the system toward encouraging initiative, analyzing mistakes as learning opportunities, and discouraging immobility.

In their 2006 Harvard Business Review article, John S. Hammond, Ralph L. Keeney, and Howard Raiffa propose an ingenious method to fight the status quo trap: start by imagining an alternative *B* to the status quo *A*, then imagine that you are in *B*. Would you change to *A*? (Hammond et al., 2006) It works for situations, but it works for mindsets as well. I witness changes in mindset every time that, during an MBA class, we do a debating exercise. As the motion (the topic) is chosen by me and teams are assigned randomly, we often have people who are either indifferent or quite cold toward what they need to argue for. I explain that arguing for something you do not believe in is a healthy intellectual exercise, and participants are happy to do it. But then the debate heats up and, at the end, I am surprised to see people adjusting their minds toward what they just argued for.

> **Exercise** The first step in countering the status quo effect is identifying it. So, as an exercise, please think of an assumption linked to your business strategy that was true in the past but that may not be valid anymore because of changes in context. Is it uncomfortable to think about it? Then you are on the right track!

Neural mechanisms (because I perceive your attempt to change my mind as a physical threat). A 2016 study led by Jonas Kaplan showed the neurobiological outcomes of trying to change somebody's mind. Functional MRI was used to see what happens in the brains of the participants when they read short essays that presented evidence against a previously held belief. The brain's response varied widely depending on the issue. For neutral issues such as the invention of the lightbulb (no, it wasn't Edison, although he would have wanted you to believe so), the contradicting evidence was analyzed in the cortex and people eventually believed the claim and changed their minds. When, by contrast, the issue was a highly political one, the brain responded in a totally different way. When supporters of gun control were presented with evidence that, when adopted, increased gun control did not lead to a decrease in violence, they did not change their minds (Kaplan et al., 2016). Predictably. This research did not look for the backfire effect, but it may have been that participants actually increased their support for gun control policies. What this study did, however, is to observe that—when reading evidence against their strong beliefs—intense activity took place in the insula and the amygdala. In the words of the researchers, "these structures are signaling threats to deeply held beliefs in the same way they might signal threats to physical safety." In short, next time you attempt to persuade people of the opposite of what they currently believe, please remember that they perceive it as if you were threatening them with physical violence.

What can we do? It is hard, but the essence is to try to separate the issue being debated from the other's identity. In organizations, the attachment we manifest for our beliefs and for the decisions that resulted from our beliefs often stems from guilt or guilt avoidance. If I change my mind, it means that what I believed and decided so far was wrong. Therefore, I instinctually prefer to stick to my beliefs, even if the price is continuing to err. A CEO I have interviewed for my research has a solution he applies when discussing an error made by an employee. He says that "the first thing to do is to take out guilt from the room, so I tell them that, if anyone is responsible, that would be me." Kindness is also a good approach. As quoted before in the chapter on debates, the famous Japanese author Haruki Murakami wrote: "Always remember that to argue, and win, is to break down the reality of the person you are arguing against. It is painful to lose your reality, so be kind, even if you are right."

> **Exercise** Please recall the last time you responded to counterarguments by engaging the fight-or-flight mode. Can you calmly assess those counterarguments now?

Sunk cost (because I have invested too much in this belief). We discussed sunk cost in the chapter on biases. Sunk cost is generally studied in relation to implementing projects, being the tendency to continue a failing project only because we have invested a lot of resources (money, time, attention, emotion) in it so far. But it works with beliefs as well. It is hard to abandon a belief for which we have sacrificed something. A touching example is the story of Sonita Alizadeh, an Afghan teen who escaped forced marriage and made a rap video, "Brides for Sale," that became a YouTube hit. With some help, Sonita eventually escaped a marriage her parents arranged and is now living and studying in the USA. Her story is famous: she is now one of the most vocal activists against forced marriage. How does Sonita's story relate to sunk cost in changing beliefs? The hardest to convince to cancel the marriage was Sonita's mother, who—in her teens—was also a subject to a forced marriage. A possible explanation is that she could not come to terms with her destiny and her sacrificed youth without fostering the belief that forced marriages are a good tradition, worth imposing on her own daughter as well.

Another good illustration is the violent rituals that must be passed to enter certain cults or similar organizations. After sacrificing something to get in, members will always tend to ignore signs that the beliefs propagated by the cult are wrong because that would mean their sacrifice was in vain.

What about a management belief? Many managers believe that they are the holders of the ultimate truth about how to conduct business, that this ultimate truth is not transferrable, and that the only way to manage is to command every little step and to control its implementation. But micromanagement comes with a series of sacrifices. For instance, micromanagers are so busy with their subordinates' daily tasks that they ignore strategic thinking and long-term planning. They also sacrifice their advancement in their career (as they do not have the bandwidth to think above their paycheck) and the development of their team. Last, but not least, a micromanager sacrifices personal and family time by staying long hours at the office or by dealing with business issues during weekends and vacations. I keep mentioning micromanagement, first because it is an important management affliction and second, because it illustrates well all kinds of mental mechanisms. The beliefs that lead to micromanagement are hard to challenge, and this is perhaps the reason why micromanagers have no idea that they are doing it.

What can we do? One option would be to counter this belief with another self-serving belief: that we are constantly growing and, therefore, that we are better today than we were yesterday. With this in mind, we may ask ourselves if, today, we would still make the same sacrifices, or—given that we are smarter—we would choose another path and a change in mindset.

Another method would be to understand the intrinsic value of the sacrifice, without linking it to our belief. For instance, many people are reluctant to change careers because of all the years spent learning and training for their current profession. They are convinced that this profession is the best fit for them and that people with their degree of specialization do not just change paths mid-life. The strength of this belief is directly proportional to the number of years of learning and training. As someone who had more than one career change, I can testify to this. But then, to free our belief from its anchoring sacrifice, we can shift our perspective. We can concentrate on the good things those years brought into our lives, so we can become free to change our mindset and our path.

> **Exercise** In order to identify a hidden belief that is based on sunk cost, you can start in reverse order. Think of a large investment (of time, effort, money) that you made, and then investigate whether this investment led to a sunk cost belief by wondering what would be different about how you think if you had not made that investment.

Lack of impulse (because I don't have the opportunity to change my mind). When do people change their minds? Often, it happens in the face of a counterexample (usually a negative outcome) or of a compelling counterargument. In other instances, insights happen during veritable "aha" moments, sparked by a transformative experience. It can also happen during formal education or training, as unlearning a wrong view of reality is a more important step than acquiring a new accurate one. The first, crucial phase of a mind change is acknowledging that we function based on a flawed assumption, on a belief that may be wrong. This involves subjecting a previously unchallenged belief to rational analysis. Until then, these assumptions and beliefs often lay unnoticed somewhere in our subconsciousness, while being perfectly able to guide behavior. As Carl Jung famously said, "Until you make the unconscious conscious, it will direct your life and you will call it fate." Unfortunately, all the situations discussed above involve a certain context or external action. We cannot, however, hope to meet these conditions too often. One cannot wake up in the morning planning for an "aha" moment or for encountering a counterexample. We often have no impulse, no catalyst for challenging an old belief.

What can we do? So how can we catalyze this process ourselves, if the context does not catalyze it for us? One solution is to encourage purposeful thinking, debate, and questioning throughout the organization, harvesting the power of many different perspectives. Another solution is to constantly question our own behavior. "Why do I do this?" and "Why do we do this?" are questions that any manager must ask from time to time. For example, let's say that a manager is open-minded and observes that he or she is always the last to leave the office. Wondering why that is the case can lead to a Google search that may, in turn, show this as a common sign of being a micromanager. If another manager mindfully observes that the company purchases service *A* by carefully comparing several offers, while traditionally purchasing service *B* from the same old supplier *X*, questioning the situation might reveal that the decision to use the supplier *X* was made many years ago when the service just appeared on the market and when *X* was the only provider.

> **Exercise** Identify one behavior in your organization that—at first sight—can only be explained by saying that "this is how things are always done around here" and look for the root cause. Also, investigate what other alternatives exist for that behavior and—if a better alternative is identified—analyze what change in mindset is necessary for adopting the new behavior. Use your team to generate multiple perspectives.

Cognitive dissonance (because I cannot contradict myself). Cognitive dissonance is the discomfort we feel while trying to hold two opposing beliefs at the same time. Some say that being able to entertain two opposing thoughts at the same time is a sign of wisdom; however, cognitive dissonance is a useful adaptive mechanism designed to help us reconsider our beliefs. If we observe a counterexample or accept a counterargument, it is dissonance that forces us to abandon our initial view. However, in the face of deep-rooted beliefs, cognitive dissonance can backfire, like in the story of the fox and the grapes. Admitting that it cannot reach the grapes would challenge its self-image, so the fox decides to change reality and to pretend that the grapes are sour. There is also a joke that illustrates how cognitive dissonance can malfunction: a psychiatrist has a patient who thinks himself to be a corpse. Running out of methods to challenge that view, the psychiatrist asks the patient whether corpses can be tickled. The patient looks non-plussed and answers "no." Then the doctor tickles him and the patient laughs. He then opens his eyes wide in amazement and admits: "Doctor, you are right! Corpses *can* be tickled!" The mechanism illustrated here is the following: faced with a counterexample to a deep-rooted belief, some people choose to hold the belief and to distrust or to explain away the counterexample.

What can we do? I can illustrate with a real example. In many markets, ridesharing services have disrupted the taxicab industry. In Bucharest, for example, the majority of tech-savvy customers prefer to use Uber or Bolt or a similar service because the cars are nicer, the drivers are nicer, because they can pay through the app, because they can see on their phone the driver approaching, and so on. Some taxi companies have tried to adapt by implementing customized apps, but they never dealt with the old cars and the (sometimes) rude drivers, so their market share declined abruptly. Some tensions have surfaced between taxi and Uber drivers: taxi drivers have organized several protests, and laws have been proposed to protect their trade. I have talked to taxi drivers and to owners of taxi companies, and they have the same explanation: "Uber is stealing our clients. And it is doing that by employing unfair methods; for instance, by ignoring the necessity to have special permits," an explanation that makes little sense. Faced with the prospect of admitting that their service is poor, they explain away the clients' preference for the alternative service. In this case, a good way out would be to ask the person to describe in writing, on a piece of paper, how things relate and cause each other in a coherent way. Eventually, they will be forced to write "Clients prefer Uber to our taxis because Uber ignores the necessity to have special transport permits." When spelled out on paper, the lack of logic will be evident and, hopefully, sufficient for reconsidering the situation.

Exercise Think about a recent negative outcome of your actions and the way you explained it to yourself. Now, write down in three phrases a clear and coherent account of this causation link.

The Dunning–Kruger effect (because I believe I am good at this). The Dunning–Kruger effect, mentioned already in the chapter on problem solving, was empirically discovered by social psychologists David Dunning and Justin Kruger in a famous 1999 paper, and it shows that people who have low ability in a domain suffer from illusory superiority, mistakenly believing that their ability is higher than it really is (Kruger and Dunning, 1999). The unfortunate cause of this misperception is the low ability itself, as the correct assessment of one's ability requires a certain level of the respective ability. In plain words, unskilled people do not have the tools to acknowledge their lack of skills. For instance, people lacking social skills will consider themselves at a decent level in this respect because assessing social skills requires social skills. In the same vein, someone who lacks artistic talent will not realize that precisely because of his lack of artistic talent.

When learning about the Dunning–Kruger effect, as is the case with most mechanisms described in this chapter, most readers will fully understand the concept and will be fully able to recognize it, albeit primarily in other people.

Exercise Let's overcome this blind spot bias with a simple and funny exercise that can show that sometimes we mistakenly think we are good at something, when in fact we are not. Do you know how a bike looks? OK! Please draw one on a piece of paper.

With few exceptions, when asked to do this, people draw Picasso-style, impossible machines. Give it a shot.

What can we do? Confidence does not grow in a linear relationship with experience and knowledge. After a brief exposure to a trade and perhaps after one or two easy wins, novices typically get the impression that they are experts, and this overconfidence leads to costly mistakes. To prevent that, organizations should implement measurable standards of performance. Overconfidence in one's own skills is also a characteristic of managers who are high on the hierarchical ladder and who mistake position for competence. I know an example that illustrates this perfectly: after hiring a very expensive specialist to deal with a niche technical task in his company, the CEO kept telling the specialist how to do her job. One (difficult to implement) way to prevent this is to design your organization so as to assign tasks and responsibility based on competence, not hierarchy.

Another danger posed by the Dunning–Kruger effect is that of hiring specialists based solely on their self-assessed skills. Most CVs are collections of exaggerated skills; however, it sometimes happens that, due to Dunning–Kruger, people honestly believe they are good at something they are not. There are numerous ways to prevent this: the easiest is to test the skills declared in a CV. Candidates for a sales position can demonstrate their ability in a staged or real sales meeting, software developers can practically prove their coding skills, and social media specialists can design a real campaign. When a new employee occupies a key position, implement—at least for a while—a group decision-making process, or a peer-validation system.

Exercise In his bestseller book, *Principles. Life & Work*, fund manager Ray Dalio (2017) explains how he introduced at his firm, Bridgewater Associates, a *baseball card* system. Unlike the collectible stickers with football players from my European childhood, U.S. baseball cards display—along with the portrait of the player—his performance statistics, which provide an accurate and objective idea of the player's strengths and weaknesses. At Bridgewater, Dalio implemented a similar system, every employee being able to consult the *baseball card* of any colleague. While the Bridgewater system—that is, aiming to reach *radical transparency*—is considered extreme, try at least to imagine it implemented in your team. If you were to be objectively assessed, what would your baseball card say? What are your main three weaknesses? What are your most important three strengths? Write them down.

Thinking in certainties (because I am 100% right). Especially in a confrontational setting, we usually have a black or white approach. We consider beliefs to be certainties, with the only possible values of confidence being 0% and 100%. Some of the mechanisms discussed above, such as the backfire effect, and features of the modern world, such as echo chambers facilitated by social media, lead us to adopt a firm and extreme position in most debates. I once asked a debate champion whether formal debating is dangerous or not to the young generation, as it trains participants to embrace and argue for an extreme point of view, without allowing for embracing a more moderate one. He smiled and, with wisdom uncharacteristic of his 18 years of age, he said that this only happens in contests, but the influence of debating on his life has been the opposite. While preparing to defend a motion, debaters always consider opposite and alternative points of view, in order to predict the strategy of the other team. Also, as the sides are assigned randomly, debaters often have to argue for opposite points of view on the same topic, in the same tournament. This, the young debater said, allowed him to understand very well the arguments around many of today's grand issues and still—if asked to venture his opinion—to have the strength to answer, "I don't know." We do not do this often. Take, for instance, a recent political debate in your country. Chances are that you have a strong opinion on one side of the battle.

Generally, we often ignore the existence of nuances, middle-ground, or alternative points of view, and we fully embrace one extreme position, especially when the debate is one that already split people in pro and con sides. Think of controversies on immigrants, vaccines, or eating meat. The same happens once sides have emerged on a business issue. Think of the last controversy that you had in your team. After fully embracing one extreme, our mind also favors the "*if you are not with me, you are against me*" approach, further transforming the debate into a duel.

What can we do? We are drawn to the extreme in two ways: black or white thinking, in which we only consider extreme points of view, and extreme adherence, in which when we adopt a point of view, we adopt it fully. In her bestselling book *Thinking in Bets*, author, psychologist, business consultant, and poker champion Annie Duke (2019) combines her different perspectives to distill principles that one can apply in management or in everyday life. She identifies the risk of thinking in extreme certainties and argues for training our minds to think in sliders. If our mind automatically considers only the extreme perspectives *A* and *B*, we should fight this by forcing ourselves to consider all the nuances on a slider from *A* to *B* and to assign a percentage to our opinion: "on this issue, I favor *B*, and my opinion is at around 80%."

If our discussion partner falls into the trap of black or white thinking, we should introduce the slider approach, but only after opening up their mind with a trick, also borrowed from Annie Duke. A wise professor and friend once told me that you cannot convince people; people always convince themselves, through dialectical inner dialogs. You can only influence these dialogs. So, when the other shows signs of *thinking in certainties* on an issue, you should ask them if they are willing to bet on it: with real money, and not a small sum. The bet does not need to be formally accepted. The question *"Want to bet on it?"* should do the trick, in an (imagined) inner dialog that could be like this:

I am certain my belief is true.

But hold on! If it is not, I can lose a lot of money. Let's at least consider the possibility of being wrong.

After opening to the perspective of abandoning certainty, the other can be nudged toward a more moderate view by being presented with the slider approach.

Exercise Think of something that is not subject to consensus but on which you have a strong opinion. What is the amount you are willing to bet on it being true? Think about the sum as a guide, and assign a value and a confidence interval to your opinion. This may, in turn, open your options. For instance, if I am 100% sure that my teaching methods are effective, I will keep doing things in the same way. Once I challenge my black or white thinking and assign a value to this belief, any value that is not 100% will prompt me to think of ways to improve my teaching.

Clearly, these 12 mechanisms are not the only ones preventing us from changing our minds. But knowing about them and trying to overcome their influence, especially on ourselves, is a good start toward flexibility. As Nassim Nicholas Taleb writes, "The person you are the most afraid to contradict is yourself." Make your strong beliefs a bit flexible! Flexibility in opinions, far from being a weakness, is a noble virtue. And every virtue requires exercising. So, at the end of this chapter, I leave you with one more challenge.

Exercise I declare this day to be the International Examine-Your-Own-Opinion Day, and we will celebrate it with an exercise. At the beginning of this chapter, I asked you to write down a strong opinion that is leading your managing style, your strategy, or your life choices. Now, in order to try to make your mindset more flexible, think of three good counterarguments against your strong opinion. Doing so is not comfortable, but it is useful. And, once you have thought about them and analyzed them, please reevaluate the strength of your opinion on a slider. If it still holds (even if it's not at 100%), your opinion will be a better decision guide now, after analysis. If not, have the courage to change your mind!

References

Dalio, R. (2017). *Principles: Life and work* (Illustrated ed.). Simon & Schuster.

Fitzpatrick, R. (2013). *The mom test: How to talk to customers and learn if your business is a good idea when everyone is lying to you* (1st ed.). CreateSpace Independent Publishing Platform.

Cohen, D. H. (2013, August 5). *For argument's sake*. [Video file]. Retrieved from https://www.ted.com/talks/daniel_h_cohen_for_argument_s_sake?language=en

Duke, A. (2019). *Thinking in bets: Making smarter decisions when you don't have all the facts* (Illustrated ed.). Portfolio.
Gottschalk, M. (2015). Volkswagen: Was it blind ambition or groupthink? *Pulse*. Retrieved from https://www.linkedin.com/pulse/volkswagen-story-groupthink-dr-marla-gottschalk/
Hammond, J. S., Keeney, R. L., & Raiffa, H. (2006). The hidden traps in decision making. *Harvard Business Review*. Retrieved from https://hbr.org
Hameiri, B., Porat, R., Bar-Tal, D., Bieler, A., & Halperin, E. (2014). Paradoxical thinking as a new avenue of intervention to promote peace. *Proceedings of the National Academy of Sciences, 111*(30), 10996–11001. https://doi.org/10.1073/pnas.1407055111
Hofstede, G. (1980). *Culture's consequences : international differences in work-related values* (Ser. Cross-cultural research and methodology series, 5). Sage Publications.
Janis, I. L. (1972). *Victims of groupthink: A psychological study of foreign-policy decisions and fiascoes*. Houghton Mifflin Company.
Kahan, D. M., Peters, E., Dawson, E. C., & Slovic, P. (2013). (2017). Motivated numeracy and enlightened self-government. *Behavioural Public Policy, 1*(1), 54–86. https://doi.org/10.1017/bpp.2016.2
Kaplan, J. T., Gimbel, S. I., & Harris, S. (2016). Neural correlates of maintaining one's political beliefs in the face of counterevidence. *Scientific Reports, 6*(1). https://doi.org/10.1038/srep39589
Kruger, J., & Dunning, D. (1999). Unskilled and unaware of it: How difficulties in recognizing one's own incompetence lead to inflated self-assessments. *Journal of Personality and Social Psychology, 77*(6), 1121–1134. https://doi.org/10.1037/0022-3514.77.6.1121
Meg Whitman Shares Learnings From China During eBay days (& HP's Strategy). (2012, May 15). [Video file]. Retrieved from https://www.youtube.com/watch?v=X_aezW5NorQ
Melby, C., Marcinek, L., & Burger, D. (2014). Fed critics Say '10 letter warning inflation still right. *Bloomberg*. Retrieved from https://www.bloomberg.com/news/articles/2014-10-02/fed-critics-say-10-letter-warning-inflation-still-right
Nyhan, B., & Reifler, J. (2010). When corrections fail: The persistence of political misperceptions. *Political Behavior, 32*(2), 303–330. https://doi.org/10.1007/s11109-010-9112-2
Ogilvy, D., & Parker, A. (2012). *Confessions of an advertising man* (Rev ed.). Southbank Publishing.
Simon, A. (2013, April 23). Why we're so afraid of change—and why that holds businesses back. *Forbes*. Retrieved from https://www.forbes.com
Tetlock, P. E., & Gardner, D. (2016). *Superforecasting: The art and science of prediction* (Illustrated ed.). Crown.
The Economist. (2009, October 20). Alfred Sloan. *The Economist*. Retrieved from https://www.economist.com
Wood, T., & Porter, E. (2018). The elusive backfire effect: Mass attitudes' steadfast factual adherence. *Political Behavior, 41*(1), 135–163. https://doi.org/10.1007/s11109-018-9443-y

15 Wrap Up

This is a book about thinking. Having a structured, rational approach to decision-making and persuasion yields better outcomes. However, throughout this book, we have discussed the limits of thinking and the many ways in which our thinking can be misleading. On the other hand, we saw that less-than-rational adaptive mechanisms such as intuition and heuristics, although they may occasionally lead to error, are usually efficient tools in any manager's toolbox.

This book ends with two pleas, one about ourselves and one about others.

First, I urge you to think about your thinking from time to time. Metathinking does not come naturally; we need to purposefully find the time and the focus to do it. Then, we need to apply to ourselves the principles of intellectual humility and to consider our thinking fallible: this is the only way we can open ourselves to improvement. We need to take a structured approach and write things down: our decisions, our assumptions, our plans for convincing others, and so on. We need to scrutinize our minds and behavior for blind spots and shift perspective by consulting with others. We need to understand our mental blockages and try to become more flexible. We need to respect our insights and train and trust our intuition. We need to test our assumptions like true scientists. And we need to come to terms with our irrationality and allow its presence, but to make sure that—for important issues—we add in a rational approach.

Second, I urge you to trust people: to have confidence that their actions, arguments, or beliefs are never of ill intent but the result of complex psychological mechanisms and of life experiences we may not know about. In our interactions, we need to purposefully put ourselves in others' shoes. In our group decision-making, we need—while structuring the process and assigning clear roles—to allow for dissent and to rather look for commitment than agreement. And when someone commits a fallacy, do not take it personally, but try—with diplomacy—to understand and educate. The empathy that I am advocating for is not only proof of

R. Atanasiu, *Critical Thinking for Managers*, Management for Professionals,
https://doi.org/10.1007/978-3-030-73600-2_15

goodwill; it will also lead to good outcomes, in our businesses and in our lives. Extended and compounded, this kind and trusting attitude toward *the other* will allow for a better business environment and a better society, as we all are *the other* for everybody else.

Printed by Printforce, the Netherlands